Isaac J. Lansing

Romanism and the Republic.

A Discussion of the Purposes, Assumptions, Principles and Methods of the Roman

Catholic Hierarchy

Isaac J. Lansing

Romanism and the Republic.
A Discussion of the Purposes, Assumptions, Principles and Methods of the Roman Catholic Hierarchy

ISBN/EAN: 9783744771566

Printed in Europe, USA, Canada, Australia, Japan

Cover: Foto ©ninafisch / pixelio.de

More available books at **www.hansebooks.com**

ROMANISM AND THE REPUBLIC.

A DISCUSSION OF THE PURPOSES, ASSUMPTIONS,
PRINCIPLES AND METHODS OF THE
ROMAN CATHOLIC HIERARCHY.

BY

REV. ISAAC J. LANSING, M.A.,
OF WORCESTER, MASS.

WITH AN

INTRODUCTION

BY

REV. LEROY M. VERNON, D.D.,
LATE SUPERINTENDENT OF MISSIONS OF THE METHODIST
EPISCOPAL CHURCH IN ITALY.

————∞◦°◦°◦∞————

BOSTON:
ARNOLD PUBLISHING COMPANY,
CONGREGATIONAL BUILDING.
1890.

PRESSWORK BY BERWICK & SMITH, BOSTON.

AUTHOR'S PREFACE.

This volume contains fourteen discourses on ROMANISM AND THE REPUBLIC, delivered in the Salem Square Congregational Church, Worcester, Mass., during the Summer and Autumn of 1888.

From the first until the last of eighteen sermons, which were delivered on consecutive Sabbath evenings, public interest was general and intense. Throngs of serious and thoughtful people crowded the Church, while great numbers sought for even standing-room in vain. Calls for the publication of the addresses as delivered were immediate, and from many quarters. As reported stenographically, they were printed from week to week in the *New England Home Journal*, which, with one other notable exception, was the only paper that gave them currency.

Repeated requests, at that time and since, that they might be preserved in a more permanent form, have resulted in the compilation of the present volume. This design was not in view originally in their preparation. Delivered extemporaneously, and reported as spoken, the preacher used no notes except memoranda, which related to the numerous books of reference which were taken to the pulpit, and from which quotations were read in the presence of the congregation. Therefore their style is that of popular address, rather than the more finished form of deliberate, literary execution. Even the rugged exclamatory passages, — which perhaps, could only be excused or justified by the impassioned earnestness of the moment of their utterance, the author has thought best to retain, that the people who heard, when they come to read, may not miss remembered and often applauded passages. For in each sermon of the entire course, a sympathetic audience encouraged and sanctioned the speaker's utterances by outbursts of assent and commendation ; which, it may be, should have been recorded in the text, as the valued expression of their sentiments.

Two discourses to men only, "On the Romish Confessional," are, of necessity, omitted from this volume, because the citations which they contained from Roman Catholic books should not be printed for general reading. With this exception the discourses are printed as delivered.

For the Title, "ROMANISM AND THE REPUBLIC," the author is indebted to an impressive article from the pen of M. Leon Bouland, the distinguished ex-priest, in *The Forum* of July, 1888.

Among authorities, I have depended mostly on Roman Catholic text-books and histories, as directly consulted by myself, and as cited by reliable authors. Such are Fredet's " Modern History," Jenkins' " Judges of Faith," Bouvier's " Dissertatio in Sextum Decalogi Præceptum," Dens' " Theology," J. P. Gury's " Moral Theology," and the " Index Expurgatorius," among Roman Catholic text-books.

H. C. Lea's " Sacerdotal Celibacy " and Lea's " History of the Inquisition," Thompson's " The Papacy and the Civil Power," Gladstone's " Vaticanism and the Vatican Decrees," Mendham's " Literary Policy of the Romish Church," Edgar's " Variations of Popery,"— all of which are especially rich in quotations from Romish authorities, —I have freely quoted.

I have found help also in the works of distinguished ex-priests and converts from Rome ; including DeSanctis, on "The Confessional," Lord Richard Montagu, "The Sower and the Virgin," Rev. Charles Chiniquy, " Fifty Years in the Church of Rome," and " The Priest, the Woman and the Confessional," Rev. James A. O'Connor, Editor of that very valuable and reliable monthly, *The Converted Catholic*, Father McGlynn's " Sermons and Addresses," Wm. Hogan, on " Popery," and others.

While of books of a more general character, I have consulted, among others : " The History of the Public School Society of New York," " Our Country " by Dr. Josiah Strong, Barnum's "Romanism As It Is," Beaudry's " Spiritual Struggles of a Roman Catholic," Van Dyke's " Popery ;" the Documents of the American Evangelical Alliance, and the Papers of Dexter A. Hawkins ; together with several lives of Loyola, and histories of the Jesuits, from both Romish and Protestant sources.

To have filled the margins or appendix with hundreds of references to these volumes, would have been easy, but this seemed superfluous.

It is believed that the facts are as alleged ; and while errors of statement may be discovered, there are no allegations submitted without ample testimony in their favor. My thanks are due to many friends who have kindly aided me with books and facts.

For the striking and comprehensive Introduction, the Author is indebted to a master of all the facts concerning Romanism, Rev. Leroy M. Vernon, D. D., founder, and for nearly eighteen years, until 1888, superintendent of the Missions of the Methodist Episcopal Church in Italy. For most of these years, Dr. Vernon has resided in Rome, under the very shadow of the Vatican. There and throughout Italy he has given profound study to Roman-ism in all its phases, gathering about him into the Church of God, some of the most extraordinary and able men of young Italy, who, under his guidance, forsook, for conscience sake, the Papacy which had honored them. For weight and trustworthiness, his statements are absolutely authoritative.

With diffidence as to form and style, but with confidence as to facts and inferences, I submit to a larger public this incomplete discussion, as a contribution to the demands of a great conflict, in which I confidently hope to see Romanism destroyed, the Roman Catholic people saved, the American Republic more firmly established, and the Kingdom of God triumphantly exalted.

I. J. LANSING.

Worcester, May 15, 1889.

PREFACE TO LATEST EDITION.

THE unexpected favor with which this effort to meet a living question has been met, and the fact that the ninth thousand of the volume is in press, though less than a year has elapsed since its publication, is a cause of profound gratitude to the author.

An Index has been added to the present edition, which will greatly enhance its value to all readers.

The recent Centennial Anniversary of the Roman Catholic Church at Baltimore has given occasion for an expression of the latest word that Romanism has to utter on the themes that most concern us as Americans. A few quotations have been given in an Appendix which show the spirit and animus of this gathering, and that the Church of Rome is, as she herself boasts, *semper eadem,* — always the same.

I. J. LANSING.

TABLE OF CONTENTS.

INTRODUCTION.

A great theme here invites the reader's attention. Macaulay says: "The polity of the Church of Rome is the very masterpiece of human wisdom. . . . The experience of twelve hundred eventful years, the ingenuity and patient care of forty generations of statesmen, have improved that polity to such perfection, that, among the contrivances which have been devised for deceiving and controlling mankind, it occupies the highest place." The animating soul of that polity is the Pope, who from Rome enforces it throughout the world, with a refined astuteness, hereditary and cumulative, unequalled in human history. The many-tongued Catholic masses, imbued with Romanist doctrines, and invested by that polity as by the shirt of Nessus, with the Pope at their head, constitute living Romanism, aggressive, imperious, and relentless as ever.

This vast power, besides assuming and exercising the most blasphemous religious prerogatives, for more than a thousand years, has dispensed crowns and dethroned kings, absolved peoples from allegiance to their rightful sovereigns, or sanctioned their bondage under tyrants, according to its own pleasure or caprice; nor has it ever formally or impliedly abandoned any of its enormous pretensions. There is not a people in the Old World whose peace it has not disturbed, whose rulers it has not embroiled, the administration of whose government it has not embarrassed, whose rights it has not usurped, and whose soil it has not drenched with blood. Its arrogant and hoary hierarchy early began from the Vatican to project its all-pervading system over our country, now by gigantic institutions commands centres of power throughout the land, has a large and rapidly increasing constituency among our people, and daily becomes more pronounced and menacing, faithful to its own traditions.

The relations of Romanism to the Republic, therefore, form a subject of supreme importance and of burning actuality, most urgently commending itself to the prompt attention of every citizen, to the dispassionate consideration especially of the patriot, the journalist, the teacher, the moralist, the divine, and the statesman, as the makers of public opinion. Wherefore nothing could be more opportune than Mr. Lansing's vigorous volume; than the weighty and fearless terms with which he eloquently invokes the public attention and developes his absorbing argument. This book is secured a very high practical value by the judicious limitation and selection of the points to be treated, and by their ample and triumphantly conclusive elaboration within modest limits.

The vastness of Romanism, with its debatable features and history, has often proven a snare to authors, especially the more ambitious. Any portrayal of Romanism always encounters two serious preliminary embarrassments: (1) it requires a statement and discussion so extended, that the public has neither the time nor the patience to follow them to the end; (2) it involves saying much that is harsh and harrowing to urbane natures, and much more quite unpresentable to decent ears or pure eyes. Hence there always remains of it, as of "the dark continent," a vast breadth and bulkiness unexplored and unknown, and an abysmal nastiness never fully uncovered or duly understood. By a skill of his own, our author has partially obviated these difficulties, and within the lids of a current volume has compressed a bold characterization and a perfectly convincing argument. Such is the nervous style, the cogent reasoning, the bow-like force of the cumulative evidence, that, though the points discussed be relatively few, and the argument comparatively brief, the irrevocable conclusion smites like a Trojan arrow, and unerringly pierces the Achilles' heel of the Papal Colossus.

The core of this work may be expressed in a single sentence: Rome's domineering imperialism, with Jesuitism its power behind the throne, together striving to centralize "all the powers on earth in the bosom of one master of souls": its essential incompatibility and inevitable unending antagonism with the Constitution and laws of our country, its relentless crusade against our public schools, its stealthy undoing of morality, and finally, its absolute irreconcilability with Protestantism — thus Romanism is irremediably hostile, politically and religiously, to our Republican Commonwealth.

Our author has an ideal temper and method for controversy; with indisputable facts, keen analysis, unimpeachable authorities, and irrefragable proofs, he advances exhaustively, never losing his rational balance, never stooping to invective nor tarrying to amuse: with sustained acumen and intensifying logical force, he bears down on the false and foreign system, and, like the mills of the gods, grinds to powder. Nor is the work impaired by any extravagance in statement or illustration, in form or coloring, in matters of fact, or in cases of opinion.

What is to-day observable and appreciable of Popery in its oldest realms and highest seats, even in its *sanctum sanctorum*, fully justifies the solemn indictment. After nearly eighteen years' residence in Rome, and familiar contact with Romanism throughout Italy, the writer bears witness that our author's testimony on all points is undeniably true. Perfectly true, indeed; but not yet the whole of the truth. The portraiture of Popery, found in her own records, and colored by her own hand, is darker, gloomier still.

The Canon Law, the undisputed, fundamental code of Romanism, is utterly incompatible with the Constitution and laws of our Republic, as witness the following leading provisions, gleaned therefrom by Dr. G. F. Von Schulte, Professor of Canonical Law at Prague, viz. : —

"I. All human power is from evil, and must therefore be standing under the Pope.

"II. The temporal powers must act unconditionally, in accordance with the orders of the spiritual.

"III. The Church is empowered to grant, or to take away, any temporal possession.

"IV. The Pope has the right to give countries and nations which are non-Catholic to Catholic regents, who can reduce them to slavery.

"V. The Pope can makes slaves of those Christian subjects whose prince or ruling power is interdicted by the Pope.

"VI. The laws of the Church, concerning the liberty of the Church and the Papal power, are based upon divine inspiration.

"VII. The Church has the right to practice the unconditional censure of books.

"VIII. The Pope has the right to annul State laws, treaties, constitutions, etc.; to absolve from obedience thereto, as soon as they seem detrimental to the rights of the Church, or those of the clergy.

"IX. The Pope possesses the right of admonishing, and, if needs be, of punishing the temporal rulers, emperors, and kings, as well as of drawing before the spiritual forum any case in which a mortal sin occurs.

"X. Without the consent of the Pope no tax or rate of any kind can be levied upon a clergyman, or upon any church whatsoever.

"XI. The Pope has the right to absolve from oaths, and obedience to the persons and the laws of the princes whom he excommunicates.

"XIII. The Pope can annul all legal relations of those in ban, especially their marriages.

"XIII. The Pope can release from every obligation, oath, vow, either before or after being made.

"XIV. The execution of Papal commands for the persecution of heretics causes remission of sins.

"XV. He who kills one that is excommunicated is no murderer in a legal sense."

After the above, as well expect concord between light and darkness, as between Romanism and the Republic. Yet the foregoing utterances are but a tithe of the like assumptions to be found in twenty folio volumes.

Within the last week Cardinal Gibbons of Baltimore has posed before the country as an advocate of religious toleration, and the press has made much of it far and wide. What swain-like simplicity! Now one of two things: either the Cardinal is sincere, and therefore antagonistic to the principles, traditions, and usages of his Church, and doomed finally to recant and reform; or he simply plays a part, winked at by the Pope, in order to ingratiate himself and his Church with the people, and to smooth the way for new encroachments. This dilemma is amply corroborated by the following paragraphs from the *Syllabus* of Pius IX., issued Dec. 8th, 1864, and subsequently by the Decree of Infallibility confirmed as truths eternal and equal in authority with the Decalogue, viz.:

"The State has not the right to leave every man free to profess and embrace whatever religion he shall deem true.

"It has not the right to enact that the ecclesiastical power shall require the permission of the civil power in order to the exercise of its authority.

"It has not the right to treat as an excess of power, or as usurping the rights of princes, anything that the Roman Pontiffs or Ecumenical Councils have done.

"It has not the right to adopt the conclusions of a National Church Council, unless confirmed by the Pope.

"It has not the right of establishing a National Church separate from the Pope.

"It has not the right to the entire direction of public schools.

"It has not the right to assist subjects who wish to abandon monasteries or convents."

Then in the same *Syllabus* the rights and powers of the Church are affirmed thus, viz. :

"She has the right to require the State not to leave every man free to profess his own religion.

"She has the right to exercise her power without the permission or consent of the State.

"She has the right to prevent the foundation of any National Church not subject to the authority of the Roman Pontiff.

"She has the right to deprive the civil authority of the entire government of public schools.

"She has the right of perpetuating the union of Church and State.

"She has the right to require that the Catholic religion shall be the only religion of the State, to the exclusion of all others.

"She has the right to prevent the State from granting the public exercise of their own worship to persons immigrating into it.

"She has the power of requiring the State not to permit free expression of opinion."

It is needless to say that the history of Romanism shows the oft-repeated application of all the foregoing claims and principles. The present Pontiff, Leo XIII., in a letter to the Bishop of Perigueux, July 27, 1884, explicitly confirms the foregoing, thus : "The teaching given by this Apostolic See, whether contained in the *Syllabus* and other Acts of our illustrious predecessor, or in our own *Encyclical Letters*, has given clear guidance to the faithful as to what should be their thoughts and their conduct in the midst of the difficulties of times and events. There they will find a rule for the direction of their minds and their works." Again, in his *Encyclical* of 1885, he approves the *Syllabus*, repudiates the idea that "each man should be allowed freely to think on whatever subject he pleases," and condemns any government in which "every one will be allowed to follow the religion he prefers."

Some years ago, Leo XIII. addressed an elaborate letter to three distinguished Cardinals of his Court, announcing his purpose soon to open to literary men the Vatican Library, on conditions to be established. Under cover of this rare token of papal liberality the Pope also invited their Eminences to take into consideration the having the history of the world re-written, since, as he alleged, the histories extant deal incorrectly and prejudicially with the history of the Church. The work was to be facilitated, and accuracy promoted, by the treasures the new historians would find in the manuscripts and tomes of the Vatican. The expulsion of Swinton's History from the Boston schools may be a sequence from the Pope's new criteria : others will follow. The Papacy, professedly in vicegerent command of mankind for fifteen centuries, has ever been making its own and guiding the world's history, filling the earth with protected fraternities of students, writers and copyists, making iniquisition into universal literature, changing and correcting much, destroying more by her *Index Expurgatorius*, condemning books and damning their authors, adorning the good with her imperial *imprimatur*, and their authors with academic degrees and patents of knighthood, burning wayward thinkers and writers at the stake with fagots of their own volumes, for ages stimulating and fostering, like a divine Mæcenas, the best genius of the Church, and magisterially dominating the pen as the sword and the sceptre, and after all is still unhappy of her achievement and of the writing that is written. Alas, alike for fallible history and infallible Pope ! The new pontifical proposal is a mystery of cunning and courage. The opening of the library was a delusion ; the recast history will remain a project. Both are signs not to be forgotten. Leo XIII. sees Romanism condemned by history; more still is it by the gospel and civilization.

The momentous, the perilous fact is the public indifference to the insidious advances and encroachments of this despotic and mighty medievalism. While it is quietly interweaving itself with the national life, and strategically preparing the basis for its future self assertion, contentious action and usurpations, almost no one takes heed or offers a serious obstruction. Were any one indeed openly and vigorously to controvert its character, its progress and grasping for power, among the Catholic population of our large cities, the result would be mob violence. There, and on this question, free speech is the ante-war free speech south of Mason and Dixon's line. The new thraldom, like the old bondage, requires to be let alone. The public peril is neglected for personal aims. Pride, pleasure and luxury, like a leash of hounds, bay on the heels of gratification. Vanity parades, ambition climbs, business hastes to be rich. The press panders, the politicians trim, the preachers doze : the priests sow tares. The country drifts, drifts, and drifts. Meanwhile duty commands every voice to cry aloud and spare not, the pen and the press to unite in impetuous sustained appeal, enforced by the priceless interests of our imperilled civil and religious liberties and institutions. When the Jesuit assassin stabbed Fra Paolo Sarpi of Venice, to end his too liberal and evangelical writing, and fled, leaving his weapon sticking in the wound, Sarpi himself plucked the bribed stiletto from his flesh, and holding it aloft, said : "The pen of the Papacy !" Contrariwise the pen is the sword of Protestantism, civil and religious, for holy war against Popery. "Awake, O sword, against" the deceiver and the destroyer ; "put up thyself into thy scabbard" only when the people are delivered by knowledge ; recognizing that ROMANISM AND THE REPUBLIC are irreconcilable opposites; that the Tiara and our starry Banner are divorced as the poles, incongruous as the Roman wolf and the American eagle.

LEROY M. VERNON.

Syracuse, N. Y., April 30th, 1889.

ROMANISM AND THE REPUBLIC.

Sermon I.

REASONS FOR CONSIDERING THE RELATION OF ROMANISM TO THE REPUBLIC.

"Again the word of the Lord came unto me, saying: Son of man, speak to the children of thy people, and say unto them, When I bring the sword upon a land, if the people of the land take a man of their coasts, and set him for their watchman; If when he seeth the sword come upon the land, he blow the trumpet and warn the people; Then whosoever heareth the sound of the trumpet and taketh not warning, if the sword come and take him away, his blood shall be upon his own head. He heard the sound of the trumpet and took not warning, his blood shall be upon him. But he that taketh warning shall deliver his soul. But if the watchman see the sword come, and blow not the trumpet, and the people be not warned; If the sword come, and take any person from among them, he is taken away in his iniquity: but his blood will I require at the watchman's hand."— EZEKIEL 33: 1-6.

The picture in this text is better understood in Eastern lands than it can be in this country. Many cities there are located on lofty heights, from which a wide survey can be made of the surrounding country. They are so located for purposes of defence ; for where enemies are likely to come in like a flood, and wandering hordes to make sudden incursions, such situations are highly favorable to safety. The watchman, placed on the walls, scans the country far and wide, and marks every sign which would suggest the presence of a coming foe. A cloud of smoke in the distance, rolling up from burning villages, attracts his watchful eye. The dust which rises above the plain, marking the march of an advancing host, is to him an occasion for alarm. The glint of the sunshine on distant, moving weapons, leads him to call the defenders to their posts, and the throng of terrified villagers, fleeing from their homes to find protection under the walls of the town, alike attests the need of watchfulness, and confirms and justifies his warning.

He does not wait until the foemen are thundering at the gates, before he announces to the garrison the danger that threatens. Should he do so, he might justly be judged a traitor, in the pay of the enemy.

So, when God's watchman, guarding the dearest interests of church and state, sees rising from other lands the clouds of desolation which betoken the ruin wrought by tyranny; when he marks the steady aggression of the enemies of truth and man; hears their threatenings and sees their weapons; when he observes the fleeing millions who, running away from oppression, seek in our freer government a refuge from their tyrants, he cannot wait until the foot of the foeman is on the threshold of our gates, his hand on our throats, and his decrees proclaimed in our market-places, before he sounds the alarm.

It is his duty to give the warning of approaching danger seen afar, and thus to protect the liberties over which he watches, rather than delay to sound his call to stand on guard, until these priceless treasures are forever lost. Such I conceive to be the duty of the Christian minister who observes the doings of the Romish church in other lands, the principles which have moved it, the methods which it has pursued, and the threats, already taking form, which it is making against the Protestant Christianity and the free government of the United States of America. Our responsibility is not merely to the present hour, but to coming ages and future times,— to those generations yet to be, who must now be protected in our persons, and defended by our fidelity. In warning you of the spirit and aggressions of Romanism, I naturally seek to justify my purpose by reasons which I submit to your calm consideration and enlightened judgment.

Why do I consider this subject? and why do I deem it my duty to God and to man, to the present and to the future, to bring this matter to the attention of this congregation and community?

1. Among the negative reasons why I consider ROMANISM AND THE REPUBLIC the first is this: I do not do it to incite religious animosity. The various branches of the Christian Church should cultivate amity, peace and brotherhood. We cannot too earnestly deprecate the spirit which awakens needless religious contention against bodies which hold approximately the common faith.

But, on the other hand, shall religion be a cloak for confessed evils, forbidding us to take account of them because they assume a religious covering? Under the pretence of religion, the grossest crimes have been committed against the state, against society, and against the faith. It ought not to shelter the immoralities of Mormonism, that Mormonism is defined as a system of religious belief. Is polygamy any more moral because it affects to be a religious ordinance and duty? By no means. Romanism can claim for its policy no exemption from attention or censure because it is a religion, any more than can any other ism.

If it is true that under the guise of the religion of Romanism a great conspiracy against liberty and truth is sheltered, it is simply fidelity to the highest obligations, and not religious animosity, that leads us to tear away the veil and show the designs which threaten our country's welfare and the progress of mankind.

2. Neither do I consider this subject in order to excite religious prejudice against any church or class of citizens. Fraternity, peace, goodwill, and a disposition to abide by rules of fairness, should animate all our relations toward our fellow-men, either in the church or state. But prejudice is the offspring of thoughtlessness and ignorance. When truth demands that we should take a strongly antagonistic attitude toward any evil, that attitude cannot be spoken of as the result of prejudice. I purpose rather to diminish prejudice by increasing intelligence; I would throw light on the methods of the Romish church, on its history and its intentions; I would cause those who are now ignorantly prejudiced to become intelligently opposed; and so would

dissipate, rather than create, intolerant and ignorant antagonism.

3. Certainly, it is far from my intention, in this discussion, to arouse or increase religious bigotry—that spirit which assumes that none are Christians except ourselves, which regards all others as in the wrong, which cannot see or tolerate anything outside of the narrow line of its own denomination. Of bigotry there is already too much, and I would that it might diminish till there were none remaining. But by this I do not mean to suggest that all creeds and opinions are equally true, nor to debar us from the definition and defence of our principles. Nor are dangerous ideas and practices in the province of religion to be exempt from examination, any more than dangerous ideas in morals or in politics. Bigotry may be increased by superstition, and often has been fostered by forbidding free discussion; but the diffusion of information on matters of common concern, in a fair spirit and by the citation of undoubted authorities, cannot nurse bigotry.

4. Still less do I discuss the subject of ROMANISM AND THE REPUBLIC in order to awaken controversy for the sake of mere controversy. We are taught in the Holy Scriptures to " follow peace with all men ;" and yet are bidden to " contend earnestly for the faith that was once delivered to the saints." There are worse evils than controversy, much as acrimonious disputation is to be deprecated. The nation that is not ready to contend for its liberties hardly deserves them, and will surely lose them. The church

which values truth so lightly that it will not in defence of the same put forth the utmost argument and persuasion, creating enlightenment by the championship of truth and the challenging of error, will soon cease to be respected, and will presently cease to respect itself.   While, therefore, I neither fear nor court controversy, and certainly do not desire to awaken it for its own sake, I would gladly welcome it in behalf of truth, if thereby the clouds might be dissipated and the dangers averted which hang over and threaten our beloved country.   And I may add, that this was the spirit of early Christianity in the primitive church.   The Epistles to the Galatians, to the Colossians and to the Corinthians, are controversial epistles, defending the Gospel, protecting the church, challenging false teachers, and assailing immoral and ungodly doctrine.   The spirit of biblical controversy is the spirit which we would cultivate, and the endeavor we make is made with the same intent.   Far be it from me to dispute the genuine piety and the deep devotion of many of the adherents of the church of Rome.   I shall not assume that its members at large, and its priests in general, knowingly hold and propagate error.   But because it demands universal and absolute allegiance, I am bound to examine the basis of its claims, before I accept or reject them.   You and I are willing that Presbyterians shall be Presbyterians, that Methodists shall be Methodists, that Episcopalians shall be Episcopalians, and so on of all Christians whose faith is a biblical faith.   And they are equally willing that we shall be Congregationalists. But Rome recognizes only heresy in every form of religion but its own; demands universal submission; endeavors to incite the fiercest hatred against all other forms of belief, and strives to overpower and destroy, by all her vast and mighty machinery, and by the anathemas of the pope, the persecution of the civil power, and the horrors of the Inquisition, which they still justify, if they cannot practice.

Before proceeding further, I desire to answer a question that may arise in your minds, why I speak on ROMANISM AND THE REPUBLIC, instead of upon Catholicism and the Republic. The reason is very clear, and one that should ever be kept in mind. I say Romanism, instead of Catholicism, because the Romish church is not the Catholic church. What is the Catholic church? The meaning of the term determines. Catholic means general, universal, the one all-embracing church. It includes all who hold to our Lord Jesus Christ in sincerity and truth. Every Christian on the face of the earth belongs to the Catholic church; but, thank God! not to the Romish church. You are Catholics because you are Christians. The devoted worshipper of the Lord Jesus in any denomination is a Catholic, because a Christian. But Rome is not the universal church; Romanism is the Latin church, a branch of the church of Christ, we may allow, but not the whole, as she falsely and impudently claims. To the arrogance of that claim, it is extremely foolish and weak for us to bow.

I shall never call them Catholic, only as I would say Methodist Catholic, Congregational Catholic, because they are not Catholics, and I advise you to more carefully define the true Catholic idea, and to call Romanism by its right name.

Secondly — I call them Romanists because they are the Roman church. Its headship is at Rome; the ruler whom it regards as infallible, who presides over and directs it with absolute authority, is an Italian by residence, a Roman, and a foreigner. And not merely is its head a Roman, but, moreover, the church is essentially Italian, and has been for centuries, in the preponderance of governing ideas, in the policy which shapes its course, in the diplomacy of its management. Sometimes, and justly, it is called Ultra montane, which, centuries ago meant, as it now means, a church governed by priests who find their homes south of the Alps. We need only to appeal to the history of the Romish church, to demonstrate the entire suitability of defining it as Romanism in its relation to the Republic, and its relation to the world; though the time is coming when to keep that name even, modern, regenerated Rome, will demand that it become a regenerated church.

Having thus cleared the way, and negatively defined my purpose, having also defined distinctly the Romish church as non-Catholic, I now desire to give you positive and direct reasons why I take up this discussion, and as a watchman who is responsible to God, to the church, to the Republic

and to the world, ask your attention to the threatening attitude and dangerous assumptions of Romanism
in our country. 1.Why do I not take up and consider the relation of other churches to the Republic?
That would be appropriate, if there were anything in
their relation startling, threatening, or especially
suggestive; but no such fact in their history exists.
The attitude of the Romish church toward the
Republic is totally different from that of any other
church.   Suppose the inquiry were raised, What is
the attitude of the Baptist church toward the Republic?   The instant and universal answer from all
Christian denominations would be, The Baptist
church is an essential and thoroughly loyal portion
of the nation.   If the question were raised, What is
the attitude of Methodism toward the Republic? we
should at once reply, that Methodism was a constitu-
ent and vital part of the life of the Republic, loyal to
the core to the principles of American liberty.

But we consider Romanism in its relation to the
Republic, rather than any of the other churches,
because its attitude is well known to be questionable,
doubtful, and, as we shall show, hostile.

2.   It acknowledges as its head a ruler who claims
the right to dictate to all rulers; who insists on his
supremacy over and above all civil powers, executive and legislative;   and who holds this theory of
his own powers, not as a theory merely, but who for
centuries has carried it out in practice, to the utmost
limits of his ability.   Every Roman Catholic dignitary, from the Pope down to the Bishop, by creed

and by oath, recognizes the Pope with an allegiance superior to that which he pays to any other power. And if the Romish power is not at present in avowed hostility, in open antagonism to the government of the United States, it is only because it chooses at present to be pacific; while really, as I shall show hereafter, holding an attitude of unqualified supremacy over us in its claims and in its purposes.

I have already said that Rome claims the right to control civil governments as no other church does. This claim of the Papacy I shall hereafter define in its own words. Recent and remarkable illustrations of this claim, in actual practice, are now before your minds. It is within the past year that, under the sanction of the Roman Catholic clergy, members of the English Parliament in this city have been honored with processions and public meetings, while they expatiated to the people on the wrongs and woes of Ireland, and the desire of the people for Home Rule, and explained the plans by which they hoped to achieve it. Vast sums of money have been collected to further their designs, and the plans of campaign on which they were working, well-known throughout all the land, received general and enthusiastic approval. But lo! a few weeks since, under the manipulations of diplomatists at Rome, there has issued from the Vatican a rescript, as it is called, of Leo XIII, condemning the action of the clergy, the agitator, the statesman and members of parliament, and forbidding them to further the civil policy which they have heretofore pursued for the emancipation of

Ireland from English rule. What is the result? A murmur of resistance and disapprobation from a few bishops and archbishops; a fiery protest from a few leading agitators: and behold! immediately following, almost absolute and universal submission! Archbishops, bishops, and clergy, statesmen, orators, agitators, all, under the threat of Roman displeasure, quietly submit to the dictation of the Pope. Now the question is not whether their methods of civil procedure were right; or whether the Pope, in censuring them, is on the right side of this political controversy. The real question is simply this: Has the Pope the right, has he the power to dictate to Roman Catholics in Ireland and America and throughout the world, what shall be their political methods, and how they shall plan and execute their political campaigns? I feel called upon at this juncture, in the name of liberty and manhood, to protest in favor of the protection of Romanists against the interference and domination of the Pope.

A farther illustration, in a more individual case and in the realm of personal opinion, of the practical interference of the Papacy in the civil allegiance of its subjects, is had in the case of Dr. McGlynn. Months ago, on the platform of a public meeting, I saw this distinguished priest of the Roman Catholic church. Modest and affable in his bearing, eloquent in his words, and vigorous and free in his thoughts, he seemed to me at the time to be a representative of the best element in the Roman Catholic church. Subsequent to that time, acting

within his undoubted rights as a citizen, guaranteed
to him by the constitution and the laws, he chose to
further certain political ideas which seemed to him in
harmony with sound principle. Forthwith, this citizen of America is cited to appear in Rome to answer
for his political opinions. He dreads to go, knowing too well the means which the mother-church
employs to secure the subordination of such of her
sons as dare to think for themselves. Declining to
go, and only affirming his rights as a free American citizen, he is put under the ban of his superiors
and deprived of the church for which he had labored
and sacrificed so heroically, and to-day is an outcast
priest, solely and only because he chose to adhere
to his own private judgment in matters secular and
political. If the Romish church, by rescript, can
destroy the political plans of Irish leaders, if by con-
sure it can dictate political views to one of its distinguished priests in America, obviously, it both
claims and exercises the right to the same jurisdiction in every country and in every case.

3. The third reason why I consider the relations
of ROMANISM AND THE REPUBLIC is, that Romanism
hates and fiercely attacks institutions especially dear
to us in this country, and which have been associated with all its prosperity from the beginning of our
history. Our fathers believed that public education
was essential to sound political and social morality;
and alongside the church, and as its offspring, they
planted the public school. This system of public
education has made, of those who come under its

benign influence, the most enlightened citizens of the most enlightened state in the world ; and it may be truly said, that the results of public education in the United States furnish one of the most striking illustrations of the wisdom of the founders of our government.   But Rome is the sworn foe of our public schools.   The most violent language in opposition to them is used, under the sanction of her prelates, by her writers, secular and clerical.   Not only in America, but in Ireland, where the British government has tried to diffuse the benefits of public education, they exhibit the same hostility.

The national schools of Ireland, carefully abstaining from giving religious instruction, but affording facilities for such instruction at designated hours, according to the preference of the parents, have been met by the fiercest antagonism on the part of the Roman power.

Great was my surprise, when a distinguished and highly educated Roman Catholic assured me that, in his opinion, it were better that the children of Ireland should grow up in densest ignorance, rather than that they should attempt to get their education in the national schools.   The determined efforts of Rome to undermine our public school system are already bearing apparent fruit.   Undertaking to falsify history, in order to build up ecclesiasticism, but recently they have demanded and have secured the explusion of certain histories from the public schools of Boston, and the dismissal of a teacher who dared to teach something contrary to their supremacy and to their preferences. In a Connecticut city, not long since, one of the young lady teachers in the High School, having, in a historical exercise, stated that the Roman Catholic church just prior to the Reformation sold indulgences, which encouraged the people to commit sin, was only able to retain her place as teacher in the school by signing a retraction or apology prepared by a Roman Catholic priest!

Has it comes to this, that the Romish church shall dictate that only such books shall be studied in our public schools as comport with her opinion of herself, and her desire to establish a universal tyranny? And are we, the offspring of the English Reformers, to bend the knee and yield? God forbid!

Remember, freemen, and Protestants of America, that where Rome has had the privilege of educating the people, more illiteracy prevails, in proportion to the population, than in any other European state. The Roman states, Italy and Spain, in their abjectness and almost universal ignorance, bear witness to this fact. Liberty of conscience and freedom of the press, dear and precious privileges of American freemen, have been pronounced by the highest authority of the Romish church, a pest and a delirium, and the Romish church, when the Pope says that, is bound to believe it, as if it were the very word of God. Surely, if these priceless privileges of conscience and discussion are of right free, we cannot too soon start up in resistance to the power which denies that freedom, and would put us in bondage to the blasphemous assumptions of mediæval tyranny.

4. My fourth reason for considering Romanism in its relation to the Republic is, that in the Romish Church is so large a portion of the criminal and dangerous classes. A distinguished ex-priest, Leon Bouland, in the July number of the *Forum*, calls our attention to the fact that, in the city of New York, probably seventy-five per cent. of the criminals are members and adherents to the Romish Catholic Church. And yet some of you, being kindly disposed, will say : Does not the Romish Church exercise a restraining influence over these dangerous classes, and, is not that influence beneficial in helping the community to keep such people in subjection? It may be true, we will not deny it, that the Romish Church has some power of restraint over these dangerous classes ; but will you not also bear in mind that the attitude of the Romish Church toward these people makes it almost impossible for Protestants to get near them, in order to teach them morality and improve their condition? She takes the whole responsibility for them. And mark this : these people who constitute our dangerous and criminal classes in America, are the offspring of those communities where Romanism for centuries has had an absolute sway. They come from countries where this church has dominated their ancestors for many generations with unresisted authority. They are, to that degree, the product of Romanism. Moreover, it ought not to be forgotten that the church which makes and which controls so large a proportion of the desperate people of society, holds over them such an absolute sway from superstition,

the dread of excommunication, and from prejudice, that she can handle them at her will, and by that means make them her agents and instruments for whatever work she chooses to set them about. I have not said that the Romish Church desires or will launch this terrific enginery against the life of the nation. The probability of that you shall determine later, when we have more carefully studied its principles. But I do say, that this army of the immoral, the dangerous and the criminal, is so abjectly under the power of Rome, and so sworn to obedience to the Pope, that if she shall choose to direct them in any course, they, on their part, are likely to obey. Will she so choose?

5. In answer, in the fifth place, I beg you to remember, that already Rome acts in this country as a political unit. These dangerous elements, with all other elements of the Papal power, in their civil capacity, are wielded by the church as an adjunct of a single political party. You and I allow the right of every man to select his political party, and to vote as he pleases; but is it not a singular fact, that the Romish Church alone, of all the churches, is politically solid? The other great political party in this country has tried to secure the allegiance of a portion of the Roman Catholic voters, but has tried with indifferent and ill success. They who manipulate the Romish vote do not intend to have it divided. They care nothing for the party with which it acts, nothing for the opposite party, nothing for America, save as it can be made the tool of the

Papacy ; and in directing this vast body of voters, do not forget that they handle them solely and only in the interest of Jesuitism, and of the purpose of the Roman Catholic hierarchy. The Romanists of America will obey the orders that come from Rome in every political action, precisely as the Romanists of Ireland and America have obeyed the Papal rescript recently issued. At least, precedent awakens our fear that such will be their course. This dangerous element, wielded as a political power, already has produced most startling conditions of municipal government in most of the great cities. They either hold the balance of power, or already constitute the the majority, in many city governments ; and they work with an adroitness and statesmanship whose purpose is as dangerous as its patience is marvelous.

6. The sixth reason why I discuss this subject is, that already the dangers which I have alleged in the fourth and fifth reasons, are very obviously at hand.

The power of the Papacy as a political force is already seen in our cities, not merely in the government of the municipality, nor in the blows which they are dealing at the public schools ; but in those open violations of the constitution of the several states and of the United States, which they have extorted from time-serving legislators, and from trembling and subservient politicians. The constitutions of most of our states forbid the appropriation on the part of the state to any sect of public moneys for its emolument or use. No religious society can justly receive, under the constitution, the public funds for its up-building and the propagation of its ideas. But this wholesome and necessary law has been so evaded, that in the city of New York the Roman Catholic Church has grasped millions of the public money. Its vast cathedral property, now occupied by one of the most magnificent churches in America, was obtained for a mere song; and it had gained, as I shall hereafter show in detail, for specifically Romanistic institutions, prior to 1870, millions of dollars from the public treasury. Already, wise and careful publicists have told us that we might look for the time when Roman Catholics will demand a division of the school fund, so that a part of it may be appropriated for the support of their parochial schools, now rapidly being founded throughout the entire country under express orders from Rome. Do you smile at this fear? Do you say, It is impossible that the time should ever come when the constitution and the principles of the states of the American Union should ever be so violated? But already the attempt has been made in our own Commonwealth. And, mark my words! the time is sure to come, and that ere long, when Romanism will have the public school moneys of our commonwealths divided, and a large share appropriated, contrary to the law and to the constitution, to their denominational institutions, *unless* freemen arouse and protect the treasuries on which they already have begun to make attacks.

I will give you two more reasons why I consider it necessary, as a conscientious watchman and defender of the liberties of the church and of the country, to consider ROMANISM AND THE REPUBLIC.

7. My seventh reason is, that the leaders of the church, a celibate priesthood and without family ties, acknowledge an allegiance to a foreign ruler superior to the United States; and are ready at his command to abjure all other fealty. We cannot overlook the peculiarity of the Roman Catholic priesthood. It tends, contrary to nature and the law of God, to debase social morality. When the iron hand of the Papacy struck down the home of the priest by forbidding the priests to marry, it was that she might secure their more absolute allegiance to the church. Without domestic ties or obligations, they look for their advancement and joys solely to the Papal power. Against the hardships of this unnatural edict there have been many protests, amounting almost to rebellion, within the Roman Catholic Church. Again and again, consequent upon observation of the damaging effects of enforced celibacy upon the morality of the church and of the priesthood, have its more enlightened members prayed and petitioned that this heavy burden might be taken from them, but up to this hour have protested in vain. We cannot appeal to history without being most certain that a celibate priesthood, as a class, has never held to high morality. And when we come to speak of the evils of this celibacy in its relation to the confessional — when we survey, from our standpoint of abundant though most painful revelations, the relation which these wifeless and childless men bear to society — you will be forced to acknowledge that they are made, by their very po-

sition and its demands, a constant menace to society
in its highest and dearest interests; as also, to a
remarkable degree, by their moral relations, the more
subservient tools of the Papal power.

8. The final reason which I present as demanding this
discussion, is that the wisest statesmen see in
Romanism and its claim, a source of great national
peril.   I can quote at this time only two or three of
them.   That distinguished son of France, himself a
member of the Gallican Catholic church, who gave
more to our country during the Revolution than any
other foreigner, who assisted in laying the foundation
of our liberties, and who is honored wherever the
American Republic is known, the Marquis de la
Fayette, said, long ago: "If the liberties of the
American people are ever destroyed, it will be by the
hands of the Roman clergy." This saying, uttered
when the Roman church was weak and small in
America, and when it seemed to threaten no disaster,
is all the more significant from the wide knowledge
and careful observation of the statesman who uttered
it.   He had seen the power of Romanism as it had
operated against the liberties of France; he knew the
strength of the hand that controlled the priests and
the people; and observing the ruinous consequences
of Papal absolutism, and the despotic way of the
Roman Curia in other lands, he anticipated that a
country so fair as this, and destined to so great
development, would become the chosen nation for the
assault of these hateful powers that had beaten back
progress in the Old World.   The most eminent

English statesman of our time, who will rank with
the greatest public men of any age and any land,
Gladstone, says : " The Pope demands for himself the
right to determine the province of his own rights, and
has so defined it in formal documents as to warrant
any and every invasion of the civil sphere . . . . .
Rome requires a convert who joins her, to forfeit his
moral and mental freedom, and to place his loyalty
and civil duty at the mercy of another." Prince
Bismarck, in a speech delivered April 16, 1875, said :
" This Pope, this foreigner, this Italian, is more
powerful in this country than any other person, not
excepting even the king. And now please to consider what this foreigner has announced as the pro-
gramme by which he rules Prussia and elsewhere.
He begins by taking to himself the right to define
how far his authority extends ; and this Pope, who
would employ fire and sword against us if he had the
power to do so, who would confiscate our property
and not spare our lives, expects us to allow him full,
uncontrolled sway." So speak the mightest statesmen of our age, and shall we not hear these warning
voices? and shall we not interpret the movements of
the Romish prelates in America on the basis of their
own vows, and according to the developments of
their plans in other lands? Can we anticipate a
brighter future for America, under the Papal tyranny,
than could have been anticipated for Spain, for Italy,
for France, for Portugal? No. The highest duty
and obligation which we recognize as Christians —
our duty to God who holds us responsible for the

preservation of our glorious heritage received from our fathers — every consideration of private right and public weal, all demand, that at a time of such great peril, we should turn aside from our customary over-sanguine hopes and optimistic views of America's certain future, to consider how we can reproduce, in time to come, the unequaled glories of the past, and against the rule of the most to be dreaded of foreign foes, maintain in the future a church without a tyrannous Papal bishop, and a state without a king.

Sermon II.

THE JESUITS AND THEIR PURPOSE.

"Watch ye, stand fast in the faith, quit you like men, be strong." — 1 Cor. 16: 13.

"If the trumpet give an uncertain sound, who shall prepare himself for the battle?" The clarion voice of our text, in the vigor with which it calls upon us to be watchful, steadfast, manly and strong, stirs our souls. They misunderstand the Scriptures who suppose that words like these apply only to the smaller details of our personal life. On the contrary, these directions have the widest range and application, defining our duty and attitude toward the great movements in which we bear a part, and on which world-wide consequences depend. "Watch ye," be alert, vigilant, observant, "stand fast in the faith," "contend earnestly for the faith once delivered unto the saints," be unyielding, adamantine in resistance, to error, "stand like a rock, and the storm and battle little shall harm you in doing their worst;" quit you like men" in active work for God and his truth; "be strong;" the result of watchfulness, steadfastness in the faith, manliness in action, is personal strength and individual power, which you should always cultivate and display. Such, in brief, is the general doctrine of the text.

In its application to the hidden and open conspir-acy of Romanism against the doctrines of God and the liberty of American Christians — the position which we should hold for the protection of our dear-est rights — no words could be more significant. " Eternal vigilance is the price of liberty," therefore " watch," lest, unexpectedly, some enemy shall take away the privileges which most you prize. " Stand fast in the faith," hold strongly, kindly, firmly, the princples of Scriptural truth and of political freedom, which, together, are the principles of Protestantism. Do not feebly consent to lose your liberties, but " quit you like men ;" and, while without the bigot's animosity, maintain the freeman's determined front. For the sake of yourselves, your country, the church, your children, " be strong," indomitable.

In the personal application of this great exhorta-tion for the government of our conduct, we cannot really perceive or understand the menace of Roman-ism, unless we review the history of the past as well as attentively survey the present. You all are some-what familiar with the facts of the great Reformation in the sixteenth century. In our blind optimism, we are inclined to believe that our liberties are secure, that our present advantages can never be for-feited, forgetful of the fact that God sometimes per-mits the hands of progress to be turned back upon the dial of history, as he permitted Rome in the century of which we speak, to weld again the fetters which the Reformation had broken, and fasten them for centuries more upon the prostrate nations.

The beginning of the sixteenth century saw the Roman Catholic church predominant over all religious, civil and social life throughout Europe. The Holy Roman Empire, with its emperor, was in subjection to the Pope of Rome. The civil rulers bowed at the footstools of the Papal power, trembled at its threats, and accepted its dictation. The leading ecclesiastic of Germany, Albert, Archbishop of Mentz, afterward cardinal, having boldly purchased his office at a great price, reimbursed himself, and poured money into the Papal treasury by securing the monopoly of the sale of indulgences, of which Tetzel was the agent and auctioneer. The priests, largely corrupted in morals and careless of the welfare of the people, were willing that the flock should be plundered, provided the spoil went into the treasury of the church. Even the Jesuit Favre, at the Diet at Worms, testified that the priests were guilty of grievous crimes. The people, shrouded in dark superstition, ignorant of the Holy Scriptures, and enslaved by their ecclesiastical masters, were still deemed worth plundering, and were yielding up their wealth to enrich the Papal court south of the Alps. That court was more interested in the revival of polite and classical learning and in gratifying its vices, than in spreading the Gospel of God. Then, when the times were ripe, Luther arose, and nailed to the door of the old church in Wittenberg those ninety-five immortal theses which became the text and proclamation of the great Reformation. The ring of his hammer startled

the Pope on his throne, and all the Roman ecclesiastics throughout the world.   Rapidly the Reformation spread throughout Germany and the northern nations, through England, Scotland, Denmark,
Sweden, Livonia, the Palatinate and part of Switzerland.   France became also penetrated with the
new doctrine; even Spain, Portugal, Italy, were
moved thereby; while it seemed that Bavaria, Hungary, Bohemia and Poland were likely to follow the
example of others in denying the assumptions of the
Pope, and accepting the word of God, rather than
the traditions of men.   "Within fifty years of the
day when Luther publicly renounced communion
with Rome," says Lord Macaulay, "Protestantism
attained its highest ascendancy, an ascendancy which
it soon lost; and which it never regained." (This
was written in 1840.)   Then arose a counter movement in the south of Europe, a reformation of
methods and of discipline in the church of Rome.
In two generations, a powerful reaction had confirmed the supremacy of the Papacy in all the uncertain territory, and France, Spain, Italy, Poland,
Hungary and Bohemia became the servile dependents
of Romanism, and so remained for nearly three
hundred years.

This counter movement in the Romish church, by
which it held almost undisputed power over these
nations for more than three centuries, is due, more
than to any other agency, to Ignatius Loyola, and the
Jesuit society of which he was the founder. The power
of this organization within the Romish church,—

an organization which through many vicissitudes is still intact, and is to-day the very core of Romanism in its principles and its policy, — claims our attention, and must be studied in its purposes and its methods, in order that we may be informed of the intentions and claims of Romanism in the United States, and that we may properly guard and protect our country against the destruction plotted against us by a sleepless and cruel foe. It is impossible to understand the Romish church of to-day or of the past three hundred years, without a knowledge of the Jesuits and their influence in the church ; and it is equally impossible to clearly apprehend the Jesuit doctrines and purposes, unless we know something of their founder. I therefore beg your attention for a little, to some facts which throw light upon the history of Ignatius Loyola, first general of the Jesuits, who created the organization, formulated its constitution, directed its beginnings, and infused into it his spirit.

1. Ignatius Loyola was born in 1491, in the north of Spain, of the family of Loyola, who were among the grandees of that country. He early became a page at the court of Ferdinand the Catholic, and was distinguished as a gallant and a courtier. He had for his dulcinea, as he tells us, " not a duchess nor a countess, but one of higher rank," and was distinguished in court at joust and tournament as one of the brave warriors and handsome courtiers of the day. At twenty-nine years of age, when the French troops of Francis I. poured over the border, Loyola was present in the little city of Pampeluna, to which

they laid siege. The governor and commander of the city resolved to yield it up. Loyola protested with vigor, secured the assistance of a single soldier, and throwing himself into the citadel, desperately resolved to defend it to the last. A few more joined him, and in their desperate resistance, while bravely fighting on the wall, Loyola was struck down by missiles which broke one of his legs. He was carried to his ancestral home and laid upon a bed of suffering. The imperfect surgery of the time, after inflicting exquisite torture, which he bravely endured, at length left one of his legs shorter than the other, destroying his fitness for the court and military exercises. At this time, while heroically suffering, lying on a sick bed, and aware that he was maimed for life, there was put into his hands a book called the " Lives of the Saints," and some simple pictorial life of Christ. Reading the " Lives of the Saints," this disappointed cavalier began to revolve in his mind visions of another knighthood in the service of the church. " Why cannot I do for the church what St. Dominic and St. Francis did?" he said. And then and there, his imagination picturing to him the glories of such a service, he devoted himself to the service of Our Lady and of the Church.

Romanist historians delight to tell how at this time St. Peter appeared and cured him of a fever; and how, praying, he saw the Virgin Mother and the Child. They also tell of an earthquake rending the walls of his room, while the rest of the castle was not shaken. Loyola's resolution was now taken;

he would become a monk; and having recovered a
degree of health, he mounted his steed and started
for the neighboring convent of Montserrat. It
shows the fierce temper of the man, that while on
his way to the convent, he overtook a Moor, with
whom he disputed about the virginity of the blessed
Mother. The Moor admitted that she was such
before the birth of the Christ, but denied that she
was afterward. The debate waxed warm, and the
Moor parted from Loyola and galloped forward.
Loyola following, resolved that if his mule, on whose
neck he laid the reins, should follow the road which
the Moor had taken, he would assail the infidel, and
stab him to the heart. Fortunately the animal took
the other road up the mountain, and Loyola was
saved the guilt of fanatical and vengeful murder.
Arriving at the convent, he gave his rich clothing to
a beggar, taking the beggar's rags in exchange,
retaining only his jewelled dagger and sword. These
he hung up before the image of Our Lady, and
through a long night, as did the ancient knights, in
vigil, devoted himself to the service of his mistress.
Next day he goes to the hospital, not far off, where,
thirsting for humility and suffering, he performs the
most menial and disgusting services for the sick.
No service was too shocking for him. But being
annoyed by those who recognized him as a noble, he
departs from the hospital, and betakes himself to the
horrible and lonely cave of Manresa, in which he
spends two years. Here he has unspeakable agony
of mind, starves himself almost to death, and sees

visions, alternately threatening and consoling. Here, at this time, he composed the only writings, with the exception of a few letters, which he wrote during his life ; the first work, A Manual of Spiritual Exercises for the creation of that society of which he afterward became the founder ; the second work, The Constitution and Rules by which that society should be governed. Filled with a visionary purpose of converting Oriental nations, he starts, at the age of thirty-one, for Palestine, begging his way. Arriving there, he is forced to return by the authorities of the church, there being no place for him. Once more in Spain, and having seen the need of education for the work which he desired to do, at thirty-three years of age he goes to school, and sitting on the bench beside little boys, studies the Latin language. About this time he is said to have seen the Holy Trinity in a vision, to have witnessed also the very fact of transubstantiation by which the bread is changed to the body of Christ in the mass, to have beheld the soul of a friend who died taken visibly to the heavens, and, still more wonderful, he is said, in a vision, to have been taught more of natural science than falls to the lot of most men to know. The Romanist biographers seriously tell how he was raised bodily from the ground while at prayer, cured incurables by a touch, and much more of the same sort. Two years later, he goes to the University of Alcala, later still to Salamanca, and at thirty-eight years of age, following an inward voice, to the University of Paris.

He is here distinguished for the intensity of his devotion, more than for any scholarly ability. At forty-four, he took his degree in philosophy, at the University of Paris. But meanwhile, steadily pursuing his purpose to found a society, he gathers its nucleus in the person of Xavier, Laynez, Bobadilla and two or three others, who, with mutual vows, resolve that they will obey the constitutions which he has formulated. Leaving Paris they go to Rome together, he seeing more visions on the way, and in 1540, after earnest solicitations of the Pope, when Loyola is forty-nine years of age, the society of Jesuits is formed. Loyola forsook all his family connections when he entered Montserrat, and with them he held scarcely any communication afterward. He left his native country, for which he never seems to have cherished further regard; abandoned, in fact, all human friends. For, though he inspired wonderful devotedness in men to his ideas, he seems never to have had a friend; unless in the person of one or two women, who followed him with almost superstitious devotion,— one of whom formed a religious house near that of the Jesuits in Rome.

I note these particulars, that you may see the character of the man, because it is reflected in his society. He is a typical Romish Ecclesiastic and Jesuit.

How different the typical Protestant, as seen in the character of Martin Luther. Born in 1483, Martin Luther at twelve attends school at Magdeburg; at fourteen goes to Eisenach, and is soon distinguished for skill in music, eloquence, and philosophy; at eighteen he enters the University at Erfurt, and becomes bachelor and master of arts at twenty-two; at twenty-five is selected, on account of his great ability and scholarship, to be professor of philosophy in the University at Wittenburg; at twenty-nine is doctor of theology, a Biblical Doctor, he says, pledged to teach the Holy Scriptures; and before he has attained the years at which Loyola left the University of Paris, Luther has propounded his theses, debated with Dr. Eck, and vanquished both Cajetan and DeVio, the Papal legates; has defied the Pope, the Church, and the Emperor, in the brave and dauntless stand which he took for the word of God, and the liberty of the church, at the diet of Worms; has translated and given to the people in their native tongue the whole New Testament; and has supervised the translation of the Old, which glorious book became not only the foundation of the Reformation but of German Literature also; and has come to be universally recognized as one of the most profound scholars, one of the most eloquent preachers, as also one of the most distinguished university professors of Germany and Christendom.

This Luther, with his broad scholarship, his love of the people, his respect for his parents, and devotion to his friends, his warm social companionships, his fond and tender home-life,— Luther, with his little children about his knees, his little daughter dying in his arms, with all the humanities of a man, with all the tenderness of a woman, with all the bravery of a reformer, and the instincts of a statesman, is as truly a typical Protestant, as the concentrated, fanatical, half-educated Loyola is a typical son of the church. So much for the root, out of which grew the society of Jesuits.

2. The first, most manifest design of the Jesuits was to exterminate Protestantism ; the second, to build up the Roman church ; included in this latter, was their purpose to diminish the power of the bishops, in favor of the supremacy, the absolutism, the infallibility of the Pope, and then to gain control of that Pope, as embodying the church, and so advancing their society. In order to the accomplishment of these purposes, the constitution of the society was formulated by Loyola ; a constitution which I cannot give you in detail only for lack of time, but some of whose salient points are as follows :

1. Every Jesuit is bound by the constitution of the society, and a solemn oath, or vow, to poverty, chastity and obedience. To these also is added, in the case of the so-called " professed," a fourth vow of absolute obedience to the Pope. Not all the Jesuits take these four vows, but only according to the grade to which they attain in the society.

Concerning *the vow of poverty*, by which they deny themselves all worldly possessions — Loyola is said to have debated and prayed forty days and forty nights. The general of the society is made the trustee of their possessions. So extreme were Loyola's views on this point, that a Roman Catholic historian tells us, that if one of the brothers plucked a flower or picked up an apple in the garden of their house, Loyola visited the offence with severe penance, as violating this rule of poverty, by possession. And yet, notwithstanding the vow, when the society was suppressed in 1772 by the act of Pope Clement XIV., they were found possessed of more than $200,000,000. It was also the law of the society correlate to this, that no Jesuit should hold any office, save in the society. Nevertheless, at this time, they had twenty-four cardinals, six electors of the empire, nineteen princes, twenty-one archbishops, and one hundred and twenty-one titular bishops; showing clearly how the lust of power gained supremacy over their vows.

The *vow of chastity*, similar to that which Romish priests now take, was to so separate them from the ordinary domestic duties of life, that their sole devotion should be given to the church. Perhaps, to a considerable extent, they have honored this vow; but a purpose so contrary to nature and the word and will of God, has never in any age warranted the assertion that the celibates of Rome were chaste.

The *vow of obedience*, however, seemed to be the strongest and most essential part of the constitution of the Jesuits. This obedience is absolute, and is to be paid to the superior. Says Loyola: " I ought to obey the superior as God, in whose place he stands." Every Jesuit's oath includes these words; " To you, the Father-General, and to your successors, whom I regard as holding the place of God, perpetual poverty, chastity and obedience, etc." Loyola's understanding of this vow is declared in his famous letter on obedience, when he writes that this obedience should be so absolutely passive that one should be like a dead body moved only by the will of another, or like a staff in the hands of an old man, or like a crucifix in the hands of a worshipper. The virtue of this obedience is in proportion to its absoluteness. When the intellect does not even raise an inquiry about the thing commanded, when the Jesuit yields without the shadow of a will or purpose of his own, then obedience attains perfection. Among the first things which happen to a novice, who is to become a Jesuit, is the entire breaking down of his will. This is systematically sought and secured. In some cases, the novice passing the first night in a Jesuit house, has been tested as follows: When he has fallen asleep, he has been awakened, commanded to rise, take up his mattress, and go to another room, and this again and again through the night. If he asks why, or raises the slightest query or objection, he is considered unfit for the society.

This rule of absolute obedience, to go anywhere and perform any service at the command of the superior, is now fully enforced. A friend of mine received the following admissions and explanation from a company of Jesuits with whom he sailed on a ship in the Mediterranean Sea a few years since. They were missionaries, going under orders. They said: " Wherever we are, in the garden, in the street, if the command comes to us to go to any part of the earth, to Asia, Africa, America, on any service, we

do not wait to enter the house for money, for clothing, or for farewells, but simply and at once start
from where we are and go."

Loyola insisted on this rule of obedience with the
utmost rigor. An old monk, who preferred wearing
his night-cap in the house to the beretta prescribed
by the rule, was dismissed. The professor of theology was sometimes commanded by Loyola to take
the place of the cook, and the cook the place of the
professor of theology; or a priest, in the midst of the
mass, was commanded to go into the street; and all
this must be done without question, however absurd.
A modest monk, coming into Loyola's presence and
told to be seated, who did not instantly comply, was
commanded to take the chair on his head, and hold
it there as long as he remained. And these are but
a few of the illustrations taken from Romish authors,
which show how completely Loyola insisted on the
fulfillment of this vow. The rigors of military
discipline to which he was accustomed in early life,
appear in all the constitutions and practice of the
society, and their head is called *the general*.

The vow of obedience to the Pope, the fourth and
last of these vows, taken by the highest members of
the profession, has been kept only when the Pope
was obedient to the will of the Jesuits. Loyola himself, by diplomacy and evasion, contended with the
Pope, and won his point too. Again and again, in the
history of the society, the clashing of the Papal
will with the will of the general of the Jesuits, has
resulted in the submission or the ruin of the Pope.

Several popes have died, apparently by poison, at the hand of this Order, who vowed obedience to them as Sixtus V., Urban VII., Clement VIII., and Clement XIV.

Turning from these Constitutions, in the next place, we call your attention to some of the methods and principles of this society. Among the first duties of a Jesuit, to which he devotes his life, is the teaching of the young. This apparently laudable purpose, made the Jesuits the school-masters of Europe. Far and wide they founded their houses of learning; as Luther before had founded them in Germany. "They possessed themselves of the pulpit, press, confesssional and the school," as says Macaulay. But never forget that the first and sole purpose of the society as a teacher, is to make submissive Roman Catholics. This determines the kind and quantity of their teaching, and this must account for the fact that, in those countries where the Papacy and the Jesuit have had completest sway, there is found to-day the most extraordinary percentage of illiteracy : as witness, Italy, where 73 per cent. of the people are illiterate, or Spain with 80 per cent.,-and Mexico with 93 per cent. Could this have been true if the Jesuits, fulfilling their vow to teach, had really opened the avenues of knowledge to their scholars? Rome educates only where she must, where Protestantism compels her to do so. From Roman Catholics have come some of the severest criticisms on the narrowness of their methods of instruction.

Secondly. The Jesuit vowed to devote himself to missions. Out of this vow, sprang the heroic devotion of Xavier and his associates, in India, of the Jesuit missions to China, to Japan, to North and South America, and Mexico. Of this mission work in China, in Japan, and in North America, there is hardly a trace remaining. In India, they prepared the way for the English power, without intending to do so. It is true that they degraded the gospel with pagan rites, so that nine popes vehemently condemned their methods and tried in vain to reform them.

In the third place, their method and principle includes the assertion and upholding of the infallibility of the pope. The statement of this doctrine in full must be reserved to a later time with all its absurd and hurtful consequences; but the word infallibility conveys its plain meaning. The pope, according to the Jesuit idea, is the church, His decisions, speaking in bulls, encyclicals and the like, are as binding as the word of God. Nothwithstanding the alleged infallibility of the pope and his absolute supremacy, they have repeatedly evaded and violated his commands. They are responsible for that recent decree of the Vatican council, which makes Papal infallibility as much a doctrine of the Romish Church as the doctrine of the existence of God; and it is a common jest in Rome, that the Jesuit general, who is known as the " Black Pope," is superior to the creature of the cardinals, who is known as the " White Pope."

Fourth, The Jesuits, among their leading principles, insist on the secular power of the pope, his right to rule as a temporal prince and monarch over all civil governors, princes, kings, rulers and legislators. They have urged on and defended him in deposing monarchs, absolving Romanists from obedience to laws, and other treasonable acts, and that within twenty-five years. The supremacy of the Papal dictum in all matters that relate to faith and morals, includes also, in their theory, all that relates remotely to the discipline of the church. And yet, notwithstanding their devotion to the secular power of the pope, they, perhaps more than any other society, have contributed to the loss of Papal influence, not only in the Roman States, but also in other countries of the world. And to show the blight of their rule and government, where pope and Jesuit were supreme in the Roman States, the morality of the people degenerated to the lowest ebb of virtue, the deepest infamy of vice.

As the last of the principles on which the society works, which I may now mention — they hold that the end justifies the means ; that if the end is good, whatever means are used thereto are good. Probably it was this conception that made Loyola join with Cardinal Paul and Cardinal Caraffa, in establishing the Inquisition in Portugal. Although some of the Jesuits deny this as a principle of their conduct, the proofs are too abundant. Gury and Busenbaum, Layman and Wagemann, in Jesuit treatises on theology and morals, distinctly avow the doctrine, and thus justify any wickedness in pursuit of the purpose of upbuilding the Church of Rome. (See Dr. Littledale in Encyc. Brit., Art. *Jesuits.*) And their practice, in the judgment of the ablest historians, proves how fully they apply their theory. Macaulay, Ranke, and Hallam, lay at their door crimes against the state, against society, and against the person, which can only be excused on the ground that blind devotion to the church had made the instigators of these crimes reckless of the means which they pursued to obtain their ends. The assassination of William of Orange, of Henry IV. of France, attempts on the life of Elizabeth of England, the Gunpowder Plot, the Massacre of St. Bartholomew, the Revocation of the Edict of Nantes, are illustrations of the wicked deeds with which history too closely connects them.

Loyola's military experience, and rigid military ideas, appear everywhere in the modes of the society and its administration. Under their general are provincials, who have charge of certain territory, and a still lower grade of officers are called rectors; and a complete system of espionage is kept up; not only on all members of the society, but on all the events of the community where they dwell, a minute report of which is regularly and carefully sent to Rome. This has been their method for centuries, and is their method to-day.

If the purpose of this society was religious, solely or mostly; if by their poverty they simply meant to separate themselves from the world; if by their chastity, they would encourage a certain ideal of purity, and if obedience only meant ready subordination to the command of a good leader, in the pursuit of a good work, how does it happen that the Society of Jesuits has incurred the suspicion, the dislike, the antagonism, the fear and the hatred of almost every ruler and every government of Europe, and of the world?

Let us speak briefly, in closing, of their work, as far as that work can be epitomized in a few words. In pursuance of their designs, scattering to all countries of Europe and of the world, the Jesuits would be supposed to have been the allies of Roman Catholic princes, and to have assisted in the diffusion of those doctrines and principles held by Roman Catholics, to the satisfaction of all faithful sons of the church. Such, however, is not the case.

For conspiracy, machinations and evil designing, the Jesuits have been banished necessarily from almost every state of Europe. Roman Catholic Portugal, in 1759, led the way; and under the leadership of one of the most enlightened statesmen that Portugal ever had, banished them from the realm. Spain followed shortly after, sending, in a single day, six thousand Jesuits from her borders to Italy; and as late as 1868, the Cortez of Spain reaffirmed its legislation against the society of Jesuits. Parma and Naples banished them; also Switzerland, Prussia and Russia; until it may be said in truth, that, saving the insignificant kingdom of Belgium, every nation of Europe has legislated against them.

But more than this: at about the time of our Revolution, the attention of Pope Clement XIV. having been called to the abuses created by the Jesuit society, after extended deliberation, in the most solemn terms, rehearsing the evils that they had done in and out of the church, in the year 1772, this Pope pronounced upon them the ban and anathema of the Roman curia, and forbade that they should reorganize or exist " to all eternity." Another pope, Pius VI., confirmed his predecessor's decree. The Jesuits fled to Protestant Prussia and to Russia also, whence they were banished again. From 1772 to 1814, still secretly cherishing their society in defiance of the Pope, and working ruin wherever they went, the Jesuits existed under the Papal ban. Then another infallible pope, Pius VII., regardless of the decree of his predecessors, reinstated and rehabilitated the society of Jesuits. The decree of Clement XIV. cost him his life. Bellarmine, a leading Jesuit of the society, prophesied that he would die within a year. That prophecy was regarded as a threat, and the pope died, with every indication of having been poisoned. The unscrupulous methods of the society, which have caused prince and pope and legislature to lay upon them their heavy hand, have never been condemned by the Jesuits, nor have they ever ceased to practice them. But where did the banished Jesuit go? Whither, when under the suspicion, and flying from the hatred of the rising spirit of freedom in Europe, does he betake himself, and where is he now? I answer, In America, in the United States.

Our country is the paradise of Jesuits. Unwarned by the experience of other lands, regardless of the bonds they weave about the limbs of liberty, we have permitted their presence in this country, until almost ready to throw off the disguise, they now threaten our institutions with ruin. It is the Jesuit who animates the attack on our public schools; the Jesuit who thrusts his hand into the public treasuries. It is the Jesuit who is endeavoring to divide the school fund, who is dictating the policy by which Romish schools shall take the place of the national schools. It is the Jesuit who is decrying free speech and liberty of conscience and a free press; who is doing his utmost in conformity with the constitutions of the society of which he is a sworn adherent, and of the Papacy of which he is at once the dictator and the slave, to reduce free America to the subjection of an absolute monarch.

What will be the result? Strange and wonderful to say, misfortune and disaster to themselves seems to follow their designs against government. In 1870, it was their influence which assembled and directed the Vatican Council, which should exalt still higher the dogmas of the church, and overthrow the growing spirit of freedom. It was their plan, at the same time, to declare the Pope infallible, and to subjugate Italy and Europe to his power. Napoleon III. of France, the favorite son of the church, whose bayonets were the guard and support of the Papal throne, was led, through Jesuit influence, to declare war upon Protestant Prussia. But behold! while they debated the infallibility of the Pope, the monarch on whom Pius IX. had shed the blight of his blessing surrendered himself, his army and his empire at Sedan, and free Italy began to march on Rome. Many prelates fled the Imperial City, and the thunder of the guns of Prussia at Sedan was answered by the cannon of free Italy, turned against the gates of Rome. Into their long degraded capital swept the hosts of freedom; the Quirinal became the palace of the King of United Italy, Victor Emanuel, and when the few hundred ecclesiastics of the Papacy, only a fraction of the Council, passed the decree which made the Pope an infallible prince, it was answered by the huzzahs of liberty throughout France and Italy. Since then, the Infallible has whined and protested, begged and threatened, but he is an Italian subject against his will, and must be, while he stays in Rome. God grant that the machinations of the Roman hierarchy may result in the emancipation of their followers from Papal tyranny in America, as in France and Italy! Let Jesuitism, which has fled to America, to found an Empire on the ruins of the Republic, having been swept by edict from the Old World, here find a grave; while American Catholic Christians, Romanist and Protestant, open the Word of God, and by it the gates of progress, here, in the free Republic of the West.

Sermon III.

THE POPE AND THE PAPAL POWER THE FOES OF FREEDOM.

"That man of sin be revealed, the son of perdition; Who opposeth and exalteth himself above all that is called God, or that is worshipped; so that he as God sitteth in the temple of God, showing himself that he is God."—2 Thess. 2: 3, 4.

Many very able commentators believe that this text prophesies and describes the Pope of Rome. I do not affirm that the sacred writer foretells the Papacy in these prophetic words; but we risk nothing in claiming that the description actually outlines the pretensions and assumptions of the Pope, and that Romanism allows to him nearly all, if not all, of the presumptuous claims that are here indicated. The lives of many of the Popes certainly correspond to the definition "the man of sin," in their scandalous wickedness and immorality. Their pride and pretensions are not unfittingly delineated in the words, "who opposeth and exalteth himself above all that is called God, or that is worshipped;" since, as I shall show, the Pope opposes all other forms of religion excepting the Roman Catholic, and exalts his claims, so that his declarations demand of Roman Catholics as absolute respect and obedience as though they were the very words of God. He certainly "sitteth in the temple of God;" and if he does not say "I am God," he presumptuously asserts, in his claims to infallibility, the possession of attributes belonging to God alone. There is no other personage in history to whom these words seem to so exactly apply; and whether they are fit to describe him you shall judge, when we have examined his demands and his government.

You will remember, that in the former discourse we enlarged upon the principles, methods, and constitution of the Jesuits, and, having seen that their policy was one of absolute imperialism, directly opposed to freedom, religious and civil, we affirmed that they now dictate, as for centuries they have controlled, the Papal policy. In further proof of this, Mr. Gladstone says ("Vatican Decrees," page 188) : " The Jesuits are the men who cherish, methodize, transmit and exaggerate all the dangerous traditions of the Curia. In them it lives. The ambition and self-seeking of the court of Rome have here their root. They supply that Roman *malaria* which Dr. Newman tells us encircles the base of the rock of St. Peter." R. W. Thompson, in his extended and admirable work on " The Papacy and the Civil Power," p. 113, says of the Jesuits : " They are simply a band of ecclesiastical office-holders, held together by the cohesive power of common ambition as compactly as an army of soldiers, and are governed by a commander-in-chief, whose brow they would adorn forever with a kingly crown, and who wields the Papal lash over them with imperial threat-

enings. All these, with exceptions, if any, too few
to be observed, are laboring with wonderful assiduity
to educate the whole membership of their church up
to the point of accepting, without hesitation or
inquiry, all the Jesuit teaching in reference to the
Papacy as a necessary and indispensable part of their
religious faith; so that, whensoever the Papal order
shall be issued, they may march their columns
unbroken into the Papal army. With blasphemous
and fulsome adulation of the Pope, applying to him
terms which are due only to God, they are all
devoted to the object of exterminating Protestantism, civil and religious, and extending the sceptre
of the Papacy over the world." And yet again, Dr.
L. DeSantis, an ex-priest, a Roman by birth, who
was once curate of the Magdalene parish in Rome,
professor of theology in the Roman University, and
qualificator of the Inquisition, thus expressed himself: "From the period of the Council of Trent,
*Roman Catholicism has identified itself with Jesuit-
ism.* That unscrupulous order has been known to
clothe itself, when occasion required, with new forms,
and to give a convenient elasticity to its favorite
maxim that the end is everything, and all the means
to attain it are good; but, by depending on the
skilful tactics of the society of Jesus, the court of
Rome has been constrained to yield to it ascendancy, confide her destiny to its hands, and permit it
to direct her interest; and of its control Jesuitism
has availed itself in the most absolute way. It has
constituted the powerful mainspring, more or less

concealed, of the whole Papal machinery." (" Rome, Christian and Papal.")

These are representative and adequate illustrations of the opinion of the best informed men of our own generation, that the Jesuits are the power behind the Papal throne. Their policy, as we know from the constitutions, is one of absolute imperialism, the subjugation of all government, all thought, all faith, and all conscience to the commands of the Pope.

1. The Pope claims to be, by divine right, absolute ruler over all men and all nations, in all things. The decree of the Vatican Council of 1870 concerning the infallibility of the Pope, now a dogma of the Romanist faith, is in the following words (" The Decrees," p. 48) : " We teach and define that it is a dogma divinely revealed, that the Roman Pontiff, when he speaks *ex cathedra,* that is, when in discharge of the office of pastor and doctor of all Christians, by virtue of his supreme apostolic authority, he defines a doctrine regarding faith and morals to be held by the universal church, by the definite assistance promised to him in blessed Peter, is possessed of that infallibility with which the divine Redeemer willed that his church should be endowed, for defining doctrine regarding faith or morals, and therefore such definitions of the Roman Pontiff are irreformable of themselves, and not from the consent of the church. But if any one, which may God avert, presume to contradict this our definition, let him be anathema." Still further, to cite the condensed form of expression used by Mr. Gladstone

("Vaticanism," p. 141) : " The council of the Vatican decreed that the Pope had from Christ immediate power over the universal church; that all were bound to obey him, of whatever right and dignity, collectively as well as individually ; that this duty of obedience extends to all matters of faith and morals, and of the discipline and government of the church ; that in all ecclesiastical causes he is a judge without appeal or possibility of reversal ; that the definitions, both in faith and morals, delivered *ex cathedra*, are irreformable in themselves, and not from the consent of the church, and are invested with the infallibility granted by Christ in the said subject-matter to the church." Surely, it is not too much to say that a convert now joining the Papal church, yielding to the claims now made upon him by the authority which he solemnly and with the highest responsibility acknowledges, is required to surrender his mental and moral freedom, and to place his loyalty and civil duty at the hand of another. Now, the expression " faith and morals," includes far more then mere ecclesiastical legislation. Let a high Roman Catholic authority tell us how much more, by implication, is included in this right of the Pope : " All, both pastors and faithful, are bound to submit, not only in matters belonging to faith and morals, but also in those pertaining to the discipline and government of the church throughout the world. This is the teaching of the Catholic faith, from which none can depart without detriment to faith and salvation. We further teach and declare, that the

Pope is the supreme judge of the faithful, and that in all causes pertaining to ecclesiastical jurisdiction, recourse may be had to his judgment; and that none may rebate the judgment of the apostolic See, than whose there is no greater authority; and that it is not lawful for any one to sit in judgment on its judgment."

Commenting on this, Mr. Gladstone says : " Absolute obedience is due to the Pope at the peril of salvation, not alone in faith, in morals, but in all things which concern the discipline and government of the church. Even in the United States, where the severance between church and state is supposed to be complete, a long catalogue may be drawn of subjects belonging to the domain and competency of the state, but also undeniably affecting the government of the church; such as, by way of example, marriage, burial, education, prison-discipline, blasphemy, poor relief, incorporation, mortmain, religious endowment, vows of celibacy and obedience. But on all matters respecting which any Pope may think proper to declare that they concern either faith or morals, or the government or discipline of the church, he claims, with the approval of a council, undoubtedly ecumenical in the Roman sense, the absolute obedience, at the peril of salvation, of every member of his communion." (" Vaticanism," p. 55.) More startling still, the Pope claims the right to define his own rights and the limits of his power; the sole unlimited power to interpret his own claims, in such a manner and by such words as he may from time to time think fit. "Against such definition of his own power there is no appeal to reason, that is rationalism ; nor to Scripture, that is heresy ; nor to history, that is private judgment. Over all these things he claims to be absolute judge." ("Vaticanism," p. 186.)

The *Catholic World* for August, 1871, one of the most influential periodicals of the Romish Church in America, thus states it : " Each individual must receive his faith and law from the church of which he is a member by baptism, with unquestioning submission and obedience of the intellect and will. Authority and obligation are correlative in end and extent. We have no right to ask reasons of the church [the Pope] any more than of Almighty God, as a preliminary to our submission. We are to take with unquestionable docility whatever instructions the church [that is the Pope] gives us." How this monstrous doctrine is understood by the Pope himself, whose understanding and words are the absolute law of the church, let us see from his own words. Has he temporal and civil power? or is he, as a man and an ecclesiastic, amenable to the laws of the country in which he sojourns? He himself says, in a Papal bull, issued by him in 1860, that his temporal power is derived from God alone, and is absolutely necessary to the church, inasmuch as it is indispensable to him that he shall possess such an amount of freedom as to be subject to no civil power ; that is, that he must be above all government and independent of them all, and have that amount of freedom and irresponsibilty to constitutions and laws which shall enable him to do as he pleases. ("The Papacy and the Civil Power," p. 137.)

In quoting, as I am about to do, another Roman Catholic authority, do not fail to bear in mind that every book published by Roman Catholics, issued by their publishing houses, and sanctioned by their prelates, has passed through the careful censorship of their ecclesiastics, and speaks therefore with authority. I now quote from a tract printed for The Catholic Publication Society, Number 46, on "The Pope's Temporal Power." After having declared that the authority of the Pope exercised at Rome is equally necessary throughout the whole world, it proceeds in form of question and answer as follows : "How can this independence of Civil authority be secured? Only in one way. The Pope must be a sovereign himself: No temporal prince, whether Emperor, or King, or President, or any legislative body, can have any lawful jurisdiction over the Pope. What right has the Pope to be independent of every civil ruler? He has it in virtue of his dignity as the Vicar of Christ. Christ himself is King of kings ; but the Pope governs the church in the name of Christ and as his representative. His divine office, therefore, makes him superior to every political, temporal and human government." But that this usurper of universal dominion may give color to these arrogant pretensions and claims, he endeavors to make it appear that he is not a foreign prince, attempting to exercise jurisdiction out of his proper realm. In the Encyclical of Pius IX., dated Jan. 5, 1873, addressed to the Armenian church, who had objected to his attempt to control the appointment of their bishops, (found in *The New Freeman's Journal and Catholic Register* April 19, 1873), the Pope declares, that " it is false that the Roman Pontiffs have ever exceeded the limits of their power, and interfered in the civil administration of states ; and that they have usurped the rights of princes. He cannot be called a " foreigner " to any Christians or any particular churches of Christians. Moreover, those who hesitate not to call the Apostolic See a foreign power, fail in the faith due to the Catholic Church, if they are of the number of her sons ; or they assail the liberty that is her due, if they do not belong to her."

By this subterfuge, he would have all Romanists, under pain and penalty, admit and affirm that he is as much a domestic imperial ruler in the United States of America, as he formerly was in the Roman States of Italy. Nor has he hesitated, nor have popes for a thousand years hesitated, to interfere with the Civil governments of various countries, endeavoring to stir up seditions, absolving subjects from their allegiance, deposing princes, and affirming absolute supremacy. Although Roman Catholic authorities, either ignorant of the facts, or wilfully perverting them, deny that the Pope assails and attempts to overturn civil government, Pius IX. professedly speaking in the name of Jesus Christ, to and concerning the governments of Italy, Germany, Spain, Switzerland and Brazil, (which governments

have deemed it expedient for their own domestic
peace and protection to adopt certain measures
which are designed to increase the liberties of the
citizen who obeys the laws of the state,) compliments
the faithful of the church on their hostility to these
laws, and commends them for refusing to obey the
laws and orders of the civil empire, rather than the
most holy laws of their God and of the church. It
was Pius IX. who, in 1855, declared absolutely null
and void all the acts of the government of Piedmont
which he held prejudicial to the rights of religion.
In the same year, because Spain had passed a law
which permitted the toleration of non-Roman worship and the secularization of ecclesiastical property, he
declared, by his own apostolic authority, those laws
to be abrogated, totally null and of no effect. So
also on the 22nd of June, 1862, in another allocution,
Pope Pius IX. recited the provisions of an Austrian
law of the previous December, which established
freedom of opinion, of the press, of belief, of conscience, of education, and of religious profession,
which regulated matrimonial jurisdiction and other
matters; and these he declared "abominable" laws,
which "have been and shall be totally void and without all force whatever." In almost identical phraseology he attempts to annul the laws of Sardinia, and
excommunicates all those who had a hand in them;
the laws of Mexico, which he judges to interfere with
his rights, and declares them absolutely null and
void. While on the 17th of September, 1863, in an
encyclical letter enumerating proceedings on the part

of the government of New Granada, which had, among
other things, established freedom of worship, he
declares these acts utterly unjust and impious, and
by apostolic authority declares the whole null and
void in the future and in the past." (Gladstone,
"Vaticanism," p. 176.) Here then, is the indictment
which we frame against this most arrogant and
tyrannical of rulers. A pontiff claiming infallibility,
who has condemned free speech, free writing, a free
press, toleration of nonconformity, liberty of conscience, the study of civil and philosophical matters
in independence of ecclesiastical authority, marriage
unless contracted in the Romish church, the definition
by the state of the civil rights of the church,— who has
demanded for the church therefore the title to define
its own civil rights, together with a divine right to
civil immunities, and a right to use physical force;
and who has also proudly asserted that the popes of
the middle ages, with their councils, did not invade
the rights of princes; as, for example, Gregory VII.
of the Emperor Henry IV., Innocent III., of Raymond
of Toulouse; Paul III., in deposing Henry VIII;
Pius V., in performing the like paternal office for
Elizabeth of England, (" Vaticanism," page 56,)—
this intruder into governments, this scourge of nations,
this enemy of independence therefore, claims, and
claims from the month of July 1870 onwards, such
plenary authority over every convert and member of
his church, that he shall place his loyalty and civil
duty at the mercy of another, that other being himself. It is needless to say to you who have been

instructed in the principles of Bible Christianity
and of civil freedom, that this is an assumption and
exercise of the most intolerable tyranny.

2.   In the Encyclical and the Syllabus of 1864,
the Pope denounces some of the dearest rights of
man, because they are opposed to Romish absolutism.
To you who are not familiar with these . terms, I
may say, that the word Encyclical is applied to a
letter or communication written to the general public,
the world at large, the church as a whole; while the
Syllabus is a similar document, containing those propositions, or heads of discourse, which sum up the
leading ideas which the Pope wishes to communicate.
Do not forget that these declarations of the Pope, by
his own definition, and the definition of Romish
councils, by the consent of Romish prelates, and
undisputed and submitted to by the Roman Catholic
church, have all the force of infallible authority and
dogma. To dispute them, or refuse obedience to
them, is to make a Roman Catholic a heretic, to put
him under the ban of excommunication, and outside
the pale of salvation.   There is no dogma of faith
or morals, no doctrine of the Holy Scriptures, that
is more binding upon the conscience and obedience of the Roman Catholic, than are these
Papal deliverances.   There is no escape from yielding to them absolutely, except to break with the
Roman Catholic church as a whole.   With fearful
epithets the Pope denounces those who insist that
governments should not inflict penalties upon such
as violate the Catholic religion.   The withholding of

this power of punishment to protect the Catholic and no other, he calls a totally false notion of social government, because it leads to very erroneous opinions, most pernicious to the Catholic religion and to the salvation of souls. These opinions he calls insanity, and then proceeds to visit with his fiercest malediction, first, those who maintain the liberty of the press; second, or the liberty of conscience and of worship; third, or the liberty of speech; fourth, those who contend that Papal judgments and decrees may without sin be disputed or differed from unless they treat of the rules of faith or morals; fifth, those who assign to the state the power to define the civil rights and province of the church; sixth, he denounces those who hold that Roman Catholic Pontiffs and ecumenical councils have transgressed the limits of their power and usurped the rights of princes; seventh, those who declare that the church may not employ force; eighth, or that power not inherit in the office of the episcopate, but granted to it by the civil authority, may be withdrawn from it at the discretion of that authority; ninth, he anathematizes those who affirm that the civil immunity of the church and its minister depends upon civil right; tenth, or that in the conflict of laws, civil and ecclesiastical, the civil laws should prevail; eleventh, or that any method of instruction, solely secular, may be approved; twelfth, or that knowledge of things philosophical and civil, should decline to be guided by divine and ecclesiastical authority; thirteenth, or that marriage is not, in its essence, a sacrament, that is, in the sense that the Romish Church understands a sacrament; fourteenth, or that marriage, not sacramentally contracted, is of binding force, [the Pope's own explanation of this is, that all marriage, so called, outside the Roman Catholic church, is *filthy concubinage.*" These are his own words, and this declaration, if generally received, as he insists it shall be, under penalty of eternal damnation, is a doctrine " horrible and revolting in itself, and dangerous to the morals of society, the structure of the family and the peace of life."] ; fifteenth, he anathematizes those who say that the abolition of the temporal power of the Popedom would be highly advantageous to the church ; sixteenth, or that any other religion than the Roman religion may be established by the state ; seventeenth, or that in countries called Catholic, the free exercise of other religions may be laudably allowed ; eighteenth, or that the Roman Pontiff ought to come to terms with progress, liberalism, and modern civilization.   (Gladstone, " Vaticanism," p. 31-2) I count it impossible that any American, on hearing these declarations first read, should realize it as conceivable that, in this generation, any ruler, especially one who pretends to stand in place of God, should have the hardihood, the insolence, the audacity to pronounce curses and anathemas on those who maintain these principles of society and government. Do you not see, that almost everything we hold dear is here assailed ? You are accursed of Rome who maintain liberty of conscience and free worship, as do all Protestants of whom I have knowledge ; or that freedom of speech which in every age has made possible the advance of nations, the redress of wrongs, and the progress of humanity.

In these documents and orders of the Pope, we have him indorsing and affirming in express terms, that the Church of Rome has the absolute authority, which no civil power should transgress, to forbid freedom of worship, and exercise force to compel men to conform to that worship. He denounces Bible societies as a pest, and would stop all their presses and burn all their books, if he had the power. He re-affirms the decree of his predecessor, Clement XII., that all his subjects be prohibited from becoming affiliated with any assembly of free-masons or rendering aid, succor, counsel or retreat to any members of that society under penalty of death, and pronounces a like penalty upon those who fail to denounce and reveal all that they know concerning that association. And here, contrary to every principle of just government, and in harmony with the most dreadful abuses and persecutions of the middle ages, the Pope affirms that Romish ecclesiastics shall not be amenable to the civil law — a direful doctrine ; and would evoke again the arm of the Inquisition, a power never repudiated by the Romish Church, and claimed and used by it wherever it is all-powerful, to blot out all other than Roman Catholic worship from the face of the earth. I confess that language is too weak to condemn these claims to power on the part of any body of men. But these are the official expositions of the constitution of Romanism, these are the dogmas of this church, this is the authority which all Romanists are bound to obey under penalty of being denounced as heretics ; to this the Romish priesthood have lent themselves ; and this power, as incapable of being reconciled to the freedom of this nation as a rattlesnake within the folds of your dress of being reconciled to the safety and health of yonr body, is the power whose advance we attempt to stay, whose pretensions we disclose, and on whose machinations we endeavor to throw the light.

3.   Perhaps you now inquire, Do Roman Catholic hierarchs and prelates realize that these are the principles of the Papacy to which they are sworn? Is it possible that men live under the Constitution and laws of this country who are believers in such tyranny, and waiting under oath to spread it? It is to be hoped that they do not all realize it ; and yet we have most adequate proof that the chief among them do.   Bishop Gilmour, in his Lenten letter of March 1873, said : "Nationalities must be subordinate to religion, and we must learn that we are Catholics first and citizens next.   God is above man, and the church above the state."   Cardinal McCloskey, who as Cardinal of Rome is a foreign prince exercising authority in the United States, contrary to the Constitution and the laws, says : " The Catholics of the United States are as strongly devoted to the sustenance and maintenance of the temporal power of the Holy Father as Catholics in any part of the world, and if it should be necessary to prove

it by acts, they are ready to do so." What does he mean by this? In a sermon preached when he was archbishop, Cardinal Manning put the following sentences in the mouth of the Pope : " I acknowledge no civil power, I am the subject of no prince, and I claim more than this ; I claim to be the supreme judge and director of the conscience of men, of the peasant that tills the fields, and of the prince that sits upon the throne, of the household that lives in the shade of privacy, and the legislator that makes laws for kingdoms ; I am the sole, last, supreme judge of what is right and wrong." He also says : " Moreover, I declare, affirm, define and pronounce it to be necessary to salvation for every human creation to be subject to the Roman Pontiff." What this subjection means we may learn from Cardinal Bellarmine. He says : " If the Pope should err by enjoining vices or forbidding virtues, the Church would be obliged to believe vices to be good and virtues bad, unless it would sin against conscience." Horrible and monstrous! Every bishop of the Roman Catholic Church in America and through-out the world, and every archbishop, has taken an oath of devotion to the Papacy, in which occur the following words : " I will from henceforward be faithful and obedient to St. Peter, the apostle, to the Holy Roman Church, and to our Lord the Pope, and to his successors canonically entering. That counsel with which they shall entrust by themselves, their messengers or letters, I will not, knowingly, reveal to any, to their prejudice : I will help them to

define and keep the Roman Papacy and the royalties
of St. Peter, saving my Lord, against all men. The
rights, honors, privileges and authority of the holy
Romish church, of our Lord the Pope and his aforesaid successors, I will endeavor to preserve, defend,
increase and advance. I will not be in any council,
action or authority, in which shall be applied, against
our said Lord and the said Roman Church, anything
to the hurt or prejudice of their persons, right,
honor, state or power; and if I shall know any such
thing to be tried or agitated by any whatsoever, I
will hinder it to my utmost, and, as soon as I can,
will signify it to our said Lord, or to some other by
whom it may come to his knowledge. The rules of
the Holy Fathers, the apostolic decrees, ordinances
or disposals, reservations, provisions and mandates,
I will observe with all my might; and cause to be
observed by others. *Heretics, schismatics and rebels
to our said Lord, or his aforesaid successors, I will,
to my utmost, persecute and oppose,*" etc. (Dowling's
"History of Romanism," pages 615-16).

Here, then, is the oath of allegiance by which
these dignitaries of the Romish church are absolutely
pledged to enforce the doctrines of the encyclical and
syllabus; to oppose and persecute all who, like you
and me, reject those doctrines, and to observe the
profoundest secrecy in all things where they think
the interests of the Pope will be subserved.

And more than this, if it were possible for conspiracy, hatred of free institutions and of Protestantism,
and antagonism to the word of God and the spirit of

progress, to go farther than these have already gone in their allegiance to this hateful and tyrannous power, they have done so in yielding themselves up to believe, that not only the *past* declarations of the Pope shall absolutely control their actions, but, if perchance at any time in the *future* he could exceed these limits of oppression, tyranny and hatred of human rights, by any mandate whatsoever, they would also obey that. The *Catholic World* of Aug. 1871, in an article upon Infallibility, sets this doctrine forth thus : " A Catholic must not only believe what the church now proposes to his belief, but be ready to believe whatever she may hereafter propose : he must therefore be ready to give up any or all of his previous opinions so soon as they are condemned and prescribed by competent authority."

It is some comfort to find that an Irish Catholic ex-Congressman of Chicago, with a manliness which we trust exists in the breasts of thousands of others of our fellow-citizens, has dared to say : " The Pope of Rome [speaking of his interference with Irish affairs of late,] has no power to damn me, or any other Catholic. His latest utterance is an outrage on Irish-Catholic manhood and womanhood. The Pope of Rome, an Italian prince, with an Italian policy to carry out, at no matter what expense to the other Catholic people, is a fair subject for Irish criticism, and it is from this standpoint I criticize him. I am a Catholic, I am a believer in the Catholic church ; but I am an Irishman and not an Italian, and I am not to be sacrificed for the needs of Italian diplomacy." Such statements would multiply, and even stronger than this, if those Romanists who have imbibed, to some extent, the free spirit of Protestant America, would intelligently consider what the demands of the Papal power are upon them, and to what they would be reduced if they submitted to the principles on which it rules.

4. I cannot leave this subject without calling your attention to the utter absurdity and blasphemy of the Papal claim. This might be done and proofs furnished at great length; but I am compelled to be brief, only for lack of time. The proofs are most ample and adequate. You have only to read the history of the Popes, as written by Hallam, Ranke, or any of the greatest historians of the world, to readily see that no class of men in the annals of time could more inappropriately assume to be infallible, much less divine, than these very Popes of Rome. Many of these infallible Popes have been as infamous for the laxity of their morals and the enormity of their crimes, as they have been for the wickedness of their pretensions. As an example of folly, Pope Urban VIII. infallibly denied the Copernican theory propounded by Galileo, that the sun is the centre of the solar system, and that the earth moves around it. The ridiculousness of this is not so great as of the Popes who have antagonized one another even to the extent of murder, all being infallible; of the Popes who have blessed what their predecessors have anathematized, and have cursed that on which their predecessors pronounced their benediction; of the Popes

who have contended and protested against each other at Rome and Avignon, when two Papal courts were being carried on at once by rival Popes. Think of Pope John XXIII., who at the Council of Constance was dethroned from the Papal chair because of the universal detestation felt for his crimes,—crimes no greater than those of Benedict VIII., or a score of others who might be named.

Yet all these, according to the law of the Roman Catholic church, however infamous their lives, are equally infallible, and are permitted to exercise their official powers over cardinals, archbishops, bishops or priests, whatever the impurity of their behavior or the wickedness of thier conduct, and after death are canonized as "saints." And as if it were not enough that the characters of so many of these Popes have been as vile as their pretensions have been absurd, it is only too true that the Papal court which has surrounded them, the advisers who have largely controlled them until the present time, have in many instances been guilty of like infamies with the worst of the Popes.

Of Cardinal Antonelli, who was prime minister of Pius IX., a French Catholic writer thus speaks: "He was born in a den of thieves; he seems a minister engrafted on a savage. All classes of society hated him equally." And of the Papacy, under his influence and direction, Gattina says, after speaking of "the thefts, the villanies, the rudeness of this cardinal": "Under Antonelli's guidance it is like the subterranean sewers of large cities; it carries all the filth. When it is stopped and filtered, it spreads infection and death." No wonder that the Roman Catholic hierarchy would forbid the study of history in the public schools, unless that history has passed through their sifting; for it must largely, if true, be a history of the infamy of the court of Rome, of the scandalous wickedness of the Popes, and of the high-handed political measures which have been suggested and advanced by the Roman Catholic Church. I close with a few reflections on the predictions of Roman Catholics as to the Romish Church in the United States, and on the growth of Romanism among us, which, considering the policy which has been out-lined, may well startle and alarm all thoughtful hearers. Father Hecker says, that "ere long there is to be a state religion in this country, and that state religion is to be Roman Catholic." The Boston *Pilot* says: "The man to-day is living who will see the majority of the people of the American continent Roman Catholics."

A former Bishop of Cincinnatti declares, that " effect-ual plans are in operation to give us a complete vic-tory over Protestantism." The Bishop of Charlestown affirms, that "within thirty years the Protestant heresy will come to an end." While Pope Gregory XVI., a half a century ago, declared : " Out of the Roman States, there is no country where I am Pope, except in the United States. (Strong's " Our Country," page 55.)

The Roman Catholic Church in the United States is growing with great rapidity. In 1800, the Romanist population was 100,000 ; in 1884, it was over six and one-half millions,— had increased sixty-fold ; at the beginning of the century there was one Romanist to every fifty-three of the population ; in 1850, one to fourteen ; in 1870, one to eight and one-half ; in 1880, one to seven and seven-tenths. Wonderful as has been the growth of the country, the Romanist church has grown more rapidly. From 1800 to 1880, the population has increased nine-fold ; the membership of all evangelical churches, twenty-seven fold ; and the Romanist population, sixty-three fold. In 1850, the Romanist church was nearly *one-half* as large as all the Evangelical Protestant churches ; let us look at their relative progress since that time. From 1830 to 1880, the population increased 116 per cent. ; the communicants of evangelical churches, one and a half times as fast, or 185 per cent. ; the Romanist population, 294 per cent., nearly two and a half times as rapidly as the population. From 1850 to 1880, the number of Evangelical churches increased 125 per cent. ; during the same period, Romanist churches increased 447 per cent., nearly four times as fast. From 1870 to 1880, a period of ten years, the churches of all Evangelical denominations increased 49 per cent., while Romanist churches multiplied 74 per cent., one and a half times as fast. During the same period the ministers of evangelical churches increased in number 46 per cent. Romish priests, 61 per cent. From 1850 to 1870, evangelical ministers increased 86 per cent. ; priests, 204 per cent., or as 2½ to 1. From 1850 to 1880, ministers increased 173 per cent., and priests 391 per cent., more than double. Rome, with characteristic foresight, is concentrating her strength in the Western territories.　As the West is to dominate the nation, she intends to dominate the West.　In the United States, a little less than one-eighth of the population is Romanist, in the territories, taken together, more than one-third.　(Dr. Strong's " Our Country.")

In the whole country there are not quite two-thirds as many Romanists as there are members of the Evangelical churches.　Not including Arizona and New Mexico, which have a large native Romanist population, the six remaining territories had, in 1880, four times as many Romanists as there were members of Protestant denominations collectively.　And including Arizona and New Mexico, Rome had eighteen times as many as all Protestant bodies.　When the Jesuits were driven out of Berlin, they declared that they would plant themselves in the Eastern territories of America; this they have done, and under the absolute dictation of the Pope, they are endeavoring to spread the intolerant, persecuting monarchy which we have reviewed.　Whoever fails to note their purpose, and whoever is indifferent to their designs, must be willing to be a slave to a foreign potentate and to see the hopes of the world uprooted in the subjugation of America to the merciless tyranny of the Inquisition.

I have stated the actual truth so mildly that I almost ought to apologize.　For every fact and citation that I have brought, for every audacious Papal claim, every authorized Romanistic principle contrary to our liberties, for every historic proof of the wickedness and immorality of Popes, I can cite, from equally unimpeachable sources, five times as many more.

Thus, before the American Christian public, as the high court of jurisdiction, I indict the Pope of Rome as the representative of the Papal policy, the representative whom they put forward to stand for the whole church in its antagonism to civil and religious freedom, against which he has committed high crimes and misdemeanors.

I impeach him in the name of liberty of conscience, whose rights he has denied ; I impeach him in the name of freedom of worship, whose temples he would close ; I impeach him in the name of a free press and free speech, whose voice he would smother in the smoke of fire and faggot ; I impeach him in the name of civil liberty, over whose just laws he has proclaimed the sovereignty of Romish councils ; I impeach him in the name of the marriage-bond of the majority of the happy households of the Christian world, which he has stigmatized as "filthy concubinage," because not contracted in the Romish church ; I impeach him in the name of Protestantism, which he calls "heresy" and against which he invokes the persecution of the civil government and the tortures of the Inquisition. In the name of progress, which he has tried in vain to stay; of modern civilization, with which he cannot be reconciled ; in the name of the free and enlightened governments of the world, against whose most beneficient laws he has hurled his anathemas; in the name of the Holy Bible, whose free circulation he has pronounced a pest; in the name of free America, whose overthrow he has plotted; in the name of Almighty God, whose prerogatives he has blaphemously usurped : in the name of all these, I impeach the Pope and the hierarchy which dominate the Roman Catholic Church, and summon them to the bar of oppressed humanity and of **Divine Justice.**

Sermon IV.

ROMANISM ANTAGONISTIC TO THE CONSTITUTION AND THE LAWS.

"Behold, I have taught you statutes and judgments, even as the Lord my God commanded me, that ye shall do so in the land whither you go to possess it. Keep, therefore, and do them; for this is your wisdom and your understanding in the sight of the nations, which shall hear all these statutes and say, Surely this great nation is a wise and understanding people. For what nation is there so great, who hath God so nigh unto them, as the Lord our God is in all things that we call upon him for ?" — Deut. 4: 5, 6.

All the earlier parts of the Christian Scriptures relate nearly as much to national as to personal life. The origin, consolidation, liberation and nationalization of the people of Israel shows the interest of Almighty God in the forms of government of great peoples. Our text exalts the character of those laws and political principles which became the basis of the Jewish state. Everywhere through both the Old and the New Testament, we find patriotic devotion to the nation mingled with profoundest reverence for God. The patriarchs who laid the foundations of the Jewish state, the law-givers, judges and prophets who came after them, all are animated with ardent devotion to their country. This is particularly noticeable in the words of the prophets, especially in the greater prophets, Isaiah, Jeremiah and Ezekiel; who, like Moses, the law-giver, were as truly statesmen as they were teachers of religious truth.   And it might truthfully be said, that the Bible is a book of patriotism. While the Jewish people were called the chosen of God, it is scarcely less evident that our own country, owing to the peculiar circumstances of its birth and the origin of its laws, is in some sense a chosen people.   When or where was ever a nation founded, or what nation has ever been so looked to by all the world as holding a providential place for the exaltation of all peoples and the advancement of liberty throughout the earth?   It may be that, like the Hebrew nation, we shall not wholly fulfill our mission; but certainly, it behooves us to put forth every endeavor so to do.   If this nation shall do as the Israelites were counselled to do; if we shall obey the statutes and judgments which God has given us; if it shall be our wisdom and understanding to make these laws and this constitution, which are praised throughout the world, the corner-stone of our future, then it can be said of us, that there is no nation so great that hath judgments and statutes so righteous as all this law which has been left us by our fathers, under which we have hitherto lived.

The Constitution of the United States is not only extraordinary in its quality, but equally so in its history.   As a basis of national life, it has received the encomiums of the most advanced and liberal statesmen throughout the world.   It could not be

called, in its origin, a theory of government merely ;
although no nation before had a constitution like it.
But it was based on the wisest maxims of political
philosophy, on the profoundest views of human
rights, on the highest law of obligation to God in
the relations of men, and was deduced from the history of other nations and other peoples in their
failure to meet the public want, and to create a
happy and free people.

Although the document which we call the Constitution of the United States is not perfect in all its
parts, and has been amended from time to time by the
wisdom of the whole body politic, yet, through the
mercy of God and his overruling providence, great
good has come out of it.   As a basis of laws, it may
be said that those of no other country furnish so
broad a foundation for universal happiness and prosperity.   If we contrast this fundamental law with
that of Russia under an absolute monarch, or of
Germany under a monarchy scarcely less absolute — if we compare it with the government of England, whose constitution is a cumbrous mass of precedents, giving privileges to a state church and a
hereditary nobility — indeed, if we compare it with
the constitution of any land, we may justly affirm in
words, what is emphatically declared by the immense
immigration which has come into this country, that
our Constitution is recognized as the best, and its
practical fruitage is the richest.   The noblest comment that can be made upon our system of government in the United States, upon its authority and its

laws, is seen in the extraordinary growth and prosperity not only of the nation as a whole, but of the states and families of the nation. Surely, such a country, created out of such laws, is worth our care. The subversion of this government, by internal foes or by external assailants, could but entail calamity upon the whole human race, and we are sure that the government can never be subverted, nor its administration overthrown, unless the principles of the Constitution are abandoned to the assaults of open enemies, or the treachery of hidden foes. Such abandonment, either through our indifference or our feebleness, must inevitably be followed by the overthrow of our privileges and the ruin of all our prosperity.

Over a single word or clause in our Constitution we fought a terrific civil war. That word was "Union." To prove ourselves a Nation, to vindicate that one idea of the constitution, we spent our thousands of millions of dollars and hundreds of thousands of lives; and yet no intelligent son of America to-day hesitates to affirm that all this expenditure was not too much to preserve and vindicate the unity of the United States. Can we doubt that other portions of our Constitution which relate to the rights of citizens and their protection, are equally worthy of defence? But no words of praise from us are needed to vindicate this all-important document, since scarcely a statesman of our country, or of any liberal government lives, but has assisted in voicing the universal judgment of freemen in praise of our Constitution.

Against this, the most open, pronounced enemy of every principle of the United States, is the Roman Catholic Church. Whether we speak of the source of political power as defined in our Constitution, of the supremacy of that law or of its several parts with their theory of human rights, or even when we speak of the formation of the executive and legislative bodies of the government as embodied in its provisions, or the administration of justice — every one of these particulars is denounced, assailed and anathematized by the Roman Catholic Church. And, since that church has come to claim supremacy over at least one-tenth, perhaps one-eighth, of our population, and to exercise political power through the manipulation of resident prelates in the interests of a foreign potentate, it is high time that we proceed to show its real hostility, and to protect, while we may, the Palladium of our liberties.

1. "We, the people of the United States," says the Preamble to the Constitution, "in order to promote a more perfect union, establish justice, insure domestic tranquility, provide for the common defence, promote the general welfare and secure the blessings of liberty to ourselves and our posterity, do ordain and establish this Constitution for the United States of America." Here is a plain declaration that the people, under God, are supreme, that they are the source of political power; that they, by their representatives and in their capacity as citizens, have the right given of God, of self-government. To this agrees the form of many of the state constitutions;

as for instance, that of the State of New York, which announces the same doctrine in these words : " We, the people of the State of New York, grateful to Almighty God for our freedom, in order to secure its blessings, do establish this constitution."

Against this first principle of our national government, the Papacy announces the Pope as the origin of the rights of states, as the supreme judge in all matters of law, and affirms, as we showed in the previous discourse, everywhere the supremacy of the church and its ecclesiastics over the state and its people. Pope Leo XIII., the present pope, says, in his encyclical ; " It is not lawful to follow one rule in private conduct and another in the government of the state : to wit, that the authority of the church should be observed in private life, but rejected in state matters." Says Pius IX., in his Syllabus : "It is an error to believe that the Roman Pontiff can and ought to reconcile himself to and agree with progress, liberalism and civilization, as lately introduced." This demand was sufficiently exposed when previously considered. Note now another particular in which the Romish church is in direct antagonism to the Constitution of the United States.

2. The Constitution is the supreme law of the land, the final test of civil duty. In substantiation of this fact, we observe that the final court of appeal in America is the Supreme Court of the United States, whose chief function is, to decide whether a law is constitutional or not. If any law made by the several states, or by any one of them, is found to

be inharmonious with the Constitution, it is pronounced null and void.   And so the most dignified
court in the world recognizes as its law our Constitution.

But Romanism confesses no such supremacy in any
civil law or in any legislation.   The only law which
shall govern the Pope is his own will, and the will
of the Pope is the law of church and state.

He can abrogate constitutions, pronounce legislative enactments null and void, call upon all Romanists to break and violate such laws, and has repeatedly commended his followers for setting the laws of
states at defiance.   In an encyclical, the Pope says :
" The Romish church has a *right to exercise its authority without any limits set to it by the civil power :
the Pope and the priests ought to have dominion over
temporal affairs :* the Romish church and her ecclesiastics have a right to immunity from civil law : in
case of conflict between ecclesiastical and civil powers
the ecclesiastical powers ought to prevail." (Strong's
" Our Country," page 50.)   " The Romish church
alone arrogates to herself the right to speak to the
state not as a subject but as a superior ; not as pleading the right of a conscience staggered by the fear of
sin, but as a vast Incorporation, setting up a rival
law against the state in the state's own domain, and
claiming for it, with a higher sanction, the title to
similar coercive means of enforcement.   The Pope
himself is foreign and not responsible to the law.
The large part of his power is derived from foreign
sources.   He claims to act, and acts, not by individ-

uals but on masses. He claims to teach them, so
often as he chooses, what to do at each point of their
contact with the laws of their country. The Pope
takes into his own hand the power which he thinks
the state to have misused. Not merely does he aid
or direct the consciences of those who object, but he
even overrules the consciences of those who approve.
Above all, he pretends to annul the law itself. The
right to override all the states of the world, and to
cancel their acts, within limits assignable from time
to time to, but not by those states, and the title to
do battle with them, as soon as it may be practicable
and expedient, with their own proper weapon and
last sanction of exterior force, has been sedulously
brought more and more into view of late years. The
centre of the operation has lain in the Society of
Jesuits. The infallible, that is virtually divine, title
of command, and the absolute, that is the unconditional duty to obey, in 1870, were promulgated to an
astonished world." (Gladstone, " Vaticanism," pages
172-74.)

The American prelates of the Romish church,
assembled in the Baltimore council, commenting on
the authority of the Papal Syllabus, affirm that it
does not appertain to the civil power to define what
are the rights and limits within which the church
may exercise authority: that its authority must be
decided upon by itself, that is, by the Pope, and
exercised without the permission and assent of the
civil government : and that, in the case of conflicting
laws, between the two powers, the laws of the church

must prevail over those of the state. They insist that the state is bound to recognize the Roman Catholic Church as the sole depository of the delegated power to decide what laws shall be obeyed and what disobeyed. To permit a church, any church, to decide upon the validity or invalidity of our laws after enactment, or to dictate beforehand what laws should or should not be passed, would be to deprive the people of all the authority they have retained in their own hands, and to make such church the governing power, instead of them. Yet, understanding this perfectly well, and evidently contemplating the time when they might possibly be able to bring about this condition of affairs, these Papal representatives directly assail a principle which has been universal in all our state governments, from their foundation : that which regulates by law the holding of real estate by churches and other corporations, and requires them to conform, in this temporal matter, to the statute laws of the states. (Thompson's " Papacy and Civil Power," pages 42 and 45.)

The Second National Council of the Roman Catholic hierarchy, was held at Baltimore in October, 1866. This plenary council, — the highest Roman Catholic authority in this country, but of course absolutely subordinate to the Pope, who dictated its policy before its session, protested against the control of ecclesiastical property by the civil laws of the several commonwealths ; and a Romanist authority remarks on one of its utterances, " The desire of gradually introducing in this country, as far as practicable, the ecclesiastical discipline prevalent throughout almost the entire church, was strongly and repeatedly expressed by the fathers of the late National Council of Baltimore. Its decrees tend both avowedly and implicitly to promote the accomplishment of this object." Here is the express declaration of principles of hostility and irreconcilable variance of the Romish church against the Constitution of the United States.

Now, while every American citizen is sworn to support the Constitution, and every Roman Catholic holding office in the United States is so obligated, the question occurs whether, as between the obligation to the Constitution of the United States and the contrary demand of the Church, they will as patriots support the State, or as Romanists support the Church.

Peter Dens, the great authority and commentator on ecclesiastical law in the Romish church, who has been a standard with them for a hundred years, defines the principles of the common law of that church, among which are the following: " The Pope can dispense with any law. The Constitutions and decrees of the Pope are explanations of the divine law, and are therefore binding as soon as known. The church does not recognize the right in any government to say whether or not the pontifical decrees shall be enforced. She is supreme and independent, and therefore can admit of no intermeddling with her authority. The Pope's temporal power is necessary to the free exercise of his spiritual authority. He derives his jurisdiction immediately from God, and imparts a share of the plenitude of his power to his bishops. Ecclesiastical property must be governed by the laws of the church. The state ought to recognize and carry into effect the laws of the church. By these, laymen have no right to property in the church, and it is against the law of God for them to dispose of its revenue.

" The coercive power of the church includes the power to punish the insubordinate, and repress the lawless, which extends to any punishment short of the shedding of blood, such as imprisonment in monasteries and other chastisements." (Thompson's " Papacy and the Civil Power," pages 608-10.) The Pope, then, can grant a dispensation as it is called, excusing any Romanist, whatever his oaths to the Constitution of the United States, from keeping those oaths, and justifying him in breaking any law, whatever that law, that the Pope shall denounce. The exercise of authority over political opinion, as we said in our first discourse, is the theory, as it is the practice, of the Roman Catholic Church. You may find in Roman Catholic bookstores a little book written by Monseigneur Segur, a Frenchman, entitled, " Plain Talk about the Protestantism of To-day." This book, which we shall have occasion to refer to several times hereafter, is highly commended by the ecclesiastics of the church, and its author has received the thanks of the Pope himself. I wish you all might read it. As concerning the point we are now making, that the Pope has absolute power to abrogate all constitutions and to command all his subjects to disobey the laws of any country in which they live, if he chooses so to do, Mons. Segur says : " The authority of the church is a guard over human understanding in whatever, directly or indirectly, affects religion ; *which means, in every kind of doctrines, religious, philosophical, scientific, political, etc.*" Please emphasize in your minds this word *political.* In connection with all else that we have secured from Romanistic sources, Archbishop Manning says : " The principles of ethics, and *therefore of politics as a branch of ethics,* all lie in the theological order." This is sufficient to establish every claim to political obedience. Hence, if the Pope shall declare that any political opinions are wrong, unjust, or immoral, the declaration must be held by all obedient children of the Church to be unerringly and indisputably true ; and to save themselves from excommunication for heresy, they must make exterminating war upon all such opinions. Hence, also, if he shall declare that any existing government is opposed to the welfare of the church, and, therefore, to the law of God, the same result must follow. And hence again, if he shall declare that the government of the United States is unjust, and an act of usurpation, because it gives license to the heresy of Protestantism ; because it repudiates the doctrine of the " divine right" of kings ; because it allows the people to make their own laws ; because it requires the Roman Catholic hierarchy to obey the laws thus made ; because it does not recognize the

Roman Catholic religion as the only true religion; because it recognizes the right of each individual to interpret the Scriptures for himself, and to entertain whatsoever religious belief his own conscience and reason shall approve, or none at all, if he shall think fit; because it has separated Church and State, and denies the right of the Church to subordinate the State to any of its laws; because it not only tolerates, but fosters and protects, free thought, free speech, and a free press; and because it is, on account of any and all of these things, in open violation of the Romish law, and therefore heretical,— does not every man of common sense see that the Papal followers must select between conformity to his opinions and excommunication? between obedience to him, and the forfeiture of eternal salvation? between resistance to the government and his pontifical curse? between treason and hierarchical denunciation? ("The Papacy and the Civil Power," page 153.)

Against the origin of our Constitution, against the principles which it sets forth, against the freedom which it provides, Rome stands, the champion of absolutism, hating republics in the principles of their government, and standing for the divine right of kings to exercise unrestricted authority over their subjects, or authority restricted only by the law of the Pope. This hostility has been shown toward the Republic of France. The descendant of the Bourbons, the Count de Chambord, was the favorite of the Papacy, and Pope Pius IX. used all his influence to elevate him to the throne which the French

Republic had thrown down; because, as Segur says:
" This descendant of kings had given solemn promise that, once on the throne of France, he will take
up the cause of the Pope; and then the sword of
Charlemagne shall spring from its scabbard and con-
voke, as of old, the Catholic peoples to the rescue
of Rome from the miserable and despicable Italian
apostates."

These apostates are Victor Emanuel, and Cavour
and Garibaldi, with all who have helped to create
modern Italy, and rescue it from Papal tyranny.
And it is to the book containing these sentiments of
hostility to republics that Pius IX. has given his
approbation and his benediction, in an affectionate
letter addressed to M. Segur as his "beloved son."
What should we say if the Pope should formally
declare the laws of the Constitution of our country
null and void, as he practically has already the First
Amendment, and other material portions of that Constitution? What should we say, were he to send his
Allocutions to North America, as he has to South
America within the last forty years, pronouncing
null and void our laws? For I would not permit
you to forget, that since 1855 the Pope, inciting
sedition in the several states, has taken upon him to
declare null and void the laws of New Granada (this
was in 1863); the laws of Mexico in 1856; the laws
of Sardinia in 1855; the laws of Austria in 1862;
those of Spain in 1855; and of Piedmont in the
same year. And in every case, the laws which he
pronounced null are essential parts of the American

Constitution and of our common law. An irrepressible conflict will exist between the Papacy and the Constitution of the United States, until one or the other is destroyed. Which shall it be? I answer, Not the constitution of the United States!

3. But Rome's antagonism to the Constitution as a whole, will be more manifest when we note how utterly irreconcilable it is with the several parts of the great document.

The First Amendment to the Constitution of the United States reads as follows: "Article 1. Congress shall make no law respecting the establishment of religion, or prohibiting the free exercise thereof; or abridging the freedom of speech or of the press; or the right of the people peaceably to assemble, and to petition the government for a redress of grievances." The Constitution of the State of New York, Article First, section third, reads: "The free exercise and enjoyment of religious profession and worship without discrimination or preference shall forever be allowed in this State to all mankind." The Constitution of Massachusetts contains the same sentiment. The meaning and cause of these enactments is obvious to every one, not only in the essential justice and righteousness of such laws, but in the dreadful history of many European states, which, in their endevor to force upon their subjects a religion or form of worship which did not commend itself to the conscience of the people, have devastated their fairest provinces, destroyed the lives of thousands of their loyal subjects, and interfered with the general prosperity of society and of the state. Mindful of these horrors, our fathers, who themselves were exiled for conscience sake, wisely decided that only that religion could control a man's life and ennoble his character which he had voluntarily received in good conscience from God; and that with this understanding they made a good law, founded on a righteous decision, the prosperity of the Church and of the State in the United States equally attests.

Hear now the contrary doctrine of the Pope. January 1, 1870, Cardinal Antonelli, in behalf of Pope Pius IX., wrote to the Bishop of Nicaraugua: " We have lately been informed here that an attempt has been made to change the order of things in that Republic by publishing programmes in which are enunciated *freedom of education and worship. Both of these principles are contrary to the laws of God and of the Church.*" Or listen to the Papal law in the letter of Pope Pius IX. to the unfortunate Maximillian in Mexico. This you may read in "Appleton's Annual Encyclopedia for 1865," p. 749: " To repair the evils occasioned by the revolution, and to bring back as soon as possible happy days for the Church, the Roman Catholic religion must above all things continue to be the glory and mainstay of the Mexican nation, *to the exclusion of every other dissenting worship.* That no person may obtain the faculty of teaching and publishing false tenets ; that instruction, whether public or private, *should be directed and watched over by the eclesiastical author-*

ity; and that, in short, the chains may be broken which, up to the present time, have held down the church in a state of dependence and subject to the arbitrary rule of a civil government." Can you find any correspondence, any harmony, any possibility of reconciliation between the Constitution of the United States and these declarations of the highest Papal authority? It is impossible. They are exactly contradictory.

Proposition 78 of the Papal Syllabus condemns the principle of toleration which allows the recognition of other religions beside the Roman Catholic. Therein the Pope anathematizes the proposition that, "It has been wisely provided by law in some countries called Catholic, that persons coming to reside therein shall enjoy the public exercise of their own religion." Thus all religious toleration is stigmatized as an error. Which shall we have in America? Which will Roman Catholics support? Which will you admit, the principle of the Constitution, that Congress shall not legislate concerning the establishment of religion; or the principle of the Papacy, that the State shall legislate in favor solely of the Romish Church?

The prohibition of the free exercise of religion, concerning which the Constitution declares Congress shall make no law, is antagonized by the express declaration of the Pope, that no other religion than the Roman Catholic may be established or tolerated by the state. We grow sick of the iteration and reiteration of this bigoted but central principle of Romanism.

In the prohibition of the free exercise of religion, the Roman Catholic Church appeals not only to law and anathema but to physical punishment, affirming the absolute duty of the civil power to use force, and the right of the Church to coerce those who choose to worship after another manner and form. Little does it matter whether the Church exercise this power immediately through inquisitors, or indirectly through a subservient state. Dr. Newman, descanting on the title of the Church to employ force, says, though he inclines to the milder side and limits the kind of force : " The lighter punishments, those temporal and corporal, such as shutting up in monasteries and prisons, flogging, and others of the same kind, short of the effusion of blood, the Church, by her own right, can inflict." The brief or letter of Innocent III. says : " We are able also, and bound to coerce." The Jesuit Shrader, with a Papal approbation, gives us the following affirmative proposition, answering to the negative condemnation of the Syllabus : " The church has the power to apply external coercion ; she has also a temporal authority, direct and indirect ;" and appends the remark : " Not souls alone are subject to her authority." — Gladstone, " Vaticanism," p. 162-4.

" Undoubtedly," says Cardinal Manning, quoting with approbation from the doctrines maintained by Bellerini, " unity with the Roman faith is absolutely necessary, and therefore the prerogative of absolute infallibility is to be ascribed to it, *and a coercive power to constrain to unity of faith*, in like manner, absolute : as also the infallibility and coercive power of the Catholic Church itself, which is bound to adhere to the faith, are absolute." And in order to most fully prove the doctrine of infallibility, and delegate to the Pope the entire authority over the Church, Archbishop Manning declares, "This infallibility and coercive power are to be ascribed to the Pope and are personal."

Here, then, as against the doctrine of the Constitution of the United States, that Congress shall not even make a law prohibiting the free exercise of religion, the Romish Church makes the law, applies it in every country,— in the United States as well as in Italy or Spain,—and affirms in addition, the right to compel by force, over the bodies as well as the souls of men, obedience to the Roman Catholic worship. And every Roman Catholic is sworn to give his obedience to the Pope as against the Constitution of the United States, under penalty of excommunication and peril of temporal and eternal damnation. When I have told you, as I shall later on, in his own words, the horrible curses which fall from the mouth of the Pope in excommunicating those who break his commands—curses that may well from their very boldness and blasphemy cause trembling in a superstitious mind — you will see in his words the black flag of that detachment of religionists calling themselves Christians, who march to the overthrow of all religious freedom.

To what extent may the Roman Catholic Church coerce? How does the Pope, how do the Cardinals

and Archbishops of to-day, understand this term as
they use it? We know what they meant by coercion
in the past. We know, in their relation to the ·
Huguenots, the Waldenses, the Albigenses, and the
Lollards, what coercion, has meant with the Romish
Church. We know what the Inquisition meant by
coercion — death by torture, by fire, by sword and ax,
by starvation, by burying alive ; and these have been
the sanctioned methods of the Romish Church, never
repudiated. Do they mean the same to-day? I
answer, There is no restriction on the degree or kind of
force that they will employ except their own cruelty.
Segur, whom I quoted sometime since, and whose
book you can purchase for a very small sum at the
Roman Catholic bookstores, justifies the Inquisition,
and in justifying it has the approval and blessing of
the Pope.   After stating that the Spanish Inquisition
was established by Roman Catholic governments as
an ecclesiastical institution, and thus agreeing that it
had the sanction and approbation of the Church, he
proceeds : " That institution you may value as you
choose : you are at liberty to condemn the abuses
and cruelties of which it has been guilty through the
violence of political passions and the character of the
Spaniard ; yet one cannot but acknowledge in the
terrible part taken by the clergy in its trials, the most
legitimate and most natural exercise of ecclesiastical
authority."   This book was not designed for Protestant readers. It was avowedly and expressly
addressed to those who were supposed to be ready
and willing listeners to the words of authority ; to

such as tamely and submissively put their manhood into the keeping of ecclesiastical superiors.

Is there any reader so ignorant that he needs to be told what the Spanish Inquisition was, which is here declared to be the most legitimate and most natural exercise of ecclesiastical authority? Of all the institutions ever known to the world, or ever invented by human ingenuity, it was the most cruel, oppressive and bloodthirsty. Its thousands of victims, whose bones were crushed with its accursed instruments of torture, and whose groans made its priestly officials laugh with a joy akin to that of the fiends of hell, still cry out of their tombs against it. Yet in the nineteenth century, while humanity has not ceased to shudder at the thought of its possible survival, the press of an American publishing house sends forth among the adherents of Roman Catholicism in the United States, with the sanction and approval of the Pope of Rome and of the Roman Catholic Bishop of Boston, the startling avowal, that this horrible instrument is " *the most legitimate and most natural exercise of ecclesiastical authority.*" And more than one of the Roman Catholic journals in the United States have taken extraordinary pains to commend this book in which this avowal is made to their readers, as does the Boston *Pilot* in its issue of February 20, 1870. ("Papacy and the Civil Power," pp. 81-83.)

The Spanish Inquisition! Jean Antoine Llorente was secretary of the Inquisition of Spain, and when that institution was suppressed, in 1809, '10, '11, all the archives were placed at his disposal. These consisted of unpublished manuscripts and papers mentioned in the inventories of deceased inquisitors. They were carefully examined, and furnished him much of the valuable information communicated in his published " History of the Inquisition." He says, that the " horrid conduct of this *holy office* weakened the power and diminished the population of Spain, by arresting the progress of arts, sciences, industry and commerce, and by compelling multitudes of families to abandon the kingdom ; by instigating the expulsion of the Jews and the Moors, and by *immolating on its flaming shambles more than three hundred thousand victims.*" He traces its history with great minuteness of detail, showing its introduction into Aragon during the reign of Ferdinand and Isabella : the punishment of the Albigenses and the Jews by its cruelties ; *its approval by Popes Sextus IV., Innocent VIII.*, and others, as the means of augmenting their power ; and gives the harsh and unprecedented rules of procedure by which it was governed. One of those rules shows how necessary it was considered to the Papacy, and that it was employed by the reverend Inquisitors both as a religious and political institution. It required all witnesses to be asked, in general terms, " If they had ever seen or heard anything which was, or appeared, contrary to the Catholic faith, or the rights of the Inquisition." (Llorente's " History of the Inquisition.")

La Maistre, in his "Letters on the Spanish Inquisition," defending the institution, says, in 1815 : " The

Inquisition is, in its very nature, good, mild and pre-
servative. It has the universal, indelible character of
every ecclesiastical institution ; you see it in Rome,
and you can see it wherever the true Church has
power." Quite true! This writer seems to be
recommending the Inquisition to Americans. He
admits that it existed in Spain by virtue of the bull
of the Sovereign Pontiff. He says that the grand
inquisitor is always either an archbishop or a bishop.
He justifies the infliction of capital punishment upon
those who attempt to subvert the established religion
of a nation ; which means, that the Pope would require
a resort to this remedy as the only means of obeying the divine law, wherever the Roman Catholic
religion is the religion of the State, as he is now
striving to make it in the United States. He says ;
" A sense of duty obliges me to say, that a heresiarch,
an obstinate heretic, and a propagator of heresy,
should indisputably be ranked among the greatest
criminals." That means, everyone who cannot be
forced into silence and submission by Romish
coercion. Again : " I by no means doubt that a
tribunal of this description, adapted to the times,
place and character of nations, would be highly use-
ful in every country." He speaks of the " demoniac
spirit of Puritanism," and of Protestantism as " nick-
named piety, zeal, faith, reformation and orthodoxy."

Now these letters of La Maistre were published by
Patrick Donahoe, Catholic bookseller of Boston, in
1843. How do you like them? What do you think

of substituting the mild Inquisition for the Constitution of the United States? And you would have to *substitute* it, since the Inquisition and the Constitution cannot live together in the same country.

And this Inquisition, somewhat modified, was made use of in the city of Rome until 1870. There religious toleration was unknown. No Protestants whatever were allowed to hold any service within the walls of Rome, as long as the Pope had power. Punishment, imprisonment and death were inflicted by the Pope, and under his express sanction and authority. I need not say, that one hour of life under the Constitution of the United States were worth an age of slavery under this revolting tyranny. And yet by every law of the Encyclical and Syllabus, by defence of past persecutions which it originated and carried forward, by the principles at present insisted on which it further advises shall speedily be made controlling, by the open and threatening declarations of its ecclesiastics, by its uncompromising hatred of all other forms of religion than its own, the Roman Catholic Church to-day would blot out the benignant Constitution of our Republic, and replace it by these accursed, blasphemous and vindictive statutes and theories, which would destroy every vestige of freedom and Protestantism from the face of the earth. I shall prove this still more fully as I proceed, out of the mouths of their own lawgivers and rulers.

4. And now I beg your attention to the specific declarations of the Constitution in favor of freedom of conscience, and the counter declarations of the

Roman Catholic law. The Constitution says, as already quoted: " Congress shall make no law respecting the establishment of religion or prohibiting the free exercise thereof, or abridging the freedom of speech or of the press." It may be possible that men shall speak so recklessly, whether by word or by printed page, that a limit must be set upon their expressions. To meet such cases, we already have laws in harmony with the Constitution, against slander, against vile and indecent language spoken or written, against those utterances in time of war that shall incite to treason or give aid and comfort to the enemy. But Congress has not, and never will violate this fundamental principle of our government, that the place and manner of worship, of speech, and of writing, shall be only limited by the laws of morality and by the safety of the State. Shall we contrast this attitude of our Constitution with that foreign power that is trying to overthrow it? You remember that we quoted Father Hecker as saying: " There is, ere long, to be a state religion in this country, and that state religion is to be Roman Catholic." While the *Catholic World* says : " Do you believe that this country will ever become Catholic ?' is changing to the question ' How soon do you think it will come to pass ? ' Soon, very soon, we reply, if statistics be correct." Bishop O'Connor says : " Religious liberty is merely endured until the opposite can be carried into effect without peril to the Catholic world." " Liberty of conscience," says Pope Pius IX., endorsing the bull of Gregory

XVI., is a most pestiferous error.   From it spring
revolutions, corruption, contempt of sacred things,
holy institutions and laws, and, in one word, that
pest of others most to be dreaded in a state, unbridled liberty of opinion."

Religious liberty he denounces, because it makes
the people disobedient to their princes ; and because,
if it should be conceded to the Italians of the Papal
States, they will soon naturally acquire political liberty, like the people of the United States.

Concerning freedom of the press, he says : " We
have been truly shocked at this most crafty device
[Bible Societies], by which the very foundations of
religion are undermined.   We have deliberated upon
the measures proper to be adopted by our pontifical
authority, in order to remedy and abolish *this pestilence*, as far as possible, *this defilement of the faith*,
so imminently dangerous to souls.   It is evident
from experience that the Holy Scriptures, when circulated in the vulgar tongue, have, through the temerity of men, produced more harm than benefit.
Warn the people entrusted to your care, that they
fall not into the snares prepared for their everlasting
ruin.   Several of our predecessors have made laws
to turn aside this scourge."   (" Papacy and the Civil
Power," pages 208-9.)

But suppose the Pope had the power in this country
that he claims ; and suppose, in violation of the
Constitution, he forbade here liberty of worship,
free speech, and a free press ; and suppose again,
which is very likely, that you should disobey this

imperial pontifical statute, what would be the result?
It may seem like repetition, and yet we think it cannot be too often or too fully impressed upon your
minds, that *death* would be the penalty of your
disobedience. For Dens, their great authority, says :
"Infidels are not to be tolerated. Infidelity is not
to be tried or proved, but extirpated." Baptized
heretics, (for they allow the legitimacy of your baptism while they affirm your heresy,) are to be visited
with excommunication, as in the case of the bull of
Pius IX., a few years ago, excommunicating all
Protestants. They are to be considered as infamous ;
their temporal goods are to be confiscated ; they
are to be subjected to corporal punishment, to exile
and impisonment. In case they remain obstinate,
they are to be dealt with as John Huss and Jerome
were, under a decree of the Council of Constance ;
that is, they shall suffer death.

Hear the emphatic and plain language of this
standard Romish authority :

"Are heretics rightly punished with death? Saint
Thomas answers 'Yes ; because forgers of money, or
other disturbers of the state, are justly punished
with death : therefore also heretics, who are forgers
of the faith, and, experience being witness, grievously
disturb the state.'" (Dens, Volume 2, Number 56,
Page 89.)

But how will these terrific penalties be executed
when the Pope has the power? The Constitution
gives every man the right of speedy trial by jury in
open court, before an impartial jury : he is to be

informed of the nature of the accusation, to be confronted with witnesses, to have compulsory process for obtaining witnesses in his favor, to have the assistance of a counsel for his defense: excessive fines shall not be imposed, nor cruel and unusual punishments inflicted. (Amendments to the Constitution, Articles VI. and VIII.) This is the mercy of a free government, which assumes the innocence of men until they are proven guilty by fair trial.

But what is the order of the Inquisition, which is the judicial enginery of the Papacy? All along they have denied that ecclesiastics shall be tried by civil court. They curse and denounce those who would subject the priests to the civil power. This curse and declaration was contrary to the declaration of Independence, which is almost as much a part of the foundation of our government as is the Constitution itself; which great instrument declares that all men are created free and equal, a doctrine against which the Pope fulminates at almost every turn. Ecclesiastics then shall not be held responsible to civil courts and constitutional laws. And by ecclesiastical courts, by secret tribunal, by inquisitor, on private information, without witnesses in one's favor, without an impartial jury, counsel being denied, the traps of fierce ecclesiastical, I had almost said devilish, law being set: by these means are heretics to be tried, and by these means condemned. This is the historic method of Romanism; its avowed policy, declared by its Popes, and by its authoritative writers, under Papal sanctions: this is actually the method pursued in the

Papal States until 1870, when the Pope lost his temporal power; and this is the condition to which they avow their purpose to subjugate us.

Do you question whether these quiet and diplomatic prelates would really execute such Papal mandates? whether kindly neighbors would become, at the Pope's command, persecutors, informers and destroyers? Hard as it is to conceive, this is exactly what has happened. So it was at the massacre of St. Bartholomew in France, where at least 70,000 Protestants were foully murdered by Papists; for which the Pope, Gregory XIII., commanded *Te Deums* to be sung in the churches of Rome, and in honor of which he ordered a medal struck with his own face on one side, and a scene of slaughter on the obverse. Though a tiger may create admiration by the symmetry of his form, and the smoothness and beauty of his skin, I prefer not to be so fascinated but that I remember that he has a tiger's nature within. I can admire the diplomatic skill, the intense devotion, and persistent patience of Romish Jesuits, but I dare not trust their heart; and therefore I arm myself and you with the truth which shall defend us from their assaults.

In your hearing, I have cited the laws and principles which claim absolute sway over Roman Catholics, and have cited also the Constitution of the United States, to which they are diametrically opposed. And now, that you may know what spirit is in those laws, whether there is a fierce and cruel heart behind them all, I shall quote to you the excommunication bestowed on Victor Emanuel, King of United Italy, by the Pope of Rome. This shocking curse was dealt out to him, not because he was immoral, or ambitious, or a fierce soldier. All these may have been his characteristics, but they call forth no Papal hate. Only when he appears amid the acclamations of emancipated Italians, the King of United Italy, does the hatred of the Pontiff burst forth against him. In the person of Victor Emanuel then, the church thus anathematizes freedom in Italy.

And remember, while I read this furious curse, that it is spoken by one whom Roman Catholics call the " Vicar of Christ," who assumes by their consent, among other titles, that of " Prince of God," " The Oracle of Religion," " Our Lord God the Pope," " The Most Holy Father," " Priest of the World," " The Divine Majesty," with other names of blasphemy. Without prejudice, make up your minds what spirit dwells in a man, or a church, that can employ the following curse :

" By authority of the Almighty God, the Father, Son, and Holy Ghost ; and of the Holy Canons, and of the undefiled Virgin Mary, mother and nurse of our Saviour ; and of the celestial virtues, angels, archangels, thrones, dominions, powers, cherubims, and seraphims ; and of all the holy patriarchs and prophets ; and of the apostles and evangelists ; and of the holy innocents, who, in the sight of the Holy Lamb, are found worthy to sing the new song ; and of the holy martyrs and holy confessors, and of the holy virgins, and of the saints, together with all the

holy and elect of God : we excommunicate and anathematize him, and from the threshold of the holy
church of God Almighty we sequester him, that he
may be tormented in eternal excruciating sufferings,
together with Dathan and Abiram, and those who
say to the Lord God, ' Depart from us ; we desire
none of thy ways.' And as fire is quenched by
water, so let the light of him be put out forever
more.   May the Son who suffered for us, curse him.
May the Father who created man, curse him.   May
the Holy Ghost which was given to us in our baptism,
curse him.   May the Holy Cross which Christ, for
our salvation, triumphing over his enemies, ascended,
curse him.   May the Holy and eternal Virgin Mary,
mother of God, curse him.   May St. Michael the
advocate of holy souls, curse him.   May all the
angels and archangels, principalities and powers, and
all the heavenly armies, curse him.   May St. John
the precursor, and St. Peter, and St Paul, and St.
John the Baptist, and St. Andrew, and all other
Christ's apostles, together curse him, and may the
rest of his disciples and four Evangelists, who by
their preaching converted the universal world,— and
may the holy and wonderful company of martyrs and
confessors, who by their holy work are found pleading to God Almighty,— curse him.   May the Choir
of the Holy Virgins, who for the honor of Christ
have despised the things of this world, damn him.   May
all the saints who from the beginning of the world,
and everlasting ages are found to be beloved of God,
damn him.   May the heavens and the earth, and all
things remaining therein, damn him.

" May he be damned wherever he may be; whether
in the house or in the field, whether in the highway
or in the byway, whether in the wood or water, or
whether in the church.   May he be cursed in living
and dying, in eating and drinking, in fasting and
thirsting, in slumbering and sleeping, in watching or
walking, in standing or sitting, in lying down or
walking *mingendo cancando*, and in all blood-letting.
May he be cursed in all the faculties of his body.
May he be cursed inwardly and outwardly.   May
he be cursed in his hair.   May he be cursed in his
brain.   May he be cursed in the crown of his head
and in his temples.   In his forehead and in his ears.
In his eyebrows and in his cheeks.   In his jaw-bones
and his nostrils.   In his foreteeth and in his grinders.
In his lips and in his throat.   In his shoulders and
in his wrists.   In his arms, his hands, and in his
fingers.   May he be damned in his mouth, in his
breast, in his heart, and in all the *viscera* of his body.
May he be damned in his veins and in his groin; in
his thighs; in his hips and in his knees; in his legs,
feet, and toe-nails.'

" May he be cursed in all the joints and articulations
of his body.   From the top of his head to the sole of
his foot may there be no soundness in him.   May the
Son of the living God, with all the glory of his
Majesty, curse him; and may heaven, with all the
powers that move therein, rise up against him —
curse him and damn him! Amen. So let it be!
Amen."

Hell is not more remote from heaven than this
from the spirit of the Lord Jesus Christ!

And I call upon all men who are witnesses to the spirit and words of Papal tyranny, on Protestants and Roman Catholics who love God and manhood, liberty and country, to register a solemn vow with God, like that in which you yielded your hearts to his service, that never, by your indifference, consent or connivance, shall the Papal power make a sepulchre beneath its curses for the Constitution and the Laws which are the glory and protection of free America.

NOTE. The form of the Excommunication of Victor Emmanuel quoted above is vouched for by A. P. Grover, Esq., in his book entitled "Romanism the Danger Ahead," from which it is cited by the author.

Sermon V.

ROMANISM ANTAGONISTIC TO THE CONSTITUTION AND THE LAWS.

My sermon is really a continuation of that of last Sunday evening, and my text is the same as then. In the book of Deuteronomy, the fourth chapter, beginning with the fifth verse: "Behold I have taught you statutes and judgments, even as the Lord my God commanded me, that ye shall do so in the land whither ye go to possess it. Keep therefore and do them; for this is your wisdom and your understanding in the sight of the nations, which shall hear all these statutes, and say, Surely this great nation is a wise and understanding people. For what nation is there so great, who hath God so nigh unto them, as the Lord our God is in all things that we call upon him for? And what nation is there so great, who hath statutes and judgments so righteous as all this law, which I set before you this day?"

You will remember, if you were here, that I showed how this might apply to the Constitution of this great country, and I also showed, in the introduction of last Sunday evening, the relation of the Constitution to the welfare and liberty of the State.

I then proceeded to point out the utter antagonism of Romanism to the Constitution and laws of the United States, and in the following particulars : First, That while the Constitution recognizes the people, under God, as the source of all authority ; the Roman Catholic Church recognizes the Pope, under God, as the source of all authority. Second, — I brought to your attention the fact that, while the Constitution is the supreme law of the land, the Roman Catholic Church insists that the will of the Pope is the supreme law of all lands. I then took up the First Amendment of the Constitution, showing that it is according to the Constitution of the United States that no religion shall be established by law; and I then showed that the Roman Catholic Church is always clamoring to have Romanism established by law. I further proved that it was contrary to the Constitution of the United States to forbid any relig-ion in this country ; and I then showed that it is according to the principles of the Roman Catholic Church to forbid every religion excepting its own.

Then I read from the Constitution of the United States, that liberty of conscience should never be abridged in our nation, and quoted from the Pope of Rome and the hierarchs to show that liberty of con-science was considered by them a pest and a delirium. I also quoted the Constitution as against abridging freedom of speech and of the press. Afterwards I quoted Roman Catholic authorities as considering liberty of speech and of the press a pestilence, as they declared in encyclicals and acts of councils. I then proceeded to show that it was contrary to the Constitution of the United States to inflict severe penalties without fair trial by jury ; and afterwards, that Roman Catholicism declares her ecclesiastical laws to be superior to all civil law, and claims the right to inflict all sorts of penalties ; and having proved all these things, I closed by reading the diabolical excommunication which was visited upon Victor Emanuel, by Pope Pius IX., to show the fierceness of the Papal spirit.

When we closed the last discourse, we had shown that Romanism, in its letter and spirit alike, was hostile to the Constitution of the United States and the laws of the country. Now we will resume where then we paused, the line of irrefutable proof that this is the fact.

In further demonstration of this, I call your attention to a remark of the most distinguished statesman of Spain, Castelar, who, in 1869, said to the Spanish Cortes : " There is not a single progressive principle which has not been cursed by the Catholic Church. This is true of England and Germany, as well as of Catholic countries. The Church cursed the French Revolution, the Belgium Constitution and the Italian Independence. Nevertheless all these principles have unrolled themselves in spite of it. Not a Constitution has been born, not a single progress made, not a solitary reform effected which has not been under the terrible anathemas of the Church."

As though to add emphasis to the very words that I have spoken, the present Pope has just issued another encyclical against liberty, of which you will find an abstract in the New York *Independent* for August 2, 1888, in which all the assaults of which we have taken note heretofore are renewed. Liberty of conscience, freedom of worship and the supremacy of the Constitution are all disallowed, and the Pope protests that the State ought to suppress any other than the Roman Catholic religion. This document is later than the infamous rescript concerning . Irish affairs, which has so effectually shut the mouths of all those enthusiastic patriots who hitherto have been doing their utmost for what they call the liberation of Ireland.

Perhaps the most capable theologian and essayist of the Roman Catholic Church in America was Orestes A. Brownson, a pervert from Protestantism. That he fully shared the sentiments of the Pope you may learn from his writings ; among which occurs the following significant assertion : " All the rights the sects have, or can have, are derived from the State, and rest on expediency. As they have, in their character of sects, hostile to the true religion, no rights under the law of nature or the law of God, they are neither wronged nor deprived of liberty if the State refuses to grant any rights at all." The New York *Tablet* says : " They have, as Protestants, no authority in religion, and count for nothing in the Church of God. They have from God no right for propagandism, and religious liberty is in no sense violated when the national authority, whether Catholic or pagan, closes their mouths and their places of holding forth."

But now I call you to notice, that Romanism in America has violated the Constitution of the United States by overt acts.

1. Note the following violation of the Constitution by Romanism, in the matter of appropriating public monies. The Constitution and the laws of the United States, and of the several States, do not warrant, but rather forbid, the appropriation of money by the States to sects, for their own specific purposes. This is a natural and necessary interpretation of the First Amendment of the Constitution, and the reason for it is obvious to all. But by threats and political influences, the Roman Catholic Church has violated this law in many cases.

Among the most conspicuous, are those in New York State and New York City. The chief authority on this matter is the late Dexter A. Hawkins of New York, who, in the New York *Christian Advocate* of January, 1880, tells us in detail how the Roman Catholics possessed themselves of several blocks in the best part of New York City, where now the Cathedral stands. Five and a-half whole blocks were stolen from the city, worth at least three millions and a-half of dollars, and no consideration was given in return. Not only this, but specifically Roman Catholic institutions, schools, churches, and so-called benevolent institutions, have been supported largely by public funds: 127 of these Romish institutions, in eleven years prior to 1879, had received six million dollars. The Tweed ring in 1869, exchanged, for the political influence of Roman-

ists, $800,000 in appropriations that year. So far
from these sectarian institutions being benevolent,
it is a notorious fact that some of them have been
made prisons for those who have thrown off the yoke
of Rome and espoused the Christian faith. Spirited
away from their homes and placed in durance vile,
some of them have never been heard from again since
they entered the walls of these institutions, the sole
purpose of which is to make, out of the young and
rising generation, converts to Rome.

But not only in the States has this flagrant violation
of the Constitution occurred. By stealth, the Roman
Catholics have secured from the national government,
appropriations to specifically Romish schools. You
may perhaps know that the Government supports, in
part, schools for the Indians, in which the various
denominations also bear a part. The Roman Catholics have a Bureau of observation and effort at
Washington, from which they bring to bear influences upon Congress to secure the lion's share of
these appropriations. Last year, of the entire
appropriations for Indian education, the Roman
Catholics, who number only one-sixth to one-tenth
of our population, received fifty-five and a-half per
cent., while all the Protestant Churches, in their
work, though they number five-sixths to nine-tenths
of the population, received only forty-four and a-
half per cent. This indicates the alarming extent to
which Rome influences even national legislatures in
the line of building up her own power.

In addition to these appropriations, thus forced

from the public treasury, Rome, with her usual greed of grain, has secured and holds vast properties in our cities and country on which she pays no taxes.

Among the principles of the Romish Church is this, that it has the legitimate right to secure, hold and use property without limit. In our country, churches and religious corporations, as well as all other corporations, can hold property only when authorized so to do by statute, and for the uses specified by statute, and then only to the amount fixed by statute. The Romish Church opposes all this, as by it they are prevented from swallowing up the property of the country.

In England, before the statute of mortmain, the Church had got possession of one-third of the property of the kingdom, and so astute were the priests in evading the laws of the realm, that it took four hundred years to so perfect them as to protect the public against the rapacity of this Church. Blackstone says, that but for these statutes, ecclesiastical corporations would soon have engulfed the whole real estate of England. After all these precautions, the civil power had finally to resort to confiscation, to restore enough of the land to the people to ensure the prosperity of the realm.

In Italy, Spain and Mexico, the civil government, for like reasons, though it was Roman Catholic, has been compelled to resort to confiscation. As a sample of Romish greed, in the year 1848, through unmitigated chicanery, the Romish ecclesiastics obtained from a feeble old man in Brooklyn, New York, a vast landed property. They secured an act of incorporation for a nominal society, The Brooklyn Benevolent Society, which simply pours its revenues into the pockets of the priests and prelates, and in the one year 1880, this property should have paid into the treasury of the city not less than one hundred thousand dollars annual taxes. They have held it without a penny of tax, and do to this day.

This is but a sample. The rapacity of the Roman Catholic Church for money is simply without bound. The Pope lives in the utmost splendor and luxury. His palace is the grandest of any sovereign in Europe. His state carriages, covered with gold, are inferior to those of no other monarch. Cardinals, archbishops and bishops, alike live in luxury, and many in gross dissipation; while the Roman Catholic people throughout the world are notoriously poor. The Romish Church is a vast system of plunder. Almost everything obtained in the way of religious consolation by her poor and superstitious people must be paid for with money. The confessional is little less than a means of extorting gold from the people. Purgatory and masses for the dead, is only another measure for the same purpose.

All Roman Catholic countries are miserably poor as compared with Protestant countries, as Romanists themselves declare. Spain, once the richest of empires, has been almost bankrupt for many years, and while Protestant countries have grown enormously in wealth, even under unfavorable circumstances, as steadily Roman Catholic nations have grown poorer. For this the church is responsible. The real trouble in Ireland is indicated by the recent interference of the Pope. The trouble is Popery. In vain the Papal power leads the Irish people to think that England is the cause of all their woes. But if Ireland was totally detached from the British Empire, that part of it that is under the domination of priests would be as Spain and Italy, it would become poorer and poorer. In Canada, in the United States, in Mexico and the South American Republics, as well as in European States, Rome must answer for the fact that her people, with all their natural gifts and advantages, which do not seem to be in any wise inferior to the providential opportunities of Protestants, are crushed to death by the extortions, the avarice, the rapacity of priestly rulers. And both by their laws and their practices, it is evident that Rome purposes nothing less in this country than to possess itself of vast wealth, at the expense of the people, for the destruction of the nation.

2.   But I pass from this violation of the Constitution and the rights of man, to some further proofs that the Romanists propose to make the Pope supreme in America.

First of all, this is their creed, their religion; this is the doctrine of their councils, the doctrine of their Encyclicals, the spirit of all their work. Their ablest theologians, whom we have cited, so expound their laws. And they are not more attached to any

principles of their religion than to this purpose to
make the Pope supreme and absolute ruler. Hear
the arrogant words in which their oracle, Brownson,
asserts this purpose: "The people need governing,
and must be governed. They must have a master.
The religion which is to answer our purpose must
be above the people, and able to command them.
The first lesson of the child is to obey; the first and
last lesson to the people, individually and collectively,
is obey. There is no obedience where there is no
authority to enjoin it. The Roman Catholic religion,
then, is necessary to sustain popular liberty, because
popular liberty can be sustained only by a religion
free from popular control, above the people, speaking from above and able to command them, and such
a religion is the Roman Catholic. *In this sense we
wish this country to come under the power of Rome.*
As the visible head of the Church, the spiritual
authority which Almighty God has instituted to
teach and govern the nation, we assert his supremacy,
and tell our countrymen that we would have them
submit to him. They may flare up as much as they
please, and write as many alarming and abusive edit-
orials as they choose, or can find time and space to
do. They will not move us, or relieve themselves
from the obligation Almighty God has placed them
under, of obeying the authority of the Catholic
Church, Pope and all." Could anything be more
definite than this, or more insolent? Nothing;
unless it is the laws and practices of the Papal
power.

To secure this end, the present Pope, Leo XIII., expressly commands American Roman Catholics to political activity. Here are his words of November 1, 1885, an extract from his Encyclical : " Every Catholic should rigidly adhere to the teachings of the Roman Pontiffs, especially in the matter of modern liberty, which already, under the semblance of honesty of purpose, leads to harm and destruction. We exhort all Catholics who would devote careful attention to public matters, to take an active part in all municipal affairs and elections, and to favor the principles of the Church in all public services, meetings and gatherings. All Catholics must make themselves felt as active elements in daily political life in the countries where they live. They must penetrate, wherever possible, in the administration of civil affairs : must constantly exert the utmost vigilance and energy to prevent the usages of liberty from going beyond the limits fixed by God's law. All Catholics should do all in their power to cause the Constitutions of States and legislation to be modeled in the principles of the true Church. All Catholic writers and journalists should never lose for an instant from view the above prescriptions." By this time, you know what the purpose of such advice and counsel is,—the suppression of liberty, the downfall of the Constitution, the ruin of the State. Do Romanists obey this Papal command? Exactly, as they obey all other Papal commands. You would hardly suppose that Roman Catholics in this or other American cities needed to be exhorted to greater political activity.

And yet under the Papal command, they are evidently aiming at supreme power over the State. For, not only have they heard the word of the Pope, and avowed as part of their creed their purpose to make him supreme, but American Romanists, in great public meetings, have promised to assist in restoring and maintaining the Pope's temporal power.

After Victor Emanuel occupied Rome, numerous great public indignation meetings were held by the Roman Catholics throughout the United States, in many of which, together with their protests against Italian interference with the Pope's temporal government, they pledged themselves to restore the Pontiff to his rightful throne ; and in denouncing the course of Italy, its Constitution and its purposes, they denounce almost every principle of the American Constitution. This was particularly the case in a great Roman Catholic meeting in Philadelphia, on the 25th of March, 1873, in which, among the terrible persecutions which they recounted as having been visited upon their fellow Catholics in Germany, they stated the following : First, the expulsion of the Jesuits ; second, the encroachment upon the Constitutional rights of the German Catholic hierarchy, by retaining in their positions and dignities the Old Catholics ; third, the encroachments upon the rights of conscience, by keeping others than Romanists in charge of the public schools ; fourth, the unchristianizing of the schools. These they call arbitrary and tyrannical measures, and yet these are the common law of the United States, to which they are equally antagonistic. In pursuance of this determination, Roman Catholic periodicals, from time to time, have threatened "political damnation," to use their own phraseology, to legislators who opposed their behests. This unseemly menace is particularly conspicuous in the Roman Catholic *Review* for November, 1885, a periodical commended by the Bishop of Brooklyn, Cardinal McClosky, Bishop of New York, Cardinal Cullen, Archbishop of Dublin, and many other prelates. Commenting on the refusal of the Legislature of New York to grant the Roman church certain favors, they boast that those legislators had been retired from political life, and affirm that they have a list of others who shall follow them, unless they yield to do the bidding of Rome. In Canada, the interference of Romish prelates in elections, their boast that the Jesuits controlled the political force of the province, have already become a matter of history, as they have of alarm. If, in the face of these threats of political overthrow, and the establishment, on the ruins of our liberties, of the Papal power, you shall reply that these Roman Catholics are American citizens, and have sworn to support the Constitution and the laws, and that you do not think that they will violate their oath, I must call upon you to remember, first of all, as the most binding of their oaths, they are sworn to obey the Pope, and that as long as they are Romanists.

3. The oaths of Roman Catholics are no guarantee of their loyalty to the Constitution. They are specifically sworn to obey the Pope in preference to

any other ruler, his law above every other law. The bishop's oath, which I have already given you in detail, unhesitatingly affirms this. The Jesuit's oath is even stronger in its utter renunciation of all other rule or government than the Papal; while the priests and laymen are bound to the same control. As a matter of fact, they profess first a supreme allegiance to the Pope.

Shortly after the decree of infallibility was announced, and this profession of primary fidelity to the Pope was made in New York, the *New York Herald*, which has always been controlled by a moderate Roman Catholic said : " There are thousands of Roman Catholics in this land who do not place Rome above the United States, and whose patriotism cannot be subverted by fealty to religious dogmas and creeds." To this patriotic utterance, which we would fain believe to be true, the New York *Tablet*, Roman Catholic, of November 1872, replied: " The *Herald* is behind the times, and appears not yet to have learned that the thousands of Catholics it speaks of are simply no Catholics at all, if it does not misrepresent them. Gallicanism, which denies the temporal power of the Pope, is a heresy ; and he who denies the Papal supremacy in the government of the universal church, is as far from being Catholic as he who denies the Incarnation, or the Real Presence. The church is more than country, and fealty to the creed God teaches and enjoins through her, is more than patriotism. We must obey God rather than man." And further it says : " Our church is God's church, and not accountable either to State or to country." Thus you see how the organ of the hierarchy denounces the doctrine of moderate Romanism, which had only insisted on loyalty to the country.

But you reply, that all Roman Catholics in office, as those who have become naturalized in this country, have taken an oath of fealty to the Constitution and the Republic,—will they not be debarred therefore from treason, even at the Pope's command, by their oath? We answer: The Roman Catholic theory of oaths permits those who have taken them, without blame, to violate any oath or obligation when the Pope commands. One of the greatest Popes, Innocent III., asserted for himself such plentitude of power as gave him right to dispense with any law. The Fourth General Lateran Council, with the approval of Alexander III., decreed, that an oath in opposition to the welfare of the Church and the enactments of the holy fathers is not to be called an oath, but rather perjury. Peter Dens, the great commentator on the laws and morality and theology of the Church, lays it down as the law of the Church, that the right of the Pope, as the ultimate superior and sovereign, is reserved in every oath; which, of course, includes the oath of allegiance. He also instructs the faithful, that the Pope has the power of withdrawing or prohibiting what is included in an oath; and that when he does so, it is no longer included. I can give you the most abundant proof, from the Roman Catholic theologians, that by the law of *mental reservation*, as they call it, any Roman Catholic is justified in taking a false oath ; in swearing that he is ignorant of what he knows to be true ; in swearing that he knows to be true that of which he is ignorant, or any other use of language which sets truth at defiance. What, then, is the oath of a Roman Catholic worth, provided his personal honor and sense of right is not greater than that of the law of his church? I do not say that Roman Catholics are not numerous whose word and whose oath are honestly made, and will be honestly kept; but I do say, that this is no part of their religion, and that the Pope may, under penalty of excommunication, command them to violate any oath.

But we go even further than this, and are unfortunately able from history to show that Roman Catholics, being wholly at the mercy of the Pope, cannot be relied on in their oaths, even when we suppose that they speak without reservation, and when, so far as we can judge, their oath is honestly taken. You may be familiar with what is known as Catholic Emancipation in Great Britain. The Roman Catholics, on account of the universal doubt entertained of their loyalty, had long been subject to civil disabilities, under which they groaned, and against which they protested. These disabilities were not imposed capriciously by the Crown or Parliament of Great Britain, but were the result of long contention with Papal usurpation, and of an honest doubt as to the loyalty of Roman Catholics. While the agitation was going on, and the measures for the relief of British Roman Catholics were pending,

English and Irish priests and laymen combined to
affirm, under oath, that " It is not an article of the
Catholic faith, neither are they required to believe
or profess that the Pope is infallible.   Second : That
their Church has no power that can directly or
indrectly injure Protestants, as all she can do is to
refuse them her sacraments, which they do not want.
And third : That no ecclesiastical power whatever can
directly or indirectly affect, or interfere with, the
independence, the sovereignty, laws and Constitution
or government of the realm."

And on the 26th of February, 1810, the English
Catholic bishops declare as follows : " The said oath,
and the declarations, objurations and protestations
therein contained, are notoriously, to the Roman Catholic Church at large, become a part of the Roman
Catholic religion, as taught us by the Bishops, and
received and maintained by the Roman Catholic
Churches in Ireland ; and as such, are approved and
sanctioned by the other Roman Catholic Churches.
The protestation was signed by two hundred and forty-
one priests, including all the vicars apostolic, by all
the clergy and laity of England of any note ; and in
1789, in a general meeting of the English Catholics
in London, was subscribed to by every person
present, and the document was deposited in the
British Museum as a proof of their loyalty and
honesty.

And yet what do we see?   We see a Council at
the Vatican, in 1870, imposing a new law upon these
Roman Catholics and their descendants, in utter and

absolute contradiction of the vow that they themselves sustained and declared, concerning which Mr.
Gladstone says, while he does not deny the honor of
the Roman Catholics that made this protest, "Either
the Papal See and Court, had at that time, abandoned
the dream of the enforcement of the infallibility of
the Church; or else, by wilful silence, they were
guilty of practicing upon the British Crown one of
the blackest frauds recorded in history." ("Vaticanism," p. 134.)

Here, then, is a historic instance, which, if
it proves anything proves this: that if all the leading Roman Catholics in this country should meet
together and solemnly swear that there was nothing
in the laws of their Church inconsistent with their
highest patriotism and devotion to the country,— if
they should swear that, according to their understanding, the Pope could not interfere with their civil
allegiance,— he might, within twenty-four hours of
that time, on his sole and only responsibility, reverse
their oaths, and command them, under pain of eternal
damnation, to take up arms against the Constitution
and laws of the United States; and their honesty of
purpose in the avowal which they had made could
not for one moment stand against the order and the
will of the infallible Pope. No wonder that an
eminent Catholic layman, in a recent periodical, with
most pathetic and sorrowful allusions, protests
against the fact that the conscience, the judgment,
the loyalty of Roman Catholics are subject solely
and only to the Pope of Rome. Thus by the evident

laws and purposes of the Romish Church, and by their history also, they are thoroughly disloyal to the Constitution of the United States, and pledged to disobedience to the laws.

I do not hesitate to say that, in all candor and reason, every Roman Catholic who confesses this allegiance to the Papacy, ought to be disfranchised in the United States, and forbidden the right to participate, as a citizen, in either holding an office or casting a ballot.

For that is exactly the attitude which we take to Mormons, who affirm primary allegiance to their hierarchy. Here is the case of a man asking to be naturalized before the court, who vows that he is not a polygamist, but does believe in polygamy; that he is a Mormon, and if a polygamist were brought before the court, he, the applicant for naturalization, would not as a juror vote to condemn his fellow-Mormon for polygamy. Whereupon the United States Court, in an elaborate, learned, and rational opinion, refused to naturalize him, on this ground, that no man who is pledged to disobedience to the laws of the United States, or who is pledged to uphold and maintain others in disobedience, can, or by right should, become a citizen of the United States. The application of the principle would disfranchise every Roman Catholic in America, and ought to. Slowly as we are awakening to our dangers, even politicians, much more statesmen, are becoming filled with alarm; while all wise publicists are recognizing with dread, as the dangerous element

in American politics, the ecclesiastical power of
Rome. There is no city but what is burdened
with it; there is no state but what is imperilled by
it: and the whole land stands in the shadow of an
impending peril, a thunderbolt in the hand of this
modern Jove of the Vatican, that may yet shatter the
nation from center to circumference.

But I must close this line of argument and proof,
in order to show finally what are the results of
Roman Catholic supremacy. They have been privileged to try the experiment of absolute government,
and what has been the consequence? I will not refer
to the misgovernment of American cities, nor point
to the degradation of South American Republics; I
will not take time to speak to you of prostrate
Mexico, of ruined Spain and Portugal, and of down-
trodden Italy, but will try to answer the question.

4. What kind of government comes from the
Papal plan, where they have absolute sway? I answer,
a government as totally unlike ours as its principles
are opposed to those of our Constitution.

In the Roman States, until Papal supremacy was
abolished, the people suffered under one of the worst
governments in the civilized world. The people
were considered as so many tenants, who occupied
and enjoyed the Papal estate on the condition fixed
by the infallible head of the church, for her welfare
and not their own. They were possessed of no civil
rights whatever, in the sense in which the world holds
them; but only such privileges as their sovereign, the
Pope, thought proper to confer upon them; and

.these could be changed, modified, or entirely withdrawn at his personal discretion, or whenever the
interests of the Church should require it. If the
government was a trust held alone for the benefit of
the Church, as Papists allowed, then the people had
no right to demand of it anything on their own
account. The government was conducted wholly
without reference to them, and they were required to
submit, whatever it did. Popular liberty was therefore unknown and impossible. The Papacy alone
was free to do as it pleased, and this was called *the
freedom of the Church*. The people, having thus no
voice in public affairs, were in a condition of vassal-
age. The government was a revival, with slight
exceptions, of the old system of feudalism, without
its redeeming features. There was no written constitution, not even a collection of precedents, from
which the citizen could learn the extent of the privileges conceded to him. So, whatever of fundamental
law there was, could be found only in the decrees,
canons, and constitutions of councils, and the bulls
and briefs of Popes, published in a language which
- no one but the educated nobility could understand.
No freedom of worship was allowed. No Bibles in
the hands of the common people.

The Consul of the United States at Rome for four
years, until 1865, W. J. Stillman, reports a condition
of persecution which beggars description. Spies were
placed at the doors of places of Protestant worship as
they were at the door of our church last Sunday night,
to see if any Roman Catholic went in. Men were

arrested in bed at night, and carried off by officers of the holy church, and never heard of again, for no offense. The system of terrorism was such that liberal Romans dared meet only in public, and never permitted a stranger to approach them in conversation. Says the Consul : " I can conceive of no system of torture worse than this terrible espionage under which every patriotic Roman lay, fearful of his own breath, one scarcely daring to speak to another, except in tropes and innuendoes. They suffered the penalty of crime for wishing merely to be free. Had it not been for the system of counter espionage kept up by the Roman committee on the government, no liberal could have lived in Rome.

The Roman government of that time (this is 1865) was the embodiment of the spirit of the middle ages. Not a Bible could be sold. Not a voice could be heard preaching Christ on any part of Italian soil. The punishment for such offence was imprisonment, or death. The few friends of freedom, sometimes in caves, sometimes in woods, were accustomed, in fear and trembling, to meet and pray. The dungeons of the Inquisition were full. The stories of their horrors are too dreadful to be told here. The testimonies of De Sanctis and Gavazzi and others, which cannot be impeached, open before us damp, dark dungeons, where men and women were starved to death ; the horrible vats where they were put alive into quick-lime to perish for their faith ; the secret trap-doors through which they were dropped, where their cries could not be heard, and their protests were unknown. Such was the condition of the people under the kind of Papal supremacy which they propose to foist upon the United States in the end of the nineteenth century.

In Spain, under Queen Isabella, in 1860, death was the penalty for heresy. But why need we go to Spain or Italy for proof that those who leave the Roman Church are subjects of fierce and violent persecution? There is not a Roman Catholic in this or any city of America that dares to leave his Church, unless he is willing to bear the fiercest imprecation, abuse, ostracism, slander and persecution; while all over this country, when men and women have confessed Christ instead of the Pope of Rome, they have been spirited away and imprisoned in Roman Catholic institutions, under the care of priests; and not a few of them have passed from within those walls, from a life of suffering, to the only place of rest which they could find — the heavens of God.

Wherever Papal power prevails, there crime in all its phases is greatly increased. There are more murders, Sabbath-breaking, drunkenness, gambling, illegitimacy, and all forms of crime, in Roman Catholic than Protestant countries. The Pastoral Letter of the Catholic Council of Baltimore in 1860, says — and here, you see, Roman Catholics are speaking for themselves — "It is a melancholy fact, and a very humiliating avowal for us to make, that a very large proportion of the idle and vicious youths of our principal cities are the children of Catholic parents."

While in Roman Catholic Ireland there were nineteen murderers to the million of population; in Roman Catholic Belgium eighteen; in Roman Catholic France thirty-one; in Austria thirty-six; in Barvaria sixty-eight; Tuscany fifty-six; while in the Papal States there were one hundred and thirteen murderers to the million; in Roman Catholic Sicily ninety; in Naples one hundred and seventy-four; at the same time there were, in Protestant England, only four murders to the million. Name any Protestant country in Europe, and let its depths of vice and immorality be measured and named, and I will name a Roman Catholic country or city whose depths of vice and immorality are lower still. (Barnum's "Romanism as It Is," chap. xxvii.)

The distinguished French Catholic Lavelaye, professor in the University of Liege, in a celebrated pamphlet on "Protestantism and Roman Catholicism in their relation to the Liberty and Prosperity of the Nation," contrasts Protestant and Roman Catholic countries in their relative progress, social condition, growth of power, education, enlightenment, morals and free institutions, and in those contrasts, confesses the diminution, degradation and weakening of Roman Catholic nations, and the education, industry, activity, expansion and power of Protestant nations. I would that I could quote his eloquent words at length. I am only denied that privilege by the space and time of which I may make use.

"A few years ago," he says, "the supremacy belonged to the Catholics. To-day, place on the one side France, Austria, Spain, Italy and South

America, and on the other side Russia, Germany, England and North America, and evidently the predominance has passed over to the heretics. Nor is it difficult to point out the causes." Can there be any soul living under the great opportunities which have been developed by Protestant Christianity in this free Republic, who would wish to see it under the influence of that power which has overwhelmed with shame and crime, with ignorance and death, the fairest portions of the world? I undertook to show that Romanism is irreconcilably hostile to our Constitution and laws, and to all other forms of religion than itself. You see what I have done. I have proved that Romanism denies the supremacy of the Constitution and laws, and affirms the supremacy of the Pope and the Church. They deny that the people under God are supreme, and declare that the Pope under God is supreme. The Constitution guarantees freedom and justice; the Pope attacks and tries to break down all Constitutional guarantees of freedom. The Constitution forbids Congress to establish any religion; the Papacy demands that it alone be established by law. The Constitution forbids legislation against any form of religious worship, the Papacy demands legislation against every form of worship but herself. The Constitution protects freedom of conscience, the Papacy pronounces it a delirium. The Constitution guarantees freedom of speech and of the press, Rome denounces both as a pest and a pestilence. The Constitution guarantees a fair and open trial by jury, the Papacy commends, urges and employs the secret tribunals of the Inquisition. The Constitution forbids cruel and excessive penalties; the Papacy demands torture and death for heretics and claims the right to inflict it. The Constitution forbids legislation and appropriations by the State to religious sects; the Romish Church already has seized millions of public money in defiance of law. The Constitution taxes justly all property; the Romish Church demands, and by fraud secures, exemption to a large degree. The Constitution demands renunciation of foreign allegiance from all citizens; the Roman Catholics boldly avow their chief allegiance to a foreign ruler. The Constitution has brought the largest liberty and the greatest prosperity; the Papacy has cursed the lands where it has ruled.

Now as a final word. Suppose that in America there were six or seven millions of Russians who were taking the same attitude toward our Government as the Roman Catholics take. Suppose that they personally avowed, as a matter of conscience and duty, their primary and eternal allegiance to the Czar,— an allegiance he should also announce himself to claim, and from which he would not absolve them. And suppose that this foreign body in our midst, took all their oaths with mental reservation of their superior devotion to the Russian Czar and the principles of his absolute monarchy. And suppose that they attacked, denounced and defied, personally, and in conclave, and through their leaders, every principle of American liberty, including the Constitution which is the foundation of our rights and our laws.

And suppose that they announced and gave it out that they were bound to obtain the supremacy in this country; that they would act as a political unit; that they would make the Czar supreme; and that nothing should stand in their way. How long would the seven or eight times as many loyal American-born citizens permit this body of foreigners to flaunt the banners of absolutism and threaten the overthrow of the State? One of two things is certain: that foreign body would be compelled either to confess primary and absolute allegiance to this government and to forego all treason in theory, speech or act; or they would be expelled from the country by an irresistible force. They would be waited on in the name of the nation, and would be compelled to make their choice, either to renounce allegiance to a foreign potentate, or to leave the country. That is the way we would treat disloyal Russians. I regard the rule of the Czar, and my inference is drawn from reason and history, as much more benevolent than the rule of the Pope and his ecclesiastics. And the foreign body which is now among us, cursing and threatening all that we hold dear, much more deserves subjugation and expulsion than the subjects of any other foreign ruler or power.

In the name of the Constitution, which I believe will hold America as the Polar Star holds the magnet,—in the name of the majesty of the law, that like the sun in the heaven has flooded this Western world with the glory of liberty,—we demand of every Roman Catholic, that he either renounce political allegiance to a foreign prince, or leave the country.

Sermon VI.

THE PURPOSE OF ROMANISM TO DESTROY OUR PUBLIC SCHOOLS.

You will find my text in the First Epistle to the Corinthians, the tenth chapter and the fifteenth verse : "I speak as to wise men; judge ye what I say." While the intense interest which attaches to a theme that is so personal to every one of us and to our country may lead us at times to a degree of earnestness, and, in denunciation, of possible severity, I propose primarily, in all these discourses, to address myself to the calm reason and understanding of wise men. Where there is no thoughtfulness, where passion holds sway, where superstition rather than reason controls the mind, it may be possible to secure temporary and indeed vigorous interest in a great theme, by merely lashing the feelings of men into a greater or less degree of earnestness or fury. But where the interests of every man and of his children to the latest generation are at stake, where the affairs of education and of the nation are deeply involved, where mistake would be almost fatal, and where vengeance and hatred would be contrary to the law of Christ and the law of the land, it is desirable that our highest wisdom be exercised and our best judgment employed.

No greater compliment can be paid to any auditory than that which the sacred writer in this epistle paid to his Corinthian brethren, when arguing with them concerning the false teachers and the false doctrines which were threatening their overthrow. He says, in effect: "I desire you to retire into the thoughtfulness of your own souls, to concentrate all your knowledge and all your wisdom upon the facts which I am discussing, and to listen to what I say as wise men, and then to judge whether what I say is true or not." I take this word as my sentiment toward this congregation; and because you are the final court before whom this and many similar questions, must be adjudicated, I call upon you all, not to awaken your prejudice against the Roman Catholic church, and particularly not to permit prejudice to move you against the Roman Catholic people; but I call upon you all to consider whether the facts that I bring to your attention are not so momentous as to deserve your most careful consideration, and to call for most responsible and vigorous action.

It is my purpose to-night to show to you that Romanism intends to destroy that system of public education which we are accustomed to speak of as *the public schools*; and in order to that, first, that you may see this as an inference, I have only to recall to your recollection the facts that have been emphasized in the last two discourses, and that have been supported by unbounded testimony from the most reliable sources. You may remember that, in these discourses, we have been considering the Constitution of the United States and the Constitution of Romanism, and that last Sunday evening, at the close of the sermon, I reviewed these points, almost a score of them, in which the Constitution of the Roman Catholic Church is diametrically and wholly opposed to the Constitution which is the basis of our government and the stronghold of our liberties. If you were not present to hear that review you should read it, for I want you to know that the summary which was made at that time showed the irreconcilable antagonism of the absolutism of Rome to the Constitution of the United States.

Now the Constitution of the United States is a political document : it is not a religious pronunciamento ; it is not a declaration of religious faith or religious creed ; but it is a declaration of those principles which can make a great Republic, and which have already made this nation, in every essential respect, the rival, if not the superior, of almost every nation on the face of the earth. When, therefore, you find that Romanism antagonizes this political document ; and when you find that the principles of civil liberty, which are necessary to every state, and which are declared in the Constitution in order to form the basis of a state, are the objects of the hostility of the Roman Catholic Church ; when you find that a document which says nothing about religion, excepting to say that it shall have free exercise, is denounced and proscribed with the fiercest hatred by the statutes of that Church, your inference must be that the Roman Catholic Church has descended from the sphere of religion to the arena of politics, and that, as a political power, it has assailed a political instrument.

There is no other church in America that has antagonized the Constitution; no other church that has pronounced against it; no other church but what cordially supports it. The Churches operate in the domain of religion; and it is their intention and purpose, by saturating the public mind with religious principles, to make the State what now it is to some extent, a Christian State. For this is historically and actually a Protestant State; there is no question about that; its history shows the fact. When, therefore, Romanism attacks our political institutions, reviles and antagonizes our national constitutions, asserts its authority over our political opinions and annuls political statutes, demands that the realm of politics, as well as of education and faith, shall be subjected to it — when the Roman Catholic Church enters the arena of political conflict as a political force, it has no right whatever to claim the immunities of a religion. It is there as a political power, and as a political power we meet it. It does not make any difference whether the political power that assails us is on the shores of the Baltic, or on the shores of the British Channel, or on the shores of the Tiber. Romanism, attacking our Constitution and our State, is simply a political engine.

Now with our politics, as embodied in the Constitution, our common schools are in direct accord, and have been since the origin of the government. If you survey the history of past times, you will find that the Constitution and the general intelligence of the country, which grew out of our schools, were contemporaneous in their origin. You will find that there has never been a time when any statesman in America, however jealous of the authority of the Constitution, has ever hinted that the common schools were unfriendly to it. You will find, on the other hand, that every American statesman, and that every student of civil government, declares that with the Constitution and the theories of the United States our common schools are in full accord; and, going farther, states, that on the general intelligence which they diffuse, must depend that Constitution for all time to come.

Moreover, you can see rationally that a system of public education must belong to a Republican government, (and I use that word exactly as I would use the word Democratic, for the two words mean the same, as I employ them now not in a partisan sense,) I say, you can see very clearly, that in a Republican government, where the citizen is a final authority, and where the voter is king, everything depends on the ability of that ruler to exercise his powers wisely and discreetly. You may see therefore, that in our form of government, under our Constitution, every voter ought to know how not only to govern himself, but to help to govern the State;

and that our schools, therefore, are of infinite importance for the common people. No doubt, in a mon-
archical or an oligarchical form of government, only a
few need to be educated, and only a few are educated. Where a few persons are to exercise all the
political authority, the more ignorant the rest are the
better the rulers like it.

You have an illustration of that in the Southern
United States of America when they were having an
oligarchical and unrepublican form of government.
They had no common schools, because they thought
that the more degraded the colored man was the
more easily he could be governed. And so, while
the upper classes of the South had the best possible
education, the lower classes had none at all. This
was not the outgrowth of our Constitutional government, nor in harmony with the principles of American
liberty, but it was the result of an abnormal form of
civilization, of a barbaric institution which was for a
time attached to our Republican Constitution. Just
as soon as Constitutional government had sway in
the South, as soon the whole people were recognized
as the source of authority in government, every
Southern State began a system of common schools,
and they are diffusing, exactly as the Northern States
have done, education among the people as an essential
of a form of Constitutional and Republican government.

Now Romanism is an absolute monarchy; it is a
despotic form of government: its idea has always
been that ignorance is the mother of devotion. I

have only to point to the States where it has had
sway to prove this, as I have done heretofore. And
Romanism, in its monarchial theory of government,
which dictates to all men instead of reasoning with
them, and which commands them instead of teaching
them to exercise self-command,— Romanism, by its
intrinsically monarchial character, can never agree
with the essentials of a free Constitution, nor uphold
its supports and bulwarks.

While, therefore, the public schools are absolutely indispensable under our Constitution, such
public schools are recognized by Rome as absolutely hostile to theirs. I shall come, ere long,
to show from their own words, that this is true;
I state it now, and prove it hereafter. No
wonder then, that when they attack our institutions,
they attack them at the point which projects farthest
out against Papal policy. No wonder that the Redan
of our civilization, (for you remember that the Redan
at Sebastopol was the great bulwark of Russia against
the might of the allied forces,)— no wonder that the
main defences of our civilization are the first object
of their assaults. Against our common schools Rome
is throwing all the weight of its power; not because
the common schools alone are the objects of its hostility, but because the Constitution which our educational system supports is the real object of their
assault.

Now so far as the benefits are concerned that
have been conferred and are being diffused over
the world by free America to-day, as compared

with those that are being conferred by the Church of Rome, there is a great deal to be said in favor of the good influence of America. Contrast any country where Rome has had sway with ours, and are you not immediately compelled to affirm, that the United States is giving more intelligence, more morality, more reverence for law, more self-government, more happiness, more wealth than Rome has ever given to any state for the last thousand years? And if I to-day were called upon, in noting the great agents which are benefitting mankind, to decide whether Romanism, or political America as we see it to-day, was the greatest benefactor of the race,—if I were called upon to decide which of the two should cease to exist,—as a lover of humanity and a lover of God, I should prefer to keep America in the world for the world's good, rather than to keep the Roman Catholic Church.

After thus much of an introduction, which shows you that Rome is unreconciled to our schools, because, as a political power, it is unreconciled to our government, I propose to show you, first, That the Roman Catholic Church denounces violently our public schools. I propose to show you, secondly, That she is threatening them with overthrow and destruction. I propose, thirdly, To bring to your attention the agencies which she has put in operation for their destruction. I propose, fourthly, To ask why? and to give you the reasons they allege why they do it; and then to give you the real reasons which they elsewhere state. And I propose at that point to close this discourse, and on next Sunday evening I design to take it up and tell you what they will put in its place: when the common schools are destroyed, what they demand shall be substituted for common schools; what has been the result of their system where it has been tried, for it has been fully tried. And then to ask you, how much you are willing to yield; and how much you are willing to do in the line of resistance.

First, then, I ask you to notice that the Roman Catholic Church, through its hierarchs and governing powers, is openly hostile to our public schools. In order to prove that, I shall quote from the following authorities: From the Encyclical of the Pope; from the declarations of the Roman Catholic press; from the opinions of their Councils; and from the words of their bishops. This book which I hold in my hand is entitled, " The Judges of Faith: Christian vs. Godless Schools." I bought it myself at a Roman Catholic book-store in Boston, and it is endorsed by a large number of Roman Catholic prelates. It is said in the preface: " It may be worthy of remark, that these pages contain the conciliar, or single rulings of no less than three hundred and eighty of the high and the highest Church dignitaries." There are brought forward twenty-one Plenary and Provincial Councils, six or seven Diocesan Synods, two Roman Pontiffs, two Sacred Congregations of some twenty Cardinals and Pontifical Officials, seven single Cardinals, who, with thirty-three Archbishops, make forty Primates and Metropolitans; finally, nearly eighty single Bishops and Archbishops deceased or living in the United States. It says, in the first page of acknowledgment: "Thanks and humble acknowledgments are due, and never to be sufficiently repaid, to His Eminence John Henry Cardinal Newman, His Grace the Most Rev. Archbishop of Baltimore, Delegate Apostolic, James Gibbons, D. D., and Most Rev. Patrick J. Riordan, Archbishop of San Francisco, of Archiepiscopal rank, and to the Rt. Rev. the Bishops: John J. Hogan of St. Joseph's and Kansas City, John J. Keane of Richmond (who was in this city the other day, I believe), John L. Spalding, of Peoria, Francis Janssens, of Natchez," and others. This then is fully sanctioned and endorsed, and represents the Roman Catholic Church.

First of all, I quote from the Papal Encyclical, to show you how the Pope, who is the infallible head of the Roman Catholic Church, regards our public schools. Says he: "The Romish Church has the right to interfere in the discipline of the public schools, and in the arrangement of studies of public schools, and in the choice of the teachers of these schools. Public schools, open to all children for the education of the young, should be under the control of the Romish Church, and should not be subject to the civil power, nor made to conform to the opinions of the age." (Encyclical XLV. and XLVII.) Those schools to-day are under the control of the civil power and are not under the control of the Roman Catholic Church; but that authority, which is as much to them as the Bible is to you, and possibly more, declares that our schools shall not be as they now are, an adjunct of the civil state, but shall come under the power of the Roman hierarchy.   In this book which I have described, and have before me, we have the declaration made that the public schools are to be destroyed, their buildings are to be deserted, and the whole system to be abandoned.

I quote from " The Judges of Faith."   On page 3 it is said : " These pages make no pretense to dictate to either state or individual in their own provinces ; neither is it expected of, or designed by a Catholic that he should aid in any secret conspiracy for the bootless enterprise of suddenly overthrowing a public legal system, *unlawful though that system be.* We bring home to the consciences of Catholics, that it is their duty to continue deserting all mere secular schools, and building schools of their own, until public opinion itself undermine what contains the source of its own downfall, (now notice this last word) and *we be relieved of unjust taxes."*   And on the sixth page it is said : " The equal advance of God-hating European societies with God-eliminating systems of popular instruction, ought to enforce co-operation with the simultaneous, energetic action of our glorious Leo," (I just read from the Encyclical what " glorious Leo "thinks) " smiting with one arm the audacious chiefs of secret revolutions, while with the other he shields the cradles and firesides of Christian homes.   And Catholics will continue build, ing schools on their own grounds ; until, like the many deserted sectarian temples which are legally acquired by inpouring children of the Church, the future state-school buildings, left empty by Catholics deserting them, and non-Catholics becoming practically disgusted with the unrepublican and unchristian system, shall also be lawfully acquired, and occupied by denominational schools." This hope, as the rest of the book, is sanctioned by the prelates indicated.

You see, then, that their purpose, their explicit purpose, is to so break down our system of common schools until the school buildings shall be deserted.

Now let me call your attention to the opinions of some of their bishops, who have made declarations along the same line. "The faithful are required, by conforming to the words of Christ's Vicegerent, their head and the head of all the militant faithful, to break down these schools; by doing their bounden duty in every country where the government, or others, publicly or privately, seek to divorce education from religion, by tearing the children of the Church from her bosom, to nurse them on the lap of the Pagan goddess of Liberty." On the eighty-sixth page we have the following declaration: " The doctrine that godless schools are good enough for Catholic children, is explicitly condemned by the authority of the Church." This is the declaration of the late Bishop Rosecrans, in Lent 1873. Then follows this remarkable statement: "The sons of the Crusaders are not yet extinct. They live, they breathe, they fight; not now for the sepulchre of Christ, for

the honor of the dead now risen to die no more, but
for his cradle, and that of His holy spouse, the
Church; for the living sons of God, foully betrayed,
robbed and plundered of goods and spiritual life by
the ruthless of the nineteenth century." That is
supposed to describe our school system. On the
eighty-seventh page it is declared, by the late Rt.
Rev. Dr. Toebbe, Bishop of Covington: " The Public
Schools are infidel and godless, and must therefore
be avoided." On the eighty-ninth page we have the
same declaration, in the following words, from the
Bishop St. Palais, of Vincennes, Indiana, who is
characterized as a saint: " We object to the public
schools on account of the infidel source from which
they originated," (there is history for you!); " we
object to those schools because the teachings of
religion is excluded from them, and such exclusion
will inevitably produce religious indifference, if not
infidelity. We object to these schools again, because
the promiscuous assembling of both sexes of a certain age is injurious to the morals of the children;
and because we dread associations which might,
in time, prove pernicious to them, and distressing
to their parents." And later, on page ninety, he
says, that duty compels him to instruct pastors to
refuse absolution to parents who permit their children to attend the public schools. On page ninety-
seven you have another important opinion of the
same spirit, wherein it is said, by the Rt. Rev.
Francis Janssens, Bishop of Natchez, " That since
the public schools were bound by Constitution to

leave out religion, and teach science without inculcating God, His doctrines, His commands; hence, the public school system should be looked upon by every Christian not only as insufficient, but as positively dangerous, promoting, of its very nature, indifferentism, if not infidelity." When you remember the authority that Romish Bishops have in their Church, and that their word is law for the priests who are under them; when you remember that these priests, carrying out the law of their Bishops, make those Bishops a most dangerous power against what they oppose; when you recall all these declarations which are unqualifiedly against our system of public education; then you can understand that their whole influence, as well as their fiercest denunciations, hurled at this method of imparting public instruction, are intending to destroy the system they denounce.

But now, suppose we turn to the public press of the Roman Catholic Church, and hear what that, as further representing the influence of the prelates, is ready to say; for the public press of the Roman Catholic Church is an organ of the dignitaries, rather than an organ of the people. In the Boston *Globe*, a representative of Rome wrote, in 1885: " We want to make our children good Catholics; which is the same as making them good Christians. We must have positive Christian schools, with entire liberty of religious instruction, even at the expense of building and supporting them, and though we should empty half the grand school-buildings in Boston, and give them to be sold at public auction to the highest bidder."

We have also a still further declaration from Roman Catholic writers, this time from the Boston *Advertiser*, wherein a Catholic priest says: " Catholics would not be satisfied with the public schools, even if the Protestant Bible and every vestige of religious teaching were banished from them. They will not be taxed either for educating the children of Protestants, or for having their own children educated in schools under Protestant control." The New York *Tablet* says: " The education itself is the business of the spiritual society alone, and not the secular society. The instruction of children and youth is included in the sacrament of Order, and the State usurps the functions of the spiritual society when it turns educator. The secular is for the spiritual, is subordinated to religion; which alone has authority to instruct man in his secular duties. The organization of the schools, their entire internal arrangement and management, the choice and regulation of studies, the selection, appointment, and dismissal of teachers, belongs exclusively to the spiritual authority."

So, one after another, the authorized agents and representatives from the Roman Catholic Church denounce our schools in the most violent language. They call them godless, infidel. The New York *Freeman's Journal* calls them " pits of destruction." It states how the little lambs of the Church fall into them, and calls them " a devouring fire." It warns parents that their children will be lost forever if they go to these schools; and in the language which is best calculated to stir the heart of a Roman Catholic,

denounces those that come under the influence of our
system of public instruction. (N. Y. *Freeman's Journal*, Dec. 11, 1869.) Now all this is intended, as
you plainly see, to discredit the public schools, and to
raise hostility against them on the part of Roman
Catholic people, and on the part of Roman Catholic
children.

But they not only declare their hostility, they
also declare their purpose to overthrow these schools.
I quote now concerning their purpose, as follows:
Mr. Parton in the *Atlantic Monthly* of May, 1860,
in an article on " Our Roman Catholic Brethren,"
said, that, judging from the past, they conclude that
in the year 1900 they will count one-third of the
population of the country, and perhaps a majority of
the controlling cities and states of it; and of the
extent to which they hope to change American institutions, should they obtain the power, the *Catholic
World* of July, 1870, gives this interesting information : " The supremacy asserted for the Church in
matters of education, implies the additional and cognate functions of the censorship of ideas, and the
right to examine and approve, or disapprove, all
books, publications, writings and utterances intended
for public instruction, enlightenment, or entertainment, and the supervision of places of amusement."
(It may be that this censorship is what is now affecting
the papers of our city and preventing their publication of stirring matters of common interest.) " The
cognate functions of the censorship of ideas and the
right to examine and approve, or disapprove, all

books, publications, writings and utterances" (perhaps that refers to me, and to all utterances of the pulpit which they would censure and suppress) "intended for public instruction, enlightenment or entertainment." In other words, their threat implies not only the overthrow of our schools, but the censorship and overthrow of all our provisions for free speech and free utterance.

I now quote from Monsignor Capel, a very distinguished Roman Catholic, who made a tour through the country, and stopped a long time in the city of New York, where he was the object of very great attention. His utterances concerning the purpose of Rome were among the boldest ever given in this country, and among them are the following. In the interview with Capel — an interview by Mr. H. A. Cram, recorded in his " Further Consideration of the So-called Freedom-of-Worship Bill," to the question " Whom must we obey, if the State should command the citizen to do one thing, and the Church should command him to do another?" Monsignor Capel replied: " Then he must obey the Church, of course." The Monsignor remarked, that the thing that was troubling him the most seriously was the school question; and he added: "I have not yet spoken upon this definitely, but I shall go to Washington when Congress is in session, and make a formal declaration which shall carry some authority with it; for I am pursuing a careful study of your whole school system. The result is, there is going to be a fight—there are a good many Catholics in this country,

eight millions, somebody says. Your public school
system is inadequate for them, and they are going
to leave it. Suppose that the Church sends out . a
command to State schools in every parish to establish
and support parochial schools and send all Catholics
to them. He says : " *It can be done by the utterance
of a word, sharp as the click of a trigger.*" Monsignor Capel ! the American people are not afraid of
the click of a trigger. We have heard it within the
past twenty-five years.

"That command," he says, "will be obeyed ; new
schools will spring up everywhere. What will be
the result of that? A fight. If it is not a downright fight, it will be at least the war-like condition,
a million or two of voting, tax-paying citizens war-
like to the Government," etc. To the prediction of
a fight, unless America submits to all the demands of
Rome, we are already accustomed. The *Catholic
Herald* of May 24, 1879, is quoted as saying,
"that a most awful conflict between the power of
good and evil is in the near future, and that the fate
of the Republic depends on the result." And so
cool and experienced an observer as General Grant
said : "If we are to have another contest, in the
near future of our national existence, it will be
between patriotism and intelligence on one side, and
superstition, ambition and ignorance on the other."
He was awake to the threatenings of Romanism, as
you see ; and he closed that memorable warning with
the words, "Keep the Church and State forever
separate."

Now, in addition to this attitude of the Roman Catholic Church, in which they are already threatening
to destroy our schools (and I have not yet read it all,
there is more to follow which will come in due order),
there is a definite demand made by them for a division of the school moneys.   I say, there is a definite
demand made by them for a division of the school
moneys.   On page 41 of " Judges of Faith," there
is an explicit demand that the schools of this country
be divided into Popish and Protestant.   Not only is
the demand made there; but the New York *Tablet*
of Nov. 27, 1866, now twenty years ago, said this :
" Appropriate to the support of Catholic schools the
proportion of the public money according to the
number of children they educate, and leave the selection of teachers, the studies, the discipline, the whole
internal management to the Catholic educational
authorities."   That demand has been often repeated
since twenty years ago.   We have also the same
demand, in almost the same language, from the Bishop
of Trenton.   On the 118th page of this book, the
Bishop of Trenton makes the following remark :
" These schools," he says, in closing up his indictment against them, " impose an enormous tax, every
year growing greater, upon the entire community.
and a very unjust and unnecessary tax upon a large
section of that community."   Bishop McQuaid of
Rochester says : " No Catholic is in harmony with the
Church who maintains opinions opposed to these
teachings against the public schools.   It is absurd to
say that one Bishop more than another insists on

the establishment of Catholic schools. It is not left to the Bishops to choose in this matter." And so he goes on still further in the same line.

The demand is in the air, that the Roman Catholics shall have a portion of the public money appropriated to their schools. In the day when our school fund is divided and is given to sects, in violation of the Constitution of the United States, in that day our school-system gets its death-blow; and in the day that our school system gets its death-blow, the intelligent citizenship of America begins to stagger under the same stroke. When the State schools in Belgium, where Rome has vast power, were crippled and nearly destroyed, this book indicates, there was almost general, universal exultation; and I presume they expect a similar degree of jubilation and gladness in this country over a similar catastrophe.

And now, as against these statements, we hear the denial of a priest of Worcester, however patriotic, who brands as bigots those who know the purposes of Rome and state them, whose eloquent voice not long since was pleading for Ireland, a voice now silenced under the authority of the Pope; whose patriotic heart was beating openly the other day for his dear Ireland, that dare now only in secret pulsate in its behalf, because of the Papal rescript! It may be worth while for him while he dares, lest Rome shall stop him as she has stopped him once,— it may be worth while for him to say that the purposes of **Rome are in harmony with the welfare of this** country ; but when the Bishops of America speak as in this book, and the Pope and the Baltimore Council, with hundreds of foreign Bishops, I am compelled, however much I respect this voice crying in the wilderness, to listen to what is the real declaration of Rome, instead of pinning my faith on the statements of a heart not yet dead, who ought not to be where he now is, under the tyranny of a power that crushes out manhood. Do not be imposed upon by your personal respect or love for any individual priest of Rome, for if he strikes for America, he turns his back on the Pope.

The Baltimore Plenary Council, we are told in this book, devoted fifty of one hundred and eighty pages to schools, and in their denunciations they traverse about the same ground that I have already gone over, making it the duty of every priest to see there is a parochial school in his parish, and making it incumbent upon him to get all the children to attend the parochial schools under threat of the displeasure of the Church, and under threat of personal displeasure also.

That brings me now to speak of the enginery they have put in operation in order to carry out their will; and I will endeavor to speak of it as briefly as I may. The power that is brought to bear on the Bishops of the Roman Catholic Church, in order that they shall destroy our system of public education, is spoken of on page 118 of this Roman Catholic book, where it is declared that there is no option with the Bishops whether they shall favor the establishment of parochial schools and the with-drawal of the children from the public schools, or not. They simply are compelled to do it. In relation to the priests, the same attitude has been taken. Every priest of the Roman Catholic Church was compelled by the Baltimore Council to do his utmost for the establishment of parochial schools, under penalty of their displeasure. This is what the Council says; and this is what it says about the priests. Hear the decree of the Council: 1. "We determine and decree, that hard by every church, where it does not already exist, a parochial school is to be erected within two years of the promulgation of this Council (January 6, 1886), and to be kept up in the future; unless the Bishop see fit to grant a further delay on account of more than ordinary grave difficulties to be overcome in its establishment. 2. That a priest who, within the aforesaid time, hinders by serious negligence the building and maintainance of a school, or does not regard the repeated admonitions of the Bishop, deserves removal from that Church."

And again they say: "The priest's promotion to an irremovable rectorate, or other dignity, will depend upon their care of their schools;" that is to say, under the fear of the displeasure of the Church, these wifeless and childless men, whose all is in the Church, are told that, unless they put forth their utmost endeavors to get all their children out of the schools of this country and put them in Roman Cath-olic schools, they shall not be promoted,— which is the darling desire of their heart.

And when it comes to their influence on the members, they bring to bear a still stronger power. Now it is a perfectly well-known fact, that there are thousands of Roman Catholics who sincerely love the public schools, and who are very reluctant to take their children out of those schools. You find that almost every Roman Catholic who has been trained in our public schools has respect for them; and you will find that he prefers that his children shall go to them rather than to the priests' schools. How is he to be prevented from sending his children to them? Why, all through this book, the threat is ringing from Bishop to Bishop, that when a Roman Catholic declines to take his children out of the public schools, he is at issue with the church; that is, in antagonism to it; and the Archbishops have given it as their opinion, and the Sacred Congregation of Rome as their opinion, and the Baltimore Plenary Council as their opinion, that in case the Roman Catholic population do not take their children out of the public schools, they shall be refused absolution at the confessional. What does that mean? Why it means this: You and I believe that God forgives our sins. We go to Him in prayer, and expect from Him not only forgiveness as he has promised, but also the conscious evidence of that forgiveness in peace in our hearts. The Roman Catholic expects his absolution at the hands of the priests. Every Roman Catholic lives in mortal terror of dying without priestly absolution. If he dies without having made confession and received that absolution, he has no hope of anything but eternal damnation, and if he lives without that absolution, he lives in mortal sin, and under the ban of the church. Now these priests are everywhere instructed—and I could read it to you over and over from this book, and quote the pages from which it is taken,—that they may refuse absolution to parents who keep their children in the public schools. Is that mortal sin? Is it a mortal sin, endangering a man's eternal future, for him to give his children the benefit of American schools?

So says the Church. Let me give you an example of that, in the declaration of the Archbishop of Boston, whom, we would suppose, on account of his living in Boston, to be a liberal-minded patriot. He is far from it. On page one hundred and thirteen of "The Judges of Faith," we have some very interesting disclosures. Before that, I will give you the benefit of the following, on page one hundred and twelve: "It is notorious among the old stock of English descendants, that New England is fast becoming New Ireland [We earnestly pray that New England may never become New Ireland, since the Ireland of the Bishop is the slave of the Pope]; and the land of the Cotton Mathers and Eliots is transforming into the inheritance of the martyred Rasles, Jogues (Jesuits), and their children, the meek sons of the Church. Schools are bound to follow their counterparts, the congregations of the faithful," and so on. Further: "Though it was thought by those more conservative that the time had hardly arrived for anything like a general reversal of former toleration of even the best common schools of Catholics, it was not long until there were discovered many more practical supporters of the change than was at all suspicioned — thanks, perhaps, to certain Roman hints." This was after many liberal-minded Romanists protested against priest Scully's brutality in Cambridge.

And here is the following from Archbishop Williams of Boston : " Any priest, however, hearing confessions, in the private tribunal of penance, is free, in the exercise of his faculties, in this as in all other cases, to give or withhold absolution, guided by the disposition of the penitent and his own judgment and discretion, and his knowledge of the facts and principles involved." (p. 115.) That is to say, if a Roman Catholic is contumacious, and tells his priest he will not take his children out of the public school, and put them into the parochial school, he may be refused absolution by the priest. This in Boston, Massachusetts. And this fearful threat hangs over every Roman Catholic. You and I laugh at priestly absolution : the Roman Catholic trembles under the lack of it, and thinks his salvation depends on receiving it. This, then, is the enginery that the Roman Catholic Church proposes to use in order to accomplish its ends. We had supposed, until we had so many of these highly enlightened people among us from over the sea, that our common schools were very good, very helpful to civilization and the community, helpful to morals, and a bulwark of the Constitution of the United States.

They have taken this highly antagonistic
attitude; we would like to know why they have
taken it.   Among the very first answers is this;
The first position that the Roman Catholics took in
this country against the schools, was, that we had
Bibles in them, and those Bibles, they said, were
sectarian books; consequently, if the schools had
Bibles in them, they were sectarian schools.   Reply-
ing, we said : First of all, the Bible is not a sectarian
book.   The translation of the Roman Catholic
English or Douay Bible is from the Vulgate, and is
notoriously a corrupted version.   And I challenge
Roman Catholic scholarship, (and remember here I
say " scholarship ;" I do not now refer to the ignorant
denunciations of priest or Bishop)— I challenge them
to show that the Bible, as we have it, is not made up
from the collation of the very best Greek manuscripts; while their Vulgate is an imperfect translation of the Holy Scriptures.   But that is of very
little account to them after all.

You remember, that even their own Douay Bible is
not in the hands of their people.   You remember
that Bible Societies have been denounced by their
Popes from the first as a pestilence.   You remember
that I have read to you here, in the language of their
Popes, that the Bible, in the hands of the common
people, is dangerous.   All this we have learned
from them ; and yet when they protested that it was
unfair to have the Bible in schools, we were willing,
for the sake of peace, in a great many cases, to let it
go out.   No sooner had the Bible been taken out of

the schools, than they specifically stated that they did not care a penny whether the Bible was in them or not. Let me read to you their exact language. The *Freeman's Journal* of November 20, 1869, says : "If the Catholic translation of the books of Holy Writ, which is to be found in the homes of all our better educated Catholics, were to be dissected by the ablest Catholic theologians in the land, and merely lessons take from it, such as Catholic mothers read to their children ; and with all the notes and comments in the popular edition, and others added with the highest Catholic indorsement ; and if these admirable Bible lessons, and these alone, were to be ruled as to be read in all the public schools, *this would not diminish in any substantial degree the objections we Catholics have to letting Catholic children attend the public schools.*" Now you know what a hue-and-cry has been made against the Bible in the schools ; but here is the authoritative declaration, that it does not make any real difference to them whether the Bible is there or not. It is the schools they wish to blot out, not merely the use of the Bible in the schools. It adds as follows : "The Catholic solution of this muddle about Bible or no Bible in the public schools, is — hands off. No state taxation or donations for any schools. You look to your children, and we will look to ours." (I notice, our police have to look to theirs.) "We don't want you to be taxed for Catholic schools ; we don't want to be taxed for Protestant or godless schools. *Let the public school system go to where it came from — the devil.*"

That is the New York *Freeman's Journal*, of Nov. 20, 1869, one of the most respectable Catholic publications in America. You understand then, do you? I think we all do.

Then, just as soon as the Bible was taken out of the schools, what did they say? " Your schools are godless. Your schools are without religion. Your schools are infidel. Your schools are immoral." I have not time to take that matter up in full detail, only I will say this; that we cannot claim that our public schools teach religion as a principal branch; but they have always taught morality and religious principle, and excepting for the opposition of the Roman Catholic Church, they would be teaching it now far more than they are; and moreover, our public schools are not more godless than the business of Christian men is godless who carry on their business on Christian principles.

The third reason alleged against our public schools, why they hate them so, is that they are immoral. The pages of this book, from the declaration of the Sacred Congregation to the declarations of the Bishops, teem with references and dark hints and subtle suggestions and open statements that our schools are terribly immoral; that it is perilous for any Catholic child to go to them, on the ground that it sinks him in the slums of immorality.

And this impeachment comes from a Church that furnishes nine-tenths of all the hoodlums in our streets. This comes from a Church that furnishes seventy-five to eighty per cent. of the crime in New

York city. This comes from a Church whose theology is so vile that it cannot be translated into
English, lest the translator be taken up for publishing
obscene literature. This comes from a Church whose
priests ask, and are compelled to ask, questions of
boys and girls in the confessional, that are not fit to
be repeated even between grown men, unless they
are physicians. Immorality, forsooth, in our public
schools! The public schools criticised as dangerous
to morality! If, for their visible immorality, on
such complaint the public schools should be sunk in
the depths of the sea as a punishment, by the same
standard of justice, the Roman Catholic Church should
be sunk into hell. "I am not mad, most noble
Festus. I speak forth the words of truth and sober-
ness." I simply draw my inference from the standard of judgment which they have made.

. But now, what are the *real* reasons why they hate
our public schools; for the above are plainly not the
real reasons. What *are* the real reasons? The first
reason is,— that they claim—Popes, Bishops and all,
—that our schools, perpetuated and patronized, would
result in the destruction of the Roman Catholic faith.

That is what they say. Here listen to "The
chief guardian of souls on earth." (That is, Leo
XIII. Thanks be to God, my soul is not under his
guardianship!) Listen to the chief guardian of souls
on earth: "The design of withdrawing primary
schools from the control of the Church, and the exer-
tions made to carry it into effect, are, therefore,
inspired by a spirit of hostility toward her, and by

the desire of extinguishing among the people the divine light of our holy faith."

That is what they say. They are afraid that the schools will extinguish the light of their Church. The schools must be destroyed to save Romanism. Listen to what is said on page 122 of this book. The Archbishop sums up,— that is Cardinal Gibbons, Archbishop of Baltimore, Administrator Apostolic, &c,— in a pastoral letter: "If no provision is made for the Christian culture of the rising youth, it is to be feared that, twenty years hence, it will be much easier to find churches for a congregation than a congregation for our churches." Again he says: "It may safely be asserted, that the future status of Catholicity in the United States is to be determined by the success or failure of our day schools."

Now you know the exact reason. The Roman Catholic Church, in antagonism to the Constitution of the United States, and in antagonism to the common schools as the support of that Constitution, endeavoring to foist its absolute tyranny upon the American people, says : We cannot do it if you have your public schools. And we answer: You will not do it, then, till the day of judgment!

Our schools teach loyalty. I have been in the public schools. I remember that little school-house on the hillside in a distant country town in Rhode Island, where a beautiful woman, now in heaven, inspired me both with respect for her sex and ambition for learning; where I went in summer-time, bare-footed, and with humble clothing, and

learned the value of education by patient strivings,
and was inspired to go further in its pursuit. I
have been in the public schools, not as you have
them here in the cities, in all their glory, but as we
had them on the hills of New England. And this
is what I remember was taught in those schools:
Loyalty and love for the State; loyalty and love for
man. I remember the day brave old John Brown was
hung (I was only a little lad,): in our school we
almost covered our faces and wept, to think that so
brave and good a man was dying that hour for his
fellowmen. We were taught there the principles of
the Constitution. We were taught that the people
were the source of political authority in the United
States, under God. We were taught that every
child had the same rights as every other, and every
citizen had the same rights as every other. We were
taught history for the sake of knowing the truth, and
there was nobody there that was afraid to have the
truth told in history. We were taught science, and
that we need not fear that what God revealed in
nature man might study in books. We were taught
the principles of religion. We were taught to
fear and reverence God; and when, on the Lord's
day, there used to come from far the Christian
people of our neighborhood, to that old, unpainted
school-house, they opened the Bible and let us read
it for ourselves, and so we learned something about
the great and good God. That seems to be very
helpful both to the State and to the person; but that
can never co-exist with Romanism, so they say
who speak for that system of ecclesiasticism.

What is all this cry of fair-play coming to ere long? For Roman Catholics are saying : "If you are fair, you will let us have our own schools, and will give us a share of the money." "If you are fair," said Jefferson Davis and Southern rebels, "you will let us alone. All we ask is, to be let alone." If you are just and patriotic, said the spirit which awoke when the guns thundered on Sumter, if you are just and patriotic, you will suppress rebellion and save the country. There is the difference in the theory of duty, the difference in the theory of fair play. If you are fair, says Rome, you will give up to us our schools, and you will help pay for them. If you love America, says the rising spirit of this country, you will save the schools, whatever the Pope says. This matter of fair play is an interesting matter, with clearly defined bounds. When everybody else rises up and wants the same kind of fair play, you see what will happen to our schools. But two or three weeks ago, in the city of Brooklyn, New York, at the commencement of one of their public schools, a little girl mounted the platform, and recited a poem against intemperance and licensing the saloon. She described in that poem, in her childish way, the poor man's wife begging the saloon-keeper that he would not sell liquor to her husband ; but he said he had a license, and went on and sold it, and she told what was the result. And as she described it in the pathetic way, which is not half so pathetic in description as in fact, she did not know what afterwards was disclosed, that there, on the platform, sat a rumseller, who was licensed and who had several children in that school. The rumseller was exceedingly disturbed and greatly excited, and no sooner were the exercises over than he began roundly to denounce the management of the public schools that had dared to insult him by having the poem repeated. He called together a lot of his associates in the saloon business, and they prepared and signed a remonstrance against having any of that kind of declaration in the public schools, because it was not fair to rumsellers. That is a matter of current news in our religious papers within the last two weeks. Now there are two hundred thousand rumsellers in the United States, and they will want everything taken out of our school books and out of our school exercises that looks towards censure of the liquor traffic; just exactly as the Roman Catholic Church wants everything taken out of our school books that does not favor the Roman Catholic Church. Now, you will be fair with liquor saloonists, will you not? Oh, do ! Now suppose here comes the Hebrew, and says : You have on all your text-books the figures 1871, 2, 3, etc., as the date of publication. That is Christianity : that is not fair to us. Our school children open their text-books and see that as they read, and they say, What does this mean? That means the birth of Jesus Christ. That is anti-Juda-ism. And suppose all our Jewish fellow-citizens should rise up and say, Do be fair with us. Give us our own text-books and our own schools. Then, after them all, the Quakers might come, and say : Your books praise the heroism and glories of war. You have in them " Sheridan's Ride," and " The Battle of Ivry," and " The Battle of Nasby," and all that kind of composition ; and that so teaches the glory of war, which we reprobate, that we want these compositions taken out, or else we want our own schools.

And then the Christian Scientist comes along, and says : Why, you have praised there, in several places, the giving of medicines by physicians, which is all a humbug, and is contrary to our conscience ; and we do not want anything of that kind in our text-books and in our schools.   Give us schools of our own, and our share of the public money.   Then the Englishmen come along and say : Now, see here ! you have some things in your public schools about England oppress-ing Ireland, and we do not believe in that ; the speech of Robert Emmet for example.   And the Home-Rule Irishman says : You have things there about the glory, greatness and beneficence of England, and we do not believe in that at all.   Come right along, gentlemen : you shall all have fair play.   Tear in pieces our whole system of schools.   Let each one take shreds and fragments of a dismembered and ruined country, and then we can all drop back into barbarism, and see what beauty there is in fair play, as you call it.   No ; the fairest of fair play, the most beneficent course of action to take to all classes of citizens, is to maintain in its integrity our common-school system, undestroyed and undivided.   I will tell you what Romanism wants in our public schools, and I shall prove it when we meet again : Romanism wants Rome dominant in our public schools ; Rome for the controlling power, with priests for the ruling agents, the Bishops for governors, and the Pope for dictator ; AND THIS ROME WILL NEVER GET !

Sermon VIII.

THE PURPOSE OF ROMANISM TO DESTROY OUR PUBLIC SCHOOLS: THEIR ALLEGED AND ACTUAL REASONS.

My discourse to-night is a continuation of that of last Sunday evening, and I resume by inviting your attention to the same text as we then used, which you will find in the First Epistle to the Corinthians, the tenth chapter and the fifteenth verse : " I speak as to wise men : judge ye what I say." Before the army of the Tennessee, in 1876, General Grant used the following weighty words : " If we are to have another contest in the near future of our national existence, I predict that the dividing line will not be Mason and Dixon's, but it will be between patriot- ism and intelligence on one side, and superstition, ambition and ignorance on the other. In this cen- ténnial year, the work of strengthening the founda- tion of the structure laid by our forefathers one hun- dred years ago, should be begun. Let us all labor for the security of free thought, free speech, free press, and pure morals, unfettered religious senti- ments, and equal rights and privileges for all men, irrespective of nationality, color or religion.

Encourage free schools, and resolve that not one dollar appropriated to them shall be applied to the support of any sectarian school: resolve that any child in the land may get a common school education, unmixed with atheistic, pagan, or sectarian teachings; Keep the Church and State forever separate." He also wrote, when President, in his message to Congress, recommending the passage of an amendment to the national Constitution, " prohibiting the granting of any school funds or school taxes, or any part thereof, either by legislative, municipal or other authority, for the benefit, or in aid, directly or indirectly, of any religious sect or denomination ; or in aid, or for the benefit of any other object of any nature or kind whatsoever." Thus this wise patriot and statesman, anticipating the very danger which we are now confronting — a demand for a division of the school funds, a part to be used for sectarian purposes — urged that an amendment should be made to the Constitution of the United States forever prohibiting such misuse. President Garfield, in his letter of acceptance, July 12, 1880, said : " Next in importance to freedom and justice, is popular education, without which neither freedom nor justice can be permanently maintained. It would be unjust to our people, and dangerous to our institutions, to apply any portion of the revenue of the nation, or of the State, to the support of sectarian schools. The separation of the Church and the State, in everything relating to taxation, should be absolute." The Republican party of that year dared to say that this

ought to be the policy of the nation. This year
they did not dare to say it. Here, then, we have
the statements of two of the greatest of the statesmen
of America in favor of the public-school system as
we have it; and you will remember that both these
men were poor boys, and if it had not been for our
system of public education, they probably would
never have arrived at the dignity which they achieved.
The public school system primarily is established for
the poor, and not for the rich. The rich can compass
an excellent education for their children at any time
by the use of their money. It is not for the sake of
the most favored class in our community that the free
schools should be maintained; but the public school
is particularly instituted to educate the children of
those who otherwise could not give their children a
good education; and because it is so instituted and
is so especially advantageous to the poor, it ought
particularly to command the suffrages of a very
large majority of this nation. Now it is against this
system of benevolent education, which is so clearly
in the interests of Constitutional liberty, that the
hierarchy of Rome is throwing all its power, as I
told you last Sunday night. To review a little; for
by their own words we prove that they endeavor to
discredit our school system by declaring their antagonism to it, and by violently denouncing it. They
have already threatened it in the strongest and most
earnest language, and have declared their purpose,
the Pope, and the Baltimore Council, and a large
number of bishops and prelates, to destroy it. I

also brought to your attention the fact, that already the attempt has been made to secure a division of the school fund, and that the tax, as now used, has been protested against in numerous cases as unjust. Then I showed you — and you have not fogotten it, and will not — that the Roman Catholic Church is using all the enginery of which it is possessed, to compel its people to abandon our free schools for the parochial schools, and that bishop after bishop had intimated that his priests would be directed, as they were already empowered, to refuse absolution to any of their people who do not take their children out of our public schools. Then we paid some attention to the alleged reasons why they take this course. First, that the Bible was in the schools. (I then showed how they repudiated that reason as soon as the Bible was taken out.) Again, that our schools were godless; and then I brought to your attention the fact that that was not the real reason. I believe, also, that I spoke in reference to their claim that our schools were immoral; and suggested that such a protest from such a source was hardly in keeping with good taste. Then I read to you what were the real reasons why they desire to destroy our school system, and I quoted from Cardinal-Archbishop Gibbons the following statement: " It may safely be asserted, that the future status of Catholicity in the United States is to be determined by the success or failure of our day schools."

Having made it perfectly plain, then, that they had drawn the lines of conflict between Romanism and the Constitution, with all that supports the Constitution, and that they were antagonizing the public schools because they were afraid that the public schools would destroy the power of the Roman Catholic hierarchy in this country, I then, for a moment, dwelt on the folly of supposing that we could divide up piece-meal our school-fund as they desire, and as the rumsellers of Brooklyn and of the country desire, and as a great many other partisans might desire, without utterly destroying the system and ruining the State. Having proceeded as far as this, I was compelled, almost abruptly, to pause.

But now, on this occasion, I wish to bring to your attention another of the alleged reasons which they urge. I want to show you that the claim that it is in violation of the conscience of Roman Catholics that we should have our system of free schools is a fallacious claim; and that the call for a division of the school funds on grounds of conscience, in case they have their own parochial schools, is also on fallacious ground. Then I want to show you, that, after antagonizing the Bible in the schools, they are with equal urgency setting themselves against true and correct history in the schools. I shall then proceed further to show that their antagonism is not confined to history, but is also against literature and science; and by the time I have closed this evening's discourse, I shall have made it plain to you, that nearly all of what we call Truth has been denounced by the hierarchy as inappropriate to be taught in our public schools.

1. Let us, then, address ourselves to the argument that is brought before us, and which is highly influential in New England, that the Roman Catholic people are violating their consciences in sending their children to our schools, and that because we believe in liberty of conscience, therefore we should grant them their own separate schools, and help to support them. Now, first of all, you remember that liberty of conscience is an utterly unknown quantity in the Roman Catholic Church. From early times and for centuries, the bulls and Encyclicals of the Popes have denounced liberty of conscience. To give you an idea of the correctness of this statement, I call your attention to the following paragraph, which I read, for the sake of brevity and accuracy: "When in this country we speak of liberty of conscience, we mean that every man shall be permitted to worship God as his own personal convictions of duty shall dictate. But the Papal hierarchy have no such meaning, and intend nothing of the sort. With them, liberty of conscience merely consists in the right to embrace, profess, and practice the Catholic religion in a Protestant country ; and not the right to embrace profess, and practice the Protestant religion in a Roman Catholic country. Protestantism cannot be tolerated or compromised without sin, and must be exterminated." ("The Papacy and the Civil Power," p. 35) Now, still further as to liberty of conscience : in the bull of Gregory XVI., of 1832, which is endorsed by Pius IX., we have denunciation and anathema upon liberty of conscience as a most

pestiferous error, from which spring revolutions, corruptions, contempt of sacred things, holy institutions and laws, and in one word, that pest of all others most to be dreaded in the State, unbridled liberty of opinion." ("Papacy and Civil Power," p. 206.) Here you have manifest proof of the fact, that the liberty of conscience which is urged upon us, as a reason why they are denouncing and would destroy our schools, is not permitted to Roman Catholics, is against their highest law, and is the object of Papal anathema. Whose conscience is it, then, that is being violated by our school system? Not the conscience of the Roman Catholic people, of whom the most intelligent part, I believe, are devoted friends of our free schools, and are very reluctant to have their children taken out of them. Not the conscience of intelligent American priests, who are being forced to establish these parochial schools or lose their standing in the Church. The only conscience that is tolerated in the Roman Catholic Church, the only conscience that can make a demand upon us is the conscience of the Pope; and I am prepared to say, that if there is a conscience under heaven that I think ought to be repudiated, both by morality and piety, it is the conscience of the Pope. I predicate this opinion on the characters of Popes that the Romish Church has had for centuries, and on the quality of the lives that they have lived, on the enactments that they have made, and on the excommunications that they have issued. Is the man who could swear so blasphemously at Victor Emanuel as did Pope Pius IX., in the bull of excommunication, a man whose conscience should dictate to America concerning its school policy? But suppose this false plea of conscience is allowed, what will it next object to? We have Bibles in our courts and in our Congress. We have chaplains also in our army. When I visited our house of correction, I found Bibles there in every cell. All Bibles and their free use are against this same conscience. How soon will they be taken out? It must be also against the conscience of the Pope, that there should rise in all the cities of America churches that are not Roman Catholic, and do not recognize any allegiance to him. As the children of Roman Catholic parents behold these churches, they are are likely to be impressed, as they are by the character of Protestant Christians, that there are good Christians in the world beside the Pope, and beside the Roman Catholics. But if our common schools, in contradicting that idea, come to be the objects of Papal hatred, and if the Papal conscience demands the destruction of the mighty fabric of our common schools because it is likely to woo their youth away from the Roman hierarchy, when will their conscience demand the levelling of our churches, because our church edifices are likely to suggest to the consciences of Roman Catholic children that their religion is not the only true religion in the world? And if we grant the right of their conscience to destroy our public schools, which are a structure vaster and grander in this nation than any piles of brick and mortar, what answer shall we make them, when the Pope of Rome demands that all Protestant structures be levelled to the ground to satisfy his conscience? Liberty of conscience must have its limitations, and those limitations have already been reached. This Papal conscience is the same which found it necessary to recognize the Southern Confederacy when this nation was being riven by rebellion. This is the same conscience that called Jefferson Davis the beloved son of the Church. Evidently, the conscience of the Pope is not a good guide for Americans.

Now when you remember that this claim to a conscientious right to overthrow our public school system is not the claim of the conscience of the Roman Catholic people, but is only the drift and purpose of the hierarchy, then you can see, that while we are loyal to the doctrine of liberty of conscience, there is no reason in the world why we should consent to the destruction of our schools.

And right along that line they raise another suggestion, namely, that of fair play : because, they say, they are taxed for the support of public schools, and that ought not to be. The tax is called unjust. Their children are going to be withdrawn from those schools, they say, and when thus withdrawn, this unjust tax must no longer be levied on Roman Catholics. So, as M. Capel said, as quick as the click of a trigger, when the Pope says it, they will all refuse to pay the tax. Now, such refusal is not fair play. Do not all these people enjoy the privileges of that Constitutional government which is supported by our public schools? Does not the diffusion of general intelligence furnish them with better surroundings than they could have elsewhere? Is not this country made a more desirable place to live in because of the tax expended for the support of public schools? If they are not deriving as great benefit from this government as they pay for in their taxes, let them emigrate to Spain or Mexico, to Portugal or Belgium, where they can have their own way. Spain is about the last state in the world of any consequence where they can have their own way. Italy and Austria and France, after ages of bondage, are having their way now, and are renouncing all allegiance to the Papacy. But I say, if any Roman Catholic priest or bishop, or any layman, feels himself defrauded when he pays his taxes in America, let him go and pay his tax in Spain or Mexico, and have all the benefits of Papal supremacy and Papal law. But even when people send no children to school should they therefore not be taxed for the support of schools and for the common good? How about that large number of people possessed of great property in the community who have no children and pay taxes for the support of schools? Is that unjust? How about many millionaires of our country whose children have never seen a day in our public schools? Shall they, because they are not sending their children to the public schools, deny the right of the State to tax them for the support of public education? I do not know about the method of distributing school monies in this city, but in some cities the taxes are paid into a common treasury. The taxes that are raised in a locality are not all spent in that locality, but the levies that are raised in one section of the state may be spent in remote localities for the support of schools there, because one county has a surplus of wealth, while another is poor. Do you suppose that every man who objects to any part of the policy of the State is going to have exemption from taxation for the support of that part of the government's policy? Suppose I, if I were a single man and not owning property, should say, I can take care of myself and do not need any police. Being alert and strong and tolerably muscular, I do not intend to be taxed for the support of the police-force of the city, because it does me no good. How about that? Now you can apply this principle far and wide, and you will find the further you reason about it the more utterly absurd is all this talk about a division of the school-fund when Roman Catholics withdraw their children and refuse to use the public schools. I tell you, my friends, there is going to be a struggle on the part of the best of the Roman Catholics before they withdraw their children from the common schools, and they ought to count on the intelligent support of every lover of his country when they make their stand against the terrors and threats of the hierarchy. That is why I bring you this argument, so that you can remember it, and help them.

When it comes to the argument of fair play, we retort and ask: Is it fair play, on account of

hostility to the best government under the sun, and
to the freest Constitution, which gives you the largest
liberty and the greatest privileges,— is it fair play, at
the mandate of a foreigner, who is no friend of liberty, and whose principal care for you is to fleece
you,— is it fair play for Roman Catholic people in
America to lend their influence to destroy the system which has given them such large benefits? No,
it is not. And when we come to the question of
fair play, the rights of fair play are all on the side of
the defence and protection of our schools. Keep
before you, then, all these fallacies thus fully
answered. The true reason was given by the Bishops,
and by Archbishop Gibbons, now Cardinal. The
real antagonist in this fight against our public schools
is the political machine which Father McGlynn has
so correctly characterized ; it is the machine of absolutism in Rome ; not love of liberty, not fair play, not
conscience, not morality, but the hierarchy of Rome.
I have always had an idea that the breaking of
machines of that sort was the best use you could put
them to.

2. Romanism not only cannot be reconciled to
the Bible, but it cannot be reconciled to history : for
the shocking iniquity of the Popes is perfectly plain
as written in the annals of the world. If I thought
it necessary, I should repeat quotations that I have
already made, to show that Bibles and Bible societies
are regarded as pestiferous by the Pope. But the
objection that the people should not read the Bible
because they do not know how to interpret it, is not

an honest objection. If the people do not know how to interpret the Bible, and therefore ought not to read it, pray tell me what books and periodicals are they able to interpret, and what shall they read? The people are not able to interpret, perhaps, the protective tariff. They may not be able to interpret fully the Constitution of the United States, according to this theory of Rome. They may not be able to interpret natural sciences. They may not be able to interpret political economy. Who is going to interpret these for them? The Pope? He claims the right. In the matter of the Bible, they say, the hierarchy shall interpret. But the truth is, this argument against the Bible in the hands of the people, and the power of the people to interpret it, is not the reason why the Roman Catholic hierarchy have tried for ages to hold in bondage the intelligence of their people. It is rather because, with an open Bible, their manhood rising up, protests against being kept in constant infancy and pupilage, and they demand the right to think for themselves.

Now the real objection to the Bible is : You cannot find in it many of the fundamental dogmas of Romanism. You cannot find in it priestly or episcopal celibacy. If the Roman Catholic people should read it, they would all see that their priests are not keeping the law of God in living without families, recognized families. The doctrine of the Immaculate Conception is not in the Bible ; nor do Roman Catholic theologians claim that it is. It was only created by Pius IX., in 1854, who said, not long before he made

it, that he did not know whether it was true or not.
The worship of Mary is not in the Bible. Purgatory is not in the Bible. The Mass is not in the
Bible. The Assumption of the Virgin is not in the
Bible. Indulgences are not in the Bible, nor Papal
infallibility, nor extreme unction, nor the Inquisition,
nor Den's Theology, nor a good deal more that they
depend on. That is the real reason why they object
to the Bible; because the open Bible, in the hands of
the people, destroys the wicked pretensions of the
hierarchy, and emancipates men from a yoke that
neither they nor their fathers have ever been able to
bear without being pressed down to the ground.

But I am coming to a central point in this matter
of controversy. The attitude that they take against
the Bible is the attitude that they take against history, and for the same reason. *Because history cannot be tortured into a justification of the ways of this
infallible Church, therefore they object to it.* Three
hundred years ago, all Germany, and all the world,
was shaken by a conflict on so-called Indulgences.
Is it not a remarkable fact, that in Boston, in this
year of grace 1888, the conflict between Romanism
and the public schools is over the very same thing?
As Luther rose up then and denounced Indulgences and their sale, so it seems once more, after
the lapse of centuries, we have got to rise up and
protest against Indulgences as a reason why a book
of history should be expelled from Boston public
schools, and why a master of those schools should be
removed from his place. I propose now to give you

some insight into that Boston incident. You know that, not long since, Boston was convulsed by the action of the school board, half of whom were Roman Catholics, in taking out of the schools Swinton's book on history, and in discharging Mr. Travis, one of the public school teachers, from his position, because he had taught concerning indulgences what the Roman Catholic Church denied, or at least the Roman Catholic people on that school board.

The following is the exact language of Swinton's History, which has been made the ground of its proscription in Boston Schools :

" When Leo X. came to the Papal chair, he found the treasury of the Church exhausted by the ambitious projects of his predecessors. He therefore had recourse to every means which ingenuity could devise for recruiting his exhausted finances, and among these he adopted an extensive sale of indulgences, which in former ages had been a source of large profits to the Church." (Here is a star, and a foot note which I will presently give you.)

"The Dominican friars, having obtained a monopoly of the sale in Germany, employed, as their agent, Tetzel, one of their own Order, who carried on the traffic in a manner that was very offensive, and especially to the Augustinian friars."

Now, after this mild statement, read the foot-note, which was most offensive to Romanists : " These indulgences were, in the early ages of the Church, remissions of the penances imposed upon persons whose sins had brought scandal on the community.

But in process of time, they were represented as actual pardons of guilt, and the purchaser of indulgences was said to be delivered from all his sins."

Now I will demonstrate to you, out of the mouth of popes and bishops and John Tetzel himself, that Swinton's History is but a mild statement of literal truth, and that the only objection that can justly be brought against it is, that he states so kindly facts which are a disgrace to Rome.

The theory of indulgences I will state in the words of Pope Leo X., in order that you may know exactly what it is, from Papal authority. Pope Leo X. explained the doctrine of indulgences thus: "The Roman Church, whom other churches are bound to follow as their mother, hath taught that the Roman Pontiff, the Vicar of Jesus Christ upon earth, possessing the power of the keys, by which power all hindrances are removed out of the way of the faithful, that is to say, the guilt of actual sin, by the sacrament of penance, and the temporal punishment due for those sins, according to the divine justice by ecclesiastical indulgence, that the Roman Pontiff may, for reasonable causes, by his apostolic authority, grant indulgences out of the superabundant merits of Christ and the saints, to the faithful who are united to Christ by charity, as well for the living as for the dead; and that in thus dispensing the treasure of the merits of Jesus Christ and the saints, he either confers indulgences by the method of absolution, or transfers it by the method of suffrage (that is, favor); wherefore all persons, whether living or dead, who really obtain any indulgence of this kind, are delivered from so much temporal punishment due according to divine justice, for their actual sins, as is equivalent to the value of indulgences bestowed and received." That is to say, indulgences are of various classes, and the classes are in several divisions; and these indulgences are supposed, by the theory of the Church, to remit the pains of purgatory, and to remit also the penalties of guilt in this life. (Dr. Barnum's " Romanism As It Is," p. 530.) Professor L. T. Townsend, of the Theological School of Boston, one of the cleanest and clearest scholars of New England, said, that after examining fifteen authorities in reference to a definition of indulgences, he found that there was nothing in Swinton at variance with their general statement.

What are the actual facts about Indulgences, when you come to the practice of their dispensation? You will find in D'Aubigne's " History of the Reformation," vol. I, book iii, chapters 1-2, what Tetzel, who was the great agent and auctioneer of indulgences in Luther's time, said about his wares; and because I want you to know what Indulgences really are, I will give you some of Tetzel's own words. " Indulgences," said Tetzel, (who had a voice like a lion and the manners of a mountebank, whose vices were infamous, and, though a monk, had two of his children with him,)—indulgences are the most precious and the most noble of God's gifts. This cross (pointing to the Red Cross) has as much efficacy as the very cross of Jesus Christ. Come, and I will

give you letters, all properly sealed, by which even
the sins that you intend to commit may be pardoned."
These are his own words. "I would not change my
privileges for those of Saint Peter in Heaven; for I
have saved more souls by my indulgences than the
Apostle by his sermons." (That was rather bad
for Peter.) "There is no sin so great, that an
indulgence cannot remit; and even if any one (which
is doubtless impossible) had offered violence to the
blessed Virgin Mary, mother of God, let him pay,
only let him pay well, and all will be forgiven him."
(The consummate indecency of the man had to come
out even in the sale of indulgences.) "Reflect,
then, that for every mortal sin, you must, after confession and contrition, do penance for seven years,
either in this life or in purgatory." (I judge that
Tetzel is in purgatory yet!) "Now, how many
mortal sins are there not committed in a day, how
many in a week, how many in a month, how many in
a year, how many in a whole life! Alas! these sins
are almost infinite, and they entail an infinite penalty in the fires of purgatory. And now, by means
of these letters of indulgence, you can, once in your
life, in every case except four, which are reserved
for the Apostolic See, and afterward in the article of
of death, obtain a plenary remission of all your
penalties and all your sins."

That is not a Protestant declaration.

Those are the exact words of John Tetzel, the
agent of the Pope, and of Albert, Archbishop of
Mainz, who went all through Germany selling

indulgences, before and after Martin Luther pronounced the ninety-five theses against them. He says also : " The very moment that the money rattles at the bottom of the chest, the soul escapes from purgatory and flies liberated to heaven." Further : we give one of these letters of absolution. I am sure you will be interested. It is worth while learning the contents of these diplomas which led to the reformation of the Church : " May our Lord Jesus Christ have pity on thee, N. H., and absolve thee by the merits of His most holy passion. And I, in virtue of the apostolic power that has been confided to me, absolve thee from all apostolic censures judgments, and penalties, which thou mayest have incurred : moreover from all excesses, sins and crimes that thou mayest have committed, however great and enormous they may be, and from whatsoever cause, were they even reserved for our Most Holy Father the Pope and for the Apostolic See. I blot out all the stains of inability and all the marks of infamy that thou mayest have drawn upon thy self on this occasion. I restore thee anew to participation of the sacraments of the Church. I incorporate thee afresh in the communion of saints, and re-establish thee in the purity and innocence which thou hadst at thy baptism. So that in the hour of death, the gate by which sinners enter the place of torments and punishments shall be closed against thee ; and, on the contrary, the gate leading to the paradise of joy shall be open. And if thou shouldst not die for long years, this grace will remain unalterable until thy last hour shall arrive. In the name of the Father, Son, and Holy Ghost. Amen." The foregoing was signed by John Tetzel "with his own hand." (D'Aubigne's "History of the Reformation," vol. 1, p. 247.) Now if that had been in Swinton's text-book, I should not have wondered if the Roman Catholic members of the school-board had been greatly exercised, but Swinton's statement was not like that. If that is not a permission to commit sin, with a guarantee that if a man does not die for long years to come the indulgence will keep him out of hell and open to him heaven — if that is not what it says, then I cannot understand language.

"A Saxon nobleman, who had heard Tetzel at Leipsic, was much displeased by his falsehoods. Approaching the monk, he asked him if he had the power of pardoning sins that men have an intention of committing. 'Most assuredly,' replied Tetzel, 'I have received full powers from His Holiness for that purpose.' 'Well, then,' answered the knight, 'I am desirous of taking a slight revenge on one of my enemies, without endangering his life. I will give you ten crowns if you will give me a letter of indulgence that shall justify me.' Tetzel made some objections; they came, however, to an arrangement, by the aid of thirty crowns. The monk quitted Leipsic shortly after. The nobleman and his attendants lay in wait for him in a wood: they fell upon him and gave him a slight beating, and took away the well-stored indulgence-chest the Inquisitor was carrying with him. Tetzel made a violent outcry, and carried his complaint before the courts. But the nobleman showed the letter which Tetzel had signed himself, and which exempted him from every penalty. Duke George, whom this action at first exceedingly exasperated, no sooner read the document than he ordered the accused to be acquitted. Duke George was a most earnest Roman Catholic, and a life-long enemy of the Reformation. Tetzel, speaking for himself, makes manifest the wickedness and folly of indulgences, to gloze over which, this very summer, textbooks are changed and teachers persecuted in Boston, Massachusetts ! Bishop Challoner, in his " Catholic Christian Instructed," defined an indulgence thus : " An indulgence is simply a remission or mitigation of those temporal punishments which the sinner still owes to the Eternal Justice, even after the forgiveness of the guilt of his offence." Now we have here a Brief of Indulgence published in Sadlier's Catholic Directory for 1870-71 : " Saint Patrick's Day. Most Holy Father : James Frederick, Bishop of Philadelphia, most humbly begs that your Holiness would deign to grant to all the faithful of his diocese who, having duly confessed and worthily approached the holy Sacrament of the Eucharist on the feast of Saint Patrick, shall visit their representative churches, a plenary indulgence, which may be accounted every year, and which may also be applied in favor, aid or assistance of the souls in purgatory." The Brief is appended thus asked for, granting the request, signed by the Pope's Secretary. I have here the translation of a prayer which Romanists state was found in the

tomb of our Lord Jesus Christ in Jerusalem, preserved by His Holiness and Charles V., in their ora-
tories, in silver cases.   After a great deal of blasphemous nonsense which you may find in that so-called
prayer, we have the following: " Whoever daily
recites three Paters and three Aves, is granted by
Pius IX. one hundred years of indulgence, corresponding with the number of drops of blood which I
shed.   And if he lives like a good Christian, he
grants him five graces, namely: (1) Plenary indulgence and the remission of all his sins.   (2) He
shall be freed from the pains of purgatory.   (3) If
he dies before reaching the age of twelve years, he
shall be as if he had reached that age.   (4) He shall
be as if he were a martyr, and had shed his blood for
the faith.   (5) I will come from heaven to earth for
his soul, and for the souls of his relations to the fourth
generation.   He who carries this prayer with him
shall not die under condemnation, nor a bad death,
nor by sudden death.   He shall be safe from con-
tagion, from plagues, from arrow-shots: shall not
die without confession: he shall be safe from his
enemies, from the power of justice, and from all mal-
evolent men and false witnesses.   In houses where
this prayer is kept there shall be no treachery nor
other evil things, and forty days before death the
inhabitant shall see the blessed Virgin Mary."   A
part is omitted as unfit for print or speech.   ("Romanism As It Is," p. 535).

The Rev. Dr. Hall, late chaplain to the American
legation in Rome, says: " On a marble slab in the

Church of St. Lawrence is this inscription: "Whosoever with devout and contrite heart approaches this cross, and the other (in the adjoining cloister), shall obtain plenary indulgence of all his sins." In the Church of St. Agostino, is this inscription; "Our Lord, Pius VII., granted in perpetuity one hundred days of indulgence, to be obtained once a day by all those who devoutly shall kiss the foot of this holy image (a statue of the Virgin and Child), reciting an Ave Maria for the necessities of Holy Church." On the gate of St. Paul is written: "Kissing devoutly the most holy cross in any place gains one year and forty days indulgence." In the church of St. Sebastian, at the entrance to the Catacombs, on a marble slab, is this inscription: "Whoever contrite and confessed shall have entered it (the Catacomb), shall obtain plenary remission of all his sins, through the merits of the 174,000 "holy martyrs" buried there. The Roman doctrine of Merit teaches, that a martyr in dying renders more to God than is necessary for the expiation of all his sins. The same is said of all saints and monks. (Bellarmine, Indulg. 1 : 2, 5). The surplus of merit of these martyrs and monks is supposed to be deposited in the treasure (or box) of the church, of which the Pope only has the key, enabling him to grant indulgences without limit, and authorizing Bishops and priests to do the same. Pierre du Moulin, ("Roman Traditions," 361) says: "These indulgences are for those who will pay for them." "There is no sin so great that the indulgence cannot remit it," said Tetzel.

I do not take you any further into this matter of indulgences; but when you compare what is in the text-book that has been taken out of the Boston schools, you will find that it does not represent one-fiftieth part of the enormity of the promises, the blasphemies, the follies that are in the extracts which I have read you from prominent and authorized representatives of the Papal Church, from the Pope down. And is Massachusetts calmly and timidly submitting to have a text-book taken out and the teacher decapitated because he dared to tell a fraction of the truth? Shades of the fathers! Would that your spirits might reanimate your sons! It is not the utter silliness of the doctrine to which I call your attention; but the question is simply this: *Shall our schools teach history; or shall they teach Romanism?* That question is going to be decided by the American public. Now Gladstone says, in his pamphlet "Vaticanism" (p. 129), that "Rome does not keep good faith with history as it is handed down to her and marked out for her by her own annals." You understand that. Let me read it again. This man who weighs every word, and I think has as remarkable power of exact statement as any man speaking the English language, says: "Rome does not keep faith with history as it is handed down to her and marked out for her by her own annals." And what is the reason? The reason is, that Romanism cannot and dare not face her own history. This is true in every essential particular relating to the Church. For instance: almost every doctrine or dogma out-

side of immediate Christian biblical doctrine, almost
every dogma of the Roman Catholic Church is
exploded by history; as for example, the Papacy, infallibility, temporal power, purgatory. All these are
wholly unsubstantial in the light of history. Take
all the assumptions of the Papacy of Rome, which
depend on the allegation that Peter was the first
Bishop of Rome. Now, from the very best evidence
that I can get on both sides, Peter was never in
Rome, and that has been the opinion of many of the
most learned theologians and historians. In a debate
in Rome some years ago, after free Italy took possession and made debate possible, all the weight of
argument and all the truth of history was on the side
of the belief that Peter was never in Rome. That
the office of Bishop was held by him is without one
bit of proof. The Bible says nothing about it, nor
does tradition for a hundred years, nor do the fathers
who came directly after the apostles. All tradition
points the other way. Take another Romish dogma:
We have in the Papacy the figment of apostolic
succession. They think that Peter was in Rome and
was the first Bishop, and handed down his power to
his successors; but to whom they do not know.
Roman Catholic historians cannot agree, for their
lives, on who the next four Popes after Peter are.
There is no concord of opinion. I have here a book,
(Edgar's "Variations of Popery,") which quotes one
hundred and seventy and more of the leading
writers, historians and fathers of the Roman Catholic
Church, and the summation of their teaching is, that

they do not know who the first four Popes were,
after Peter, who never was a Pope! Where is your
unbroken apostolical succession? Nowhere. There
is no such thing in history.

And now further. In this apostolic succession
there are many Popes, of some of whom it is
altogether uncertain whether they were legally Popes
or not.   There are at least four periods where there
were two Popes at once, and how they did curse each
other! I never heard or read such cursing, except
as between Popes. You remember what a gift at
that Pius IX. had. Well, from the first,— and that is
one reason why we know Peter was never a Pope,—
from the first, these Popes have used the most diabolical language toward one another when there happened
to be two of them. And on two separate occasions
there were three Popes. Now which of the three
was Pope, when all claimed to be? They were all
cursing,— if that is any mark of a Pope,— every man
of them anathematizing and denouncing the others.
At the time known as the great schism, occurring
from and after 1378, there was a period of seventy
years in which there was a Pope at Avignon over in
France, and a Pope in Rome, and they surely did not
hold each other in good estimation. There were
seventy years in which the air was blue with their
mutual anathemas, and the apostolic succession was
wholly unsettled. Now, you remember that these
Popes were all infallible. I affirm to you that, by
the authority of Roman Catholic historians, many of
these Popes were guilty of the most infamous crimes,

and that the Councils of the Roman Catholic Church itself have characterized many of the Popes in language so dreadful that it is hardly fit to be read before any audience. What did the Council of Constance say concerning John XXIII., who was a Pope of Rome? I will read as much as I dare to you. " The Council, seeing no other alternative, resolved to depose John for immorality. The Sacred Synod of Constance, in the twelfth session, convicted His Holiness of schism, heresy, incorrigibleness, simony, impiety, immodesty, unchastity, fornication, adultery, incest, rape, piracy, lying, robbery, murder, perjury and infidelity." This was John XXIII., Pope of Rome; and that is what the Council of Constance said of him, the very same Council that burned John Huss and Jerome of Prague. Nor was he an exception either; for what do they say concerning another of the Popes? Benedict VIII., the Council convicted of " schism, heresy, error, pertinacity, incorrigibility, and perjury." At the same time, the Popes had their opinion of the Councils too, as you will find; for the Council of Basil incurred the displeasure of Eugenius, who was Pope at that time; and you ought to know what an infallible Pope thought of an infallible Council. This assembly he called " blockheads, fools, mad-men, barbarians, wild beasts, malignants, wretches, persecutors, miscreants, schismatics, heretics, vagabonds, renegades, apostates, rebels, monsters, criminals, a conspiracy, an innovation, a deformity, a conventicle, distinguished only for its temerity, sacrilege, audacity, machinations, impiety,

tyranny, ignorance, irregularity, fury, madness and
the dissemination of falschood, error, scandal, poison,
pestilence, desolation, unrighteousness and iniquity."
That is what he said. If the Pope told the truth,
the Council was indeed a fearful set of villains ; if he
told a lie, he was a fearful villain himself. Eugenius
proceeded then to expel a pernicious pestilence and
a gross impiety from the Church, by disabling all the
members of this Council, the Doctors, Archbishops,
Bishops and Cardinals, of all honor, office, benefit,
and dignity : in excommunicating and anathematizing
the whole assembly, with their patrons and adherents
of every rank and condition, civil and ecclesiastical ;
and consigned " that gang of all the devils in the universe, by wholesale, to receive their portion in con-
dign punishment and in eternal judgment, with Korah,
Dathan and Abiram." The pontifical and synodical
denunciation extended to the Basilian magistracy, as
well as sheriffs, governors, officials and citizens.
These, if they failed in thirty days to expel the Council from the city, Eugenius subjected to interdict and
confiscation of goods. Their forfeited property might,
by pontifical authority, be seized by the faithful, or by
any person who could take possession, This edify-
ing sentence is infallibly pronounced in the plenitude
of apostolic power, and subjected all those who should
permit any infringement on his declaration, constitution, condemnation and reprobation, to the indignation of Almighty God and the blessed apostles Peter
and Paul. This was the act of the general, apostolic, holy Florentine Council, and was issued with due

solemnity in a public synodical session. (Romish Historians, quoted by Edgar, pp. 96-7.) Now after that, another Pope — Pope Nicholas — cursed the Council, and having cursed to his satisfaction, he took it all back; Nicholas, in the plenitude of apostolic power, and in a bull which he addressed to all the faithful, rescinded, in due form, all the suspensions, interdicts, privations and anathemas which had been issued against Felix and the Council of Basil; while at the same time he "approved and confirmed all their ordinations, promotions, elections, provisions, collations, confirmations, consecrations, absolutions and dispensations." He denied all that was said or written against Felix and the Basilian Convention. Now when one infallible Pope exhausts language to denounce, and gets as good as he sends from an infallible Council; and when another infallible Pope takes it all back, and calls the Council a lot of good men; I want to ask you where the infallibility of the Pope comes in?

Can Romanism appeal to history for sanction of Papal Infallibility? Shall I have time to tell you of the monsters of iniquity that some of these Popes were? "But the Roman Catholic hierarchs of the middle and succeeding ages exhibited a melancholy change. Their lives displayed all the variations of impiety, malevolence, inhumanity, ambition, debauchery, gluttony, sensuality, deism and atheism. Gregory the Great seems to have led the way in the career of villany. This well-known pontiff has been characterized as worse than his predecessors, and better than his successors; or, in other terms, as the last good and the first bad Pope. The flood-gates of moral dissolution appeared, in the tenth century, to have been set wide open, and inundations of all impurity poured on the Christian world through the channel of the Roman Catholic hierarchs.

Awful and melancholy indeed is the picture of the Popedom at this era, drawn as it has been by its warmest friends. Platina, Petavius, Luitprand, Genebrard, Baronius, Hermann, Barclay, Binius, Giannone, Vignier, Labbe, and Du Pin. (Edgar's "Variations of Popery," pp. 108-9).

"Fifty Popes," says Genebrard, "in one hundred and fifty years, from John VIII. to Leo IX., entirely degenerated from the sanctity of their ancestors, and were apostatical, rather than apostolical. Forty pontiffs reigned in the tenth century. The successor, in each instance, seems demoralized even beyond his predecessor." Baronius, a famous Roman Catholic historian, in his annals of the tenth century, seems to labor for language to express the degeneracy of the Popes, and the fearful deformity of the Popedom. "Many shocking monsters," he says, "intruded into the pontifical chair, who were guilty of murder, assassination, simony, dissipation, tyranny, sacrilege, perjury, and all kinds of miscreancy." "The Church," says Giannone, "was then in a shocking disorder, in a state of iniquity." The greatest of the Popes was Gregory VII., known as Hildebrand. Now concerning Gregory VII. we have an opinion, and we have a declaration from Roman Catholics of the highest standing in those times, that he was elected through force and bribery and without the concurrence of the emperor or clergy. He obtained his supremacy, in the general opinion, by gross simony ; but he had the hardihood to pretend that his dignity was intruded on him against his will. The Councils of Worms and Brescia depicted his character with great precision. The Council of Worms, comprehending forty-six of the German prelacy, met in 1076, and preferred numerous imputations against Gregory. This Synod found His Holiness guilty of usurpation, simony, apostasy, treason, schism, heresy, chicanery, dissimulation, fornication, adultery and perjury. His Holiness, in the sentence of the German prelacy, preferred harlots to women of character, and adultery and incest to just and holy matrimony. The Council of Brescia, which was composed of thirty bishops, and many princes from Italy, France and Germany, called Gregory a fornicator, an impostor, an assassin, a violator of the canons, a disseminator of discord, a disturber. He had sown scandal among friends, dissensions among the peaceful, and separation among the married. The Brescian fathers then declared His Holiness guilty of bribery, usurpation, simony, sacrilege, vain-glory, ambition, obstinacy, perverseness, sorcery, divination, necromancy, schism, heresy, infidelity, assassination and perjury." These are the words of Councils of the Roman Catholic Church concerning the character of the greatest Pope — unless Innocent III. disputes that eminence with him—that ever sat in the Papal chair in Rome. Boniface III. was as bad, or worse. Sixtus IV., in 1471, just before the discovery of America, is characterized in terms as horrible. Of one of the Popes it is said, he was convicted of forty crimes. The Fathers of Trent found him guilty of—I will not read the list. You are getting quite familiar with it; and there are some parts of it that you never will get familiar with from my reading.

Alexander VI., Pope of Rome, was a Borgia, and the very name is associated with the wickedness of wickedness. If ever there was a monster on earth who was guilty of every imaginable crime that could belong to a person that had disgraced human nature by the vilest uses, Alexander VI. was one of those men.

Now, my friends, I will give you a morsel that is more remarkable than anything yet said. I hold in my hand a modern History, which I suppose the Romish Church intends to put in the place of Swinton's. This modern History is written by Peter Fredet, D. D., and was published by J. Murphy & Co., of New York, in the year 1886. On the 511th page of this History, I find the following declaration about these Popes: "It is true, a few among them gave great scandal to the Christian world in their private character and conduct; but it ought to be *remembered at the same time, that, through a special protection of Divine Providence, the irregularity of their lives did not interfere with their public duty, from which they never departed. The beneficial influence of sacred jurisdiction does not depend on the private virtue of the persons invested with it;* but on their divine mission and appointment to feed the Christian flock. Nor did Christ promise personal sanctity to its chief pastors ; but gave to them authority to teach and govern the faithful." That is Roman Catholic history. Monstrous ! Monstrous !! The Popes who, by Roman Catholic authority, are characterized in terms that carry with them the utmost condemnation, are declared by a Roman Catholic historian, in 1886, to be so correct in their administration that it makes no difference how they live ! They are equally infallible, whatever their vices and crimes ! I am reminded of what was said once by a man who was told, in the case of a Bishop of scandalous character, that the Bishop did not sin ; it was the man that sinned. The Bishop was sinless, though the man was wicked. He simply asked : " Pray tell me, what will become of the Bishop when the devil gets the man ?"

Let me ask you, now, what history will give us in defense of the doctrine of purgatory, through which Rome wrings, from superstition, countless millions of money. I have here a letter from the late Chaplain of the American legation in Rome, who has given close attention to the study, and who writes also in regard to indulgences. After stating that " the Pope can give a living man indulgence of his sins ;" we have the following citations, which are of very great interest : " The doctrine of purgatory was declared to be an article of faith in the Roman

Church, by the Council of Florence, only in the year 1439." (That is, up to that time, for 1450 years nearly, either purgatory was undiscovered, or the souls of Catholics and everybody else went to it, and nobody knew it! And are they there yet?) "In the latter part of the fifteenth century, Pope Alexander VI. was the first to declare that indulgences delivered souls from purgatory." (*In the latter part of the fifteenth century*, you see!) Cardinal Cajetan, before whom Luther was summoned, said in a tract on indulgences: "We have no certain knowledge in regard to the origin of indulgences; and we possess in writing no authority on this subject, nor in Holy Scripture, nor in the writings of the ancient fathers, nor of the Greek and Latin doctors." Cardinal Fisher, in confuting Luther, said: "As to indulgences, it is uncertain by whom they were instituted; and as to purgatory, no mention is made of it by the ancients; so that belief in indulgences and in purgatory has not been necessary to the primitive Church." Take away purgatory, and no one will need indulgences, or seek them. Purgatory and indulgences are all a modern invention; and when you come to study and read history, you will find that the Roman Catholic dogmatic system cannot stand in the face of history for a day or an hour.

And what of Mariolatry and other similar blasphemies? I declare to you that now, when it is time to close, I am not half through this line of thought, and I am not going to try to finish it to-night. Such is the abundance of evidence proving that the pretensions of Romanism are inconsistent with all truth, and with all open study of what is necessary for men to know, that our contempt for the false claims of this infallibility increases with proof, until it piles up an indictment which disannuls forever the claims of Rome, and which seems to say to every citizen of this Republic : Against Roman usurpation, based on falsehood in the name of truth, yield not for one hour, not for one moment!

I have not told you how she changes history. It it is only a question of time with me that I should. But I have to add one thing that is more startling than anything that I have hitherto said : By the dogmas of the Roman Catholic Church, as laid down by Cardinal Manning, *the Pope is the judge of what history is*; and if he says that a thing did not exist, notwithstanding the world knows it did, — if he says that certain facts are not historical, the Church is bound to believe him !

" History is a wilderness into which infallibility will allow no one to wander without guilt of his own appointment, and it denies to every man the right to exercise his own reason or common sense in separating the true from the false." ("Papacy and the Civil Power.")

" If any one say," says Cardinal Manning, ("The Vatican Council and its Definitions," page 121,) — "If any one say that there is no judgment but right reason, or common sense, he is only reproducing in history what Luther applied to the Bible. Again, in Catholics such a theory is simply heresy."

Why? He answers thus: "The only source of revealed truth is God: the only channel of that revelation is the Church. No human history can declare what is contained in that revelation. The Church (the Pope) alone can determine its limits, and therefore its contents. And when the Pope, acting for the Church, *does determine what are its limits and contents, no difficulties of human history can prevail against it.* The Church is its own evidence, *anterior to its history, and independent of it. Its history is to be learned of itself.*" It is under his dictation that they are telling Boston schools what shall be taught as history. And they are coming to Worcester to tell you; and what are you going to say to them? I can imagine. I have faith for the future. I had laid out here, in my discourse, to read to you from Fredet's History, of 1886, a precious lot of things that are as far from the truth as the poles are apart. I had intended to tell you how intolerant they are of nearly all our books; to bring before you an incident not yet four weeks old, where the Papal power, after having sanctioned a book and said that the faithful might read it, has now resolved that the book ought not to be read, and put its leading proposition on the *Index Expurgatorius.* I had intended to tell you of the *Index Expurgatorius,* and in what attitude the Papal Church stands toward all literature and science. But I have only time at this moment to draw to an abrupt close, deferring these revelations to another day. I want you to know them all. I cannot bear that you shall go into this conflict half equipped. I do not want the insolent and arrogant priests of Rome to tell you, either in their papers or in their churches, a mass of lies, that are lies in the face of their own history, and have you believe them. I am simply giving you ammunition. I am only bringing before you a variety of facts of the utmost importance for you to know before you advance to the attack. Let us put on the shield of truth, against which every Romish pretence is shivered; as are shivered the javelins of hate on the bucklers of Almighty God. We know what correct history is. Did our ancestors persecute the Quakers? We know it, and are ashamed of it. Did they hang the witches? We admit it, and say, It never shall be so again! No matter what the imputation, if it be truth, admit it. An honest man, or Church, or State, has no reason to deny a frank, fair declaration of fact. But if we professed to be an infallible Church, and were resolved that all was perfect, and had always been, and had resolved to stand up for everything we and our ancestors had done, we would be compelled, either to deny the truth, or else to bend it in justification of the enormities of former days.

That giant among men of thought, Victor Hugo, said, in a marvellous paper, which I shall read in your hearing yet one day, that after all the mischief they had done elsewhere, Rome was now assailing France. "But," he said, with that singular felicity of expression which characterizes his writings, "France is a lion, and is alive." And here—in the presence of these confessed and hostile designs with which Romanists assail our national policy and free institutions, counting on our acquiescence and the effects of hidden treachery — I take up the words of that herald of freedom in France, and say, for the benefit of the hierarchy wherever they are, whether in Worcester or in Rome : " Beware ! AMERICA IS A LION, AND IS ALIVE ! "

Sermon VIII.

THE PURPOSE OF ROMANISM TO DESTROY OUR PUBLIC SCHOOLS.

"I speak as to wise men; judge ye what I say:" these have been the words of my text for two consecutive Sunday evenings, and because the three sermons on our public schools are practically one, these are the words of my text to-night. You find them in 1 Corinthians, 10: 15. I have no time for introductory remarks, save for a word in review. I greatly desire that as wise men you shall keep distinctly in mind exactly what I propose to show. I have shown you that the Roman Catholic Church is hostile to the constitution of the United States, and to our public schools, which are an adjunct and a necessity to that Constitution. I have shown you that its hostility to the common schools has been exhibited by disparaging them, by threats against them, by the expressed determination to ruin them if possible, by demands for a division of the school fund, by protests alleged, though falsely, to be founded on conscience and on fair play, by opposition to the Holy Scriptures, and also by opposition to correct history. When we closed our review on last Sunday night, I was showing that the Roman Catholic Church, in its fear that public education would work its destruction, and in

its determination to destroy the common schools, not
only objects to the Bible and to history, but that it
carries its objections against almost everything that
we call truth.

Turning to this book, "Judges of the Faith" (which
I described to you before, the Roman Catholic book
which is endorsed by hundreds of prelates from the
Pope down), I call your attention next to the fact,
that on the 11th, 21st and 24th pages, not only the
Bible and History are declaimed against, but also the
Readers that are used in our public schools, and all
our school literature, in general.   Here are objections
offered not only to Swinton, but to Wilson, Hume and
Hallam, to Peter Parley, and many other historians;
and the most contemptuous characterizations are
given to a great variety of other school literature.   On
the 24th page, they speak very contemptuously of a
History which contains the following allusions, as they
quote : " Indulgences sold for profit" (we fortunately
know something about that) ; "actual pardons of
guilt ;" the Murder of Mary, Queen of Scots, justified,
and herself vilified (see Froude's late researches) ;
the Thirty Years' War put upon Ferdinand II., endeavoring to extinguish Protestantism ; Philip II.'s
schemes "principally actuated by bigotry ;" "the glori-
fication of Garibaldi, the famous Italian patriot."
All these phrases are held up as though erroneous
and wicked.   And yet they are true !

What does Italy think of Garibaldi, whom they refuse to acknowledge as an Italian patriot?   I will tell
you.   If you visit the Hall of Representatives in Rome,

where gather the men who now legislate for free
Italy, you will find that one seat is taken away, and
in the place where that seat formerly was is a silver
plate, on which we read that Garibaldi once sat there,
and because they think no man is worthy to be his
successor, they have removed his chair. While
Romanism hounds Garibaldi, Italy reveres him as a
patriot.

The objections of Romanists to our school books
are so general, that in Cincinnati, in the year 1869,
Archbishop Purcell, (who gained great notoriety
in this country by stealing a million or two of dollars from the Roman Catholic Church—if, indeed, it
could be called stealing, for the Bishop has a right
to all he can get in the Roman Catholic Church, and
holds in his own name all the church property of the
diocese)—Archbishop Purcell objected to the books
of general reading and reference in the libraries of
the schools in Cincinnati; and the school committee,
disposed to make peace, permitted him to take a
catalogue of the library books and indicate what
works should be removed from those libraries. That
was witnessed in 1869, in Ohio. Will it be a happy
day for America, for literature and for general intelligence, when the Roman Catholic Church takes out of
all our school libraries the books that it objects to?
We wonder what will be left. They claim and
expect the censorship of all literature, and all utterances of the press, platform and pulpit, as I read to
you from the *Catholic World* last Sunday night.

Now the censorship of Rome over all this literature, not only biblical and historic, but scientific also, is a part of the machinery of that church. They have in Romanism, exercising authority throughout the world, what is called The Sacred Congregation of the Index, over which a Cardinal, and sometimes a Pope presides, and which meets every Monday in Rome. It is the duty of this committee of the Roman Catholic Church to determine what books shall be permitted to be published, read and studied throughout the Roman Catholic world, and what shall be forbidden. When a book is objectionable to them, they refuse to have it printed and circulated ; when a book is favorable to Romanism, they consent to its circulation. So fierce is the antagonism of the Roman Catholic Church to books that are obnoxious to them, that, long centuries ago, an edict of excommunication was issued against all persons who either printed, or possessed, or read heretical books. I will read you from that bull. The earliest one published is that by Gregory XII. in 1411, which was renewed, with additions, by Pius V. His bull was renewed under the same name by Urbane VIII. in 1627, and finally as a bull of excommunication by Pius IX., on the twelfth of October, 1859. The first article of this bull is as follows : " We excommunicate and anathematize, in the name of God, Father, Son, and Holy Ghost, and by the authority of the blessed apostles, Peter and Paul, and by our own, all Wickliffites, Hussites, Lutherans, Calvinists, Huguenots, Anabaptists, and all other heretics, by whatsoever name they are called, and of whatsoever sect they be; and also, all schismatics, and those who withdraw themselves, or recede obstinately from the obedience of the Bishop of Rome; as also their adherents, receivers, favorers, and generally any defenders of them; *together with all who, without the authority of the Apostolic See, shall, knowingly, read, keep or print any of their books which treat on religion, or for any cause* whatever, publicly or privately, on any pretence or color, defend them." That is to say, we have a bull endorsed by at least five Popes, of excommunication against those who shall dare to publish, circulate, read or possess books that are forbidden by the Sacred Inquisitorial Congregation of Rome.

And what is the penalty pronounced by the congregation and church against those who have violated this bull of the Pope? You will find, when you come to study the history, that very heavy fines and penalties have been denounced upon persons who shall publish, and even those who shall possess, such books. Under a King of Spain, by Papal direction and sanction, *death* was the penalty for those who possessed books forbidden by the Sacred Congregation of the Index.

The Roman Catholic Church does not merely object to the Bible, and to history; but it also objects to science, it objects to literature, it objects to every department of knowledge that is contrary to its pretensions; and that objection is carried so far, that the curse of excommunication is pronounced on any who shall dare to have books which they have proscribed, and shall presume to study books which they have denounced. You will be interested at the citation of one sample of how their policy worked in a matter of science and scientific investigation. On the fifth day of May, 1616, The Sacred Congregation of the Index denounced and forbade the Copernican theory that the earth moves round the sun. They denounced it as a heresy; cursed those that taught it, anathematized those that printed it, and threatened those that believed it. There has been a great deal of wriggling on the part of the Roman Catholic Church to avoid the responsibility of this act, but truth is strong; and when the Roman Catholic Church grapples with the truth of history, history is ultimately sure to win in the conflict. Later, in 1620, they denounced Copernicus by name. Then they denounced Galileo, and arrested him, and threatened him, and imprisoned him, and made him affirm that the earth *did not* move around the sun; and when he said it, he muttered under his breath, "But it *does* move." Galileo's book appeared in 1632, and was condemned in 1634. That edict of the Roman Catholic Church left the Copernican theory on the list of forbidden books in the *Index Expurgatorius* until 1835. Every man, therefore, who dared, up to 1835, to believe that the earth moved round the sun, or dared to teach it or print it, or who had a book in his house or in his possession which stated it,—every such man was excommunicated and damned by the Pope of Rome and The Sacred Congregation. Do you propose to take your science from an authority like that? Yet if in the public schools the movement of the earth round the sun had been taught any time before 1835, Romanists would have objected just as strongly to this Copernican theory that the earth moves round the sun as they object to Swinton's History ; and I suppose that some cowards would have let them forbid the book in the public schools. I do not believe we are ready to have our text-books assorted by such scientists. In 1835, from the *Index Expurgatorius,* (of which, fortunately, I happen to have through the kindness of a friend two copies), and without a word of apology, the books on the Copernican theory, for the first time in two centuries, were omitted from the list of forbidden publications.

In the year 1844, there was formed in the City of Montreal the Montreal Institute,—a company of young men mostly Roman Catholics, who desired to improve themselves through association and through literature. They gathered together a library of about nine thousand volumes ; and at length it began to be noised abroad that there were heretical books in the library. The Bishops interfered, and endeavored to break up the Montreal Institute. The gentlemen composing that Institute handed out their catalogue and said : " What is there here that is obnoxious ?" There was no answer. Hostility did not take the form of debate. It was understood that Milton's " Paradise Lost " and Dante's " Inferno" and " Paradiso " were among the books objected to. An edict of ecclesiastical censure was pronounced on

the Montreal Institute, and that Institute appealed
to Rome.   Among the leading men of the Institute
was Joseph Guibord, a printer, a man of great intelligence, who became the object of distinct hostility
because of his desire to perpetuate the Institute and
keep their library intact.   While the matter was
pending, Joseph Guibord died, and the attempt was
made to bury him in what is known as " sacred
ground," where he owned a lot, somewhere about the
last of November, 1869.   The attempt was met by the
resistance of a mob of Roman Catholics, inspired by
the leading church officials, who so far hindered and
forbade that poor body being laid to rest in the lot
which he had purchased, that the remains were taken
to a Protestant cemetery, and temporarily placed in
the vault.   Then began litigation in the courts, to see
whether the body of Joseph Guibord should lie in
his own lot.   What was his offence?   He belonged
to the Montreal Institute which had not instantly
yielded when the hand of the Bishops was laid upon
it ; because it was seeking for intelligence, and, to a
degree, for freedom of thought.   An appeal was
made to the courts to permit the body to be buried.
Some courts decided one way, and some another.
Meanwhile, Mrs. Guibord, who was a brave and
earnest woman and a Roman Catholic, gave her
effort to the work of securing the right to bury her
husband in his own cemetery lot, and dying, left her
estate for that purpose.   At length an appeal was
taken to the privy council of Great Britain, and it
was decided that the body should be buried in

sacred ground. Then followed mobs, disturbances and denunciations, the like of which even Canada, priest-ridden as it is, had hardly seen. The grave was prepared; and finally, guarded by the military, in the presence of a howling mob, the body of Joseph Guibord was laid in the grave, and cement of the strongest sort, mixed with iron, was poured in over it, in order to keep it safe from the fury of the enraged Romanists. Then the Bishop of Montreal apostolically cursed the ground where this man's remains lay — cursed it with mocking tones, as if the voice of Joseph Guibord was speaking from the ground. Some one inquired how far down his curse went, as the wife's body was laid in the same grave, and she was a good Catholic and not excommunicated! He cursed it with the remarkable facility for cursing which priests have, in the presence of the Roman Catholics of Montreal, and went unrebuked by his fellow-bishops, and by the Pope of Rome. What was the offence for which Joseph Guibord's dust was cursed? That he belonged to a library association which dared to think without priestly and papal repression, and to own Milton's "Paradise Lost" and Dante's "Paradiso" and "Inferno." I should think that the Bishop of Montreal might well take Dante's "Inferno" and read in it a description of his own future habitation, if he dared to curse a man for loving truth and freedom. Now the Roman Church blesses, and now again curses, and it is a little doubtful when and why.

Forty or fifty years ago, Rosmini, a distinguished

ecclesiastic of the Roman Catholic Church, a man of learning, who was an intimate friend of three of the Popes, published certain scientific books. These books were repeatedly attacked, and came three times before The Congregation of the Sacred Index. Every time they came, the Congregation said there was nothing in them contrary to the theology or doctrines of the Roman Catholic Church. But the Jesuits were busy. They kept insisting that these books ought not to be circulated. The Sacred Congregation insisted that they should ; and finally, the Pope issued an edict that there should be nothing more said about it. The Jesuits worked on as they always do, Pope or no Pope, and within the last few months The Sacred Congregation have taken forty of the leading propositions of Rosmini's book, condemned them, and demanded that those shall be taken out of the books, if they are circulated. When you yield your Swinton's History in the public schools, when you yield your Bible, you are simply on the line of yielding everything. There is no limit or stopping-place at which Rome says : You may permanently have these books in your schools.

I want you to notice this ; because, when our Massachusetts committees, in their desire to be kind and fair, begin to yield, they begin to slide down an inclined plane with accelerated velocity, and they do not know where they will stop. You never can satisfy Rome until you are her absolute slave. This is the point at which I purposed to close my last Sunday evening's sermon.

I was hoping to get as far as this. Then I meant to show you that, in order to satisfy Roman Catholics, you must take out of the public schools all our Bibles; all books that speak disrespectfully of those Popes of whom I read you so many interesting facts last Sabbath evening; all books that condemn any doctrine that has been praised by Rome, or praise any doctrine that has been condemned by Rome; therefore, all works on political economy according to the principles of the Constitution of the United States; all books on natural science that are obnoxious to the priests of The Sacred Congregation. And, by the way, how long will they allow us to teach Chemistry? since chemistry proves that the " Sacrifice of the Mass" is folly, and that the wafer is no more the body and blood of Jesus Christ, after the priest has spoken over it, than it was before.

So our scientific books and our Bibles, our histories and our literature, are to be taken out of the schools, and you want to know what we shall have in their place. What kind of a system of public education does Rome intend to give us? What do they want taught in our schools? and if we yield to them what shall we have? When we know this, then we shall know the plans of this Church, and what we can rely upon for the future. To answer these important questions, I have so much to say that I can adorn it very little, and must speak with great directness concerning the general system of Roman Catholic education. In this first book, "Judges of the Faith," page 139, I read the following words

from The Sacred Congregation of Rome, endorsed
by The Third Baltimore Plenary Council : "Reserv-
ing *the exclusive right of the priest as regards, particularly, the appointments and dismissal of teachers*, the
discipline of the school, and superintendence in spir-
ituals." We are, then, to have a system of education
as far as the Roman Catholic Church goes, that is
exclusively presided over by priests ; and they, as
you know, are compelled to further this scheme of
parochial schools, for the sake of their own prefer-
ment ; which they will lose, unless they do further it.
The duty of the laity is also prescribed in this
book, in the following words : "Nor with less zeal
and prudence is the erroneous opinion to be
uprooted from the minds of the laity ; viz., that the
solicitude for the school is to be confined to that
portion of the congregation actually and directly
making use of it for their children. It must be
plainly demonstrated, that the profits and blessings
accruing from the preservation of faith and morals
in parochial schools redound to the benefit of the
whole community." That is to say, if Roman Catholic parents have no children in the parochial schools,
The Third Plenary Council of Baltimore expressly
insists that those parents shall pay their money into
those schools for their support, and shall do all they
can for their prosperity. But, remember, it is a matter of *conscience* with many Roman Catholics that
they shall *not* support parochial schools. What
then ? We heard them claim, that because their consciences demand parochial schools, therefore we must

yield our system to them. And now this is their demand, within their own communion, that those who have no children in the parochial schools, and who do not believe in the parochial schools, shall be compelled to support them. How about conscience? Is this freedom of conscience? I tell you, the Roman Catholic Church never says Conscience when it has any other meaning than submission to the Pope. Never!

We have it indicated here in this book, on page 141, that the preferred teachers of Rome are monks and nuns. We have the statement of Father Chiniquy, who was fifty years in the Romish Church, and who has written one of the ablest books on this question that we have, that Jesuits are always preferred as teachers in Roman Catholic schools. I noticed in one of our papers in this city, yesterday or the day before, a list of the professors in the Roman Catholic College of the Holy Cross in this city for the ensuing year. Every one of those gentlemen had after his name the letters S. J. What does that mean? Society of Jesus — Jesuits. In other words, they are all Jesuits, every man of them. And that paper which is just now fondling the Roman Catholic Church, and may be assumed to be accurate on Romanist matters — the paper that is giving us columns of Roman Catholic news, and scarcely a reference to any other church — is responsible for the statement that all the teachers in this Worcester College are Jesuits. We learned something about the Jesuits not very long ago. Here is a little more.

In the Jesuit oath (for you want to know what kind of men are preferred for this teaching) you find the following words: " I do renounce and disown any allegiance as due to any heretical king, prince or state named Protestant, or obedience to any of their inferior magistrates or officers. I do further declare, that the doctrine of the Church of England, the Calvinists, Huguenots, and others of the name of Protestants, to be damnable; and they themselves are damned, and to be damned, that will not forsake the same." (I wish they were a little freer with salvation, and not so free with damnation. It seems to me that they know more about that subject than I ever heard before.) "I do further declare," says the Jesuit, who is to be the chief teacher in these schools, " that I will help, assist and advise all or any of His Holiness' agents in any place wherever I shall be, in England, Scotland or Ireland, or in any other territory or kingdom I shall come to; and do my utmost to extirpate the heretical Protestant's doctrine, and to destroy all their pretended powers, legal or otherwise. I do further promise and declare that, notwithstanding I am dispensed with to assume any religion heretical," (that is, he may come and join this church and lie all through, even at God's altar, provided there is some Jesuit end to be attained by it,) " for the propagating of the Mother Church's interests, to keep secret and private all her agents' councils from time to time, as they intrust me, and not to divulge, directly or indirectly, by word, writing or circumstance whatsoever, but to execute all that shall be proposed," etc. (See "Romanism," A. P. Grover, Chicago, 1887, page 116.) These are the favorite and choice teachers, the chosen teachers, of the Roman Catholic Church; men who have announced their hostility to every form of government, of teaching, and of religion, except the Church of Rome; and men that swear absolute devotion to her in all that they do, and are privileged to do; and play the hypocrite in any assembly, and join any church, for the purpose of finding out its secrets; and vow solemnly to act wholly in the interests of the Pope and the papacy. And yet the Roman Catholic Church prates about morality in schools, and thinks our teachers are not teaching morality enough, and fears that their youth, their tender youth, will be corrupted by our teachers, and wants to put them under the care of the Jesuits, men that are perjured, as is everyone who has sworn allegiance to the Constitution of this country and has sworn oaths of papal obedience against it; she wants these men to be the leading educators of America!

Toward what are they aiming? What is their purpose, and what do they mean by education? This is a most interesting query. I shall answer you in their own words, for I am very much interested to know from their own lips what they do mean. I find the following declaration of their idea of education, which I want you to contrast with ours. The *Catholic World* for April 1871, gives the Roman

Catholic idea of education as follows : " Education is the American hobby—regarded, as uneducated or poorly educated people usually regard it, as a sort of panacea for all the ills that flesh is heir to.   We ourselves, as Catholics, are as decidedly as any other class of American citizens in favor of universal education, as thorough and extensive as possible—*if its quality suits us.* We do not indeed prize as highly as some of our countrymen appear to do the ability to read, write and cipher. *Some men are born to be leaders, and the rest are born to be led.*   (Who is born to be led ; and who is born to be a leader? is a fair question.)   " The best ordered and administered state, is that *in which the few are well educated and lead, and the many are trained to obedience, are willing to be directed, content to follow, and do not aspire to be leaders.*   In extending education, and endeavoring to train all to be leaders, we have only extended presumption, pretension, conceit, indocility, and brought incapacity to the surface.   *We believe that the peasantry, in old Catholic countries, two centuries ago, were better educated; although for the most part unable to read or write, than are the great body of American people to-day.*" Now you understand that this theory of education states that the few shall be educated and shall be leaders ; that the many shall be educated, whether they know how to read and write or not, and shall be led.   That is Roman Catholic education.   Do you say that this is only my statement of it? No ; it is their own. And do you want it emphasized? Look at Italy, and France, and

Spain, and Portugal, and Austria, and Mexico, and South America, if you desire illustrations. What is their idea of education? The few to be taught and lead, the many to do what tyrants have made their subjects do through all the years of this suffering world's history — to grind in their prison-houses for the enrichment of despots. That is their theory; and they want to transplant it here. I do not think I ever heard a statement more utterly contrary to the American policy concerning the rights of man than this.

What is our theory of American education? It is, to teach every man all he can learn. It is, that the boy on the tow-path shall come to be President, if he knows enough. It is, that the tanner-man shall lead the greatest armies of history in the grandest of all struggles for human rights. It is, that the boy from the shoemaker's bench in Natick shall preside over the Senate of the United States, which is the grandest House of Lords in the world. It is Garfield, and Grant, and Henry Wilson. This is American education. What is Roman Catholic education? The few to lead, the many to be slaves. Now the Roman Catholics know this. The more intelligent among them know it. Their leaders know it. The beating hearts of many American citizens that protest, although within the Roman Catholic Church, against this type of education, affirm it. And what does the *Freeman's Journal* say? Fortunately, I have just a little extract from that. The New York *Freeman's Journal and Roman Catholic Register*, for March 12,

1881, describing parochial education, says: "A smattering of the catechism (in parochial schools) is supplied to fit them for the duties of life;" and intimates that these schools and their policies, then, are only "apologies, compromises, systemless pretenses" for education. That is what the *Freeman's Journal* thinks of parochial schools. Dr. O. A. Brownson, who was a great authority in the Roman Catholic Church for twenty years, and whose *Review* was published in New York, and republished in London during that time,—Dr. A. O. Brownson tells what he thinks, from inside the Roman Catholic Church, concerning Roman Catholic education. In the number for January, 1862, *Brownson's Review* thus spoke of the quality of Roman Catholic schools and colleges. (Now remember that Brownson had more power as a Roman Catholic writer in this country than any other man, so far as power of statement and power of definition could give it.) He says: " These schools practically fail to recognize human progress. As far as we are able to trace the effect of the most approved Catholic education of to-day, whether at home or abroad, it tends to repress, rather than quicken the life of the pupil; to unfit, rather than prepare him for the active and zealous discharge either of his religious or social duties. They who are educated in our schools seem misplaced and mistimed in the world; as if born and educated for a world that has ceased to exist. Comparatively few of them [Catholic graduates] take their stand as scholars, or as men on a level with the Catholics of non-Catholic colleges; and those

who do take that stand, do it by throwing aside nearly all they learned at their own colleges, and adopt-
ing the ideas and principles, the modes of thought
and action, they find in the general civilization of the
country in which we live. The cause of the failure
of what we call Catholic education is, in our judgment, in the fact that we do not educate for the present or the future, but for the past. We do not mean
that the dogmas are not scrupulously taught in all
our schools and colleges ; nor that the words of the
catechism are not duly insisted upon. We concede
this. There can be no question that what passes for
Catholic education in this or any other country, has
its ideal of perfection in the past, and that it resists
as un-Catholic, irreligious and opposed to God, the
tendencies of modern civilization." (Go on, Mr.
Brownson. I wish you were here to say this as you
could say it. But I suppose he is in purgatory !)

"The work it gives its subjects, or prepares them to
perform, is not the work of carrying it forward, but
that of resisting it, driving it back, anathematizing it,
as at war with the Gospel ; and either of neglecting
it altogether, or taking refuge in the cloister, in an
exclusive or exaggerated asceticism, always border-
ing on immorality (Hear that again ! He says,
they are driving back progress, and either neglecting
the Gospel, or taking refuge in the cloister, in an
exclusive or exaggerated asceticism, always border-
ing on immorality) ; or of restoring a former order
of civilization, no longer a living order, and which
humanity has evidently left behind, and is resolved

shall never be restored." *Brownson's Review*, January and April, 1862. A truthful confession !

You have then from Roman Catholic authorities, what their idea of education shall be ; and you have the opinion of one of their leading men as to what its effect is. He goes on further, and says, it is a foreign education, and that the Roman Catholic people by it are made a foreign people in the land where they live. Father Chiniquy says (and he had a Roman Catholic education in their very best schools in Canada) : " The purpose of Rome is to educate a man just enough so he will kiss the toe of the Pope." And further he says, speaking of the repression of inquiry : " You are told that you must not question your superior in any matter, but yield implicit obedience to him, and the only liberty allowed is the liberty of obedience." He is well qualified to speak, and in no degree discredited because his mind and conscience were too well educated to permit him to remain a Romish satellite. So much for the general idea of Roman Catholic education.

Priests and monks, nuns and Jesuits for teachers ; a type of education that ignores the masses, while it makes the few leaders ; a type of education that gives a smattering of the the catechism ; a system of the past, and not for the future ; a method that prostrates the intellect, instead of lifting it up ; a type of education that makes the peasants of two hundred years ago more an ideal community than the people of this enlightened commonwealth, who have had the education which America has given throughout all its history !

But now what do they demand shall be taught in our public schools? for I must hasten in order to bring this to your attention.

First of all, they demand that Romanism shall be taught ; and I will read this demand from the opinion of the Bishops of the Netherlands, who speak for all the Bishops, found on the seventy-second page of the " Judges of Faith ": " It is further necessary that the schools teach the children and make them practice the Catholic religion." The worship of the Virgin must be taught ; that is stated on the 132d page in this book. Papal infallibility must be taught : that is exactly, in so many words, what the Roman Catholics of Germany said after the Vatican Council, and what the government refused to have done ; and after 1870 laws of Germany were made, in order that the Papal infallibility should not be established, and the authority of the emperor overthrown. They profess the right to teach the most unqualified sectarianism. Some of the text-books that they have already used in this country, in schools where they have the power, are sectarian to the very last degree.

You recollect that they call our schools " godless schools." Godless schools ! Then I suppose they would call their schools godly schools. Would you like to hear what they teach in these " godly " schools? Let me take time to tell you. Fortunately, a text-book is occasionally issued which discloses the spirit of their teaching without disguise.

There is a volume, one of a series, entitled, " Familiar Explanation of Christian Doctrine, adapted for the family and more advanced students in Catholic schools and colleges," published in 1875, by Kreuzer Brothers, Baltimore, and sanctioned by Archbishop Bayley. Lesson XII. is called, " No salvation outside of the Roman Catholic Church." The questions and answers run thus (this is what they want to use instead of Swinton's History) : " Q. Since the Roman Catholic Church alone is the true Church of Jesus Christ, can any one who dies outside of the Church be saved? A. He can not. Q. Did Jesus Christ himself assure us most solemnly, and in plain words, that no one can be saved out of the Roman Catholic Church? A. He did; when he said to his Apostles, ' Go and teach all nations,' etc." (I confess, I don't see the connection.) " Q. What do the Fathers of the Church say about the salvation of those who die out of the Roman Catholic Church? A. They all, without any exception, pronounce them infallibly lost forever." A little farther on may be found the following : " Q. Are there any other reasons to show that heretics, or Protestants, who die out of the Roman Catholic Church are not saved; A. There are several. They cannot be saved because, (1) They have no divine faith ; (2) They make a liar of Jesus Christ, of the Holy Ghost, and of the Apostles ; (3) They have no faith in Christ. (4) They fell away from the true Church of Christ. (5) They are too proud to submit to the Pope, the vicar of Christ. (6) They cannot perform any good works whereby they can obtain heaven. (7) They do not receive the body and blood of Christ. (8) They die in their sins. (9) They ridicule and blaspheme the mother of. God and his saints. (10) They slander the spouse of Jesus Christ, the Catholic Church." Again, page 97: "Q. Now do you think that God, the Father, will admit into heaven those who thus make liars of his son, Jesus Christ, of the Holy Ghost, and the Apostles? A. No ; he will let them have their portion with Lucifer in hell, who first rebelled against Christ, and who is the father of liars. Q. Have Protestants any faith in Christ? A. They never had. Q. Why not? A. Because there never lived such a Christ as they imagine and believe in. Q. In what kind of a Christ do they believe? A. In such a one of whom they can make a liar, etc., etc. Q. Will such a faith in such a Christ save Protestants? A. No sensible man will assert such an absurdity. Q. What will Christ say to them on the day of Judgment? A. I know you not, because you never knew me." Again, page 104: "Q. Are Protestants willing to confess their sins to a Catholic Bishop, or priest, who alone has power from Christ to forgive sins?" (I could answer that myself, without looking on the book), "'Whose sins you shall forgive, they are forgiven them.' A. No ; for they generally have an utter aversion to confession, and therefore their sins will not be forgiven throughout all eternity. Q. What follows from this? A. That they will die in their sins, and are damned." These are the lessons instilled by Romish teachers in the minds of American youth. A child goes to one of the Roman Catholic schools, and soon learns of parents, brothers and sisters, that the Christ in whom they believe is no true Christ, and that they will all die in their sins and be damned, and not Romanists. This is not the teaching of an obscure priest, but of Archbishop Bayley.

Would you rather have a godly school or a godless school, according to their definition? I confess that I begin to see why they think and talk so much about being damned. It is because people who tell lies like those above quoted deserve to be. Here is a text-book teaching hatred, hatred of all other religions except that of Rome. Says Rev. Louis N. Beaudry, a very gentle and sweet-spirited man, who came out of a very pious Romish family : " The first lesson that I learned as a Catholic child was to hate Protestants." Says a gentleman in this city, who is a convert from the Roman Catholic Church, and who is now a minister of the French Baptist Church : "When I was a little boy, in Canada, at school, we were encouraged in dislike of our Protestant fellow-pupils, so that we thought it right to throw missiles at them, and abuse them ; and often they went bleeding from the encounter, having committed no offence against us, only they were Protestants." Such a spirit as that of the text-book above quoted will not assist to the improvement or elevation of education ; nor will teaching of that kind be likely to give us civilization, but rather barbarism.

I read to you the other night from Fredet's History, and only refer to it now. This is a History that justifies the Inquisition; that justifies the Popes of Rome in the villanies of which I read you last Sunday night: that justifies the massacre of Saint Bartholomew, and the act of the Pope who struck a medal on that occasion to celebrate it. This is a History having the date of publication 1886, which tells Roman Catholics, and tells us that, no matter how vile the Pope may be, he is still as infallible as if he were good. And to learn this is education! Already, in some schools, they have images, and the confessional. I am told there is a school in Boston where they have introduced them.

Now what is the consequence of education like this? I am not theorizing. I am not telling you of what has not been tried. We have nations for our text-books, and ages for the leaves that we turn, when we inquire what Roman Catholic education has done, and will do again. Survey the world and see what has been produced by the Roman Catholic education, which they would substitute for ours in schools. What a revelation does history disclose of their policy? It has produced illiteracy, pauperism, degradation and crime. To learn what Roman Catholicism has done, I turn to the Report of the Minister of Instruction in Italy for the year 1864. I have not time to read it all; but this distinguished man says: " Of every thousand males in the old provinces and Lombardy, 539 were able to read, and 461 did not know their letters. Of every thousand females, 426 could read, 574 could not. In Naples and Sicily, of every thousand males, 165 were able to read, 835 could not. Of every thousand females, 62 could read, 938 could not. That is, in every hundred of the population in these Neapolitan provinces, about ten only were able to read. The ratio of pupils to inhabitants was, in the old provinces and Lombardy, one pupil for every thirteen inhabitants; in the central region, one for forty-two; in Naples and Sicily one for seventy-three; while the number of pupils in Connecticut was one to *five*. Compare that with one to seventy-three and one to forty-two, as you have it in regions where Rome has its sway. Out of twenty-one million people in 1864 in Italy, three and one-half millions could read and write, and the rest could not. We have the statement that in Spain seventy-five, and some authorities say eighty per cent., cannot read nor write. In regard to Switzerland, in the year 1842, a Romish priest, Franscini, of the Canton of Ticino, showed how much superior in every respect the Protestant cantons were, giving among the reasons the fact that Roman Catholic education prevails in Romish cantons, and Protestant education prevails elsewhere. We have also a picture of Ireland, showing us what the condition of Ireland was in the territory where the Romish Church was dominant, and what it was outside of the Romish counties, revealing the same lessons as Switzerland. In the Protestant countries of Great Britain and Prussia, in 1869, where twenty can read and write, there are but thirteen in the Roman Catholic countries of France and Austria. In European countries, one in every ten are in schools in the Protestant countries, and but one in one hundred and twenty-four in the Roman Catholic countries. In six leading Protestant countries in Europe, one newspaper or magazine is published to every 315 inhabitants, while in six Roman Catholic countries there is but one newspaper to every 2,715 people. It was estimated, in 1850, that at least seven-eighths of the twenty millions of people in Spanish America (Mexico, Cuba, Central America, and the north and west parts of South America, etc.) were unable to read. See Barnum's "Romanism As It Is," pp. 14-17. That is what the Romish system has done on a large scale. In Mexico, 90 per cent. of the people cannot read and write.

Now I want to ask one question: If the Roman Catholic Church is animated by a desire to educate, if they really desire to spread sound learning, why, in the name of all that is good and kind, do they not leave their children in the schools of our country to be educated as they ought to be, and spend their money in Mexico, in South America, in Spain, in Italy, in teaching Roman Catholics there to read and write? Why do they not? The answer is plain enough. There is no desire for general education in their minds, but only the desire to advance the Roman Catholic Church.

I now invite your careful attention to what is perhaps the most convincing fact on the effects and dangers of Romish schools. I shall show you, from plain figures, that Romish education in our country brings forth illiteracy, pauperism and crime in a startling degree of increase, as compared with education in our public schools. We have some figures concerning this that I think you can carry away with you in mind. Do you know that parochial schools in Boston have, as they claim, over 60,000 Roman Catholic children? And do you know what the effects of Roman Catholic parochial education are? There are furnished to every 10,000 inhabitants by Roman Catholic schools 1,400 illiterates; that is to say, where there are 10,000 people whose children go to the parochial schools, there are furnished 1,400 illiterates from such population; by the public schools of 21 states 350 illiterates, only one-quarter as many; by the public schools of Massachusetts 71, while the Roman Catholic schools in the same proportion furnish 1,400. And how about paupers? Every 10,000 people sending their children to parochial schools furnish 410 paupers as the result of that form of education; by the public schools of 21 states, 170 paupers to 10,000 (compare with 410); by the public schools of Massachusetts 69 paupers to every 10,000, against 410 paupers furnished by the parochial schools. Do we want more parochial schools at that rate?

And how about criminals? By the Roman Catholic parochial schools, to every 10,000 of the population, there are furnished 160 criminals; by the public schools of 21 states 75, not half as many; by the public schools of Massachusetts there are furnished only 11 criminals to every 10,000 inhabitants, compared with

160 criminals furnished by every 10,000 who send their children to the parochial schools. That is, the parochial schools furnish about fifteen times as many criminals as the public schools of Massachusetts. There are more children now in school than there ever were, and still an increase of crime. In France, two or three years ago, were reported in 10,000 lay schools 5.55 crimes, 22.29 offences ; in 10,000 church schools 65.10 crimes and 90.50 offences. The whole world furnishes proof of the evils of parochial schools. What seems to be the inference ? There is a kind of schooling that is not a safeguard against crime. (Dexter A. Hawkins in Doc. XX. Evangel. Alliance p 42, and elsewhere.)

I have one final and very important matter to state to you here to-night before I close this discourse. It is this : Where the state furnishes money to Roman Catholic institutions,—which is, you know, contrary to the genius of our country and contrary to the constitution of the United States,—the increase of pauperism is enormous. Why ? Because the institutions get an appropriation according to the number of persons that they have in their orphanages, protectories and schools for juvenile delinquents ; so much for each child. Just as soon as they get money from the state they begin to take in children whose parents are both living. They get the state appropriations, so much per capita ; then make the support of these children come down to the very lowest figure ; and pour the balance of the money into the treasury of the church. You want some proof of that? I will give it to you. There is plenty of it; I can assure you of that. The " Report on the Institutions for the Care of Destitute Children of the City of New York," Nineteenth Annual Report State Board of Charities, pp. 78, 79, transmitted to the Legislature, Jan. 28, 1886, shows, that in Kings County there were, in August, 1875, about *three hundred children in the Nursery*, a branch of the alms-house. These were at that time transferred to sectarian institutions, and the number of dependent children at once increased wonderfully. In August of each of the succeeding five years, the number in the county was as follows : 1876, 670 ; 1877, 784 ; 1878, 1169 ; 1879, 1304 ; 1880, 1479. *This is an increase of five hundred per cent. in six years*, dating from and including 1875.

In Kings County, during the five years referred to, the cost to the people of the County from this pauperizing of children, *seven hundred and twenty of whom were found to have both parents living*, was reported as having risen from $40,000 to $172,000, at a price for each child so large that Commissioner Ropes said that the over-crowded asylums farmed out those whom they had no room for. The proportion in different asylums, as reported, was : ROMAN CATHOLIC, 1,298 ; *all Protestant denominations*, 266 ; *Jewish*, 17. Do not forget these figures. Just as soon as the state opens her treasury to the Roman Catholic Church, just so soon, by means as dexterous as they are dishonest, they pauperize their children and their people to aggrandize their Prelates, their Bishops, their Cardinals and their Church. Here is the demonstration of the incomparable superiority of our system of education to theirs. Illiteracy, pauperism, crime, degradation follow on the Roman Catholic methods. And what follows on ours? Let the proud position of our country among the nations of the earth demonstrate. I close to-night by reading something as perfect in language as it is accurate in fact, which, though extended, I am sure will be interesting to the very last word. The following was written by Victor Hugo when the priests were striving to obtain control of education in France :

" Ah, we know you. We know the clerical party ; it is an old party. This it is which has found for the truth those two marvellous supporters, ignorance and error. This it is which forbids to science and genius the going beyond the Missal, and wishes to cloister thought in dogmas. Every step which the intelligence of Europe has taken has been in spite of it. Its history is written in the history of human progress ; but it is written on the back of the leaf. It is opposed to it all. This it is which caused Prinelli to be scourged, for having said the stars would not fall. This it is which put Campanella seven times to the torture, for saying that the number of worlds was infinite, and for having caught a glimpse at the secret of creation. This it is which persecuted Harvey for having proved the circulation of the blood. In the name of Jesus, it shut up Galileo. In the name of St. Paul, it imprisoned Christopher Columbus. To

discover a law of the heavens was an impiety, to find
a world was a heresy. This it is which anathematized Pascal in the name of religion ; Montaigne in
the name of morality ; Moliere in the name of both
morality and religion. For a long time the human
conscience has revolted against you, and now
demands of you : 'What is it that you wish of me ?'
For a long time, already, you have tried to put a gag
upon the human intellect ; you wish to be the masters of education, and there is not a poet, not an
author, not a thinker, not a philosopher that you
accept. All that has been written, found, dreamed,
deduced, inspired, imagined, invented by genius, the
treasure of civilization, the venerable inheritance of
generations, the common patrimony of knowledge,
you reject.

There is a book — a book which is for the world
what the Koran is for Islamism ; what the Vedas are
for India — a book which contains all human wisdom
illuminated by all divine wisdom — a book which the
veneration of the people calls The Book — The Bible.
Well, your censure has reached even that — unheard
of thing ! Popes have proscribed the Bible ! How
astonishing to wise spirits, how overpowering to
simple hearts, to see the finger of Rome placed upon
the book of God ! And you claim the liberty of
teaching. Stop ; be sincere ! let us understand the
liberty which you claim. It is the liberty of not
teaching. You wish us to give you the people to
instruct. Very well. Let us see your pupils. Let
us see those you have produced. What have you

done for Italy? What have you done for Spain?
For centuries you have kept in your hands, at your
discretion, at your schools, these two great nations,
illustrious among the illustrious. What have you
done for them? I shall tell you. Thanks to you,
Italy, whose name no man who thinks can any
longer pronounce without inexpressible filial emotions
— Italy, mother of genius and of nations, which has
spread abroad, over all the universe, all the most
brilliant marvels of poetry and the arts, — Italy,
which has taught mankind to read, now knows not
how to read! Yes, Italy is, of all the states of
Europe, that where the smallest number know how to
read.

"Spain, magnificently endowed Spain, which
received from the Romans her first civilization; from
the Arabs her second civilization; from Providence,
and in spite of you, a world, America — Spain,
thanks to you, a yoke of stupor, which is a yoke of
degradation and decay, — Spain has lost the secret
power which it had from the Romans; this genius of
art which it had from the Arabs; this world which it
had from God; and in exchange for all that you have
made it lose, it has received from you the Inquisition — the Inquisition which certain men of the party
try to-day to re-establish; which has burned on the
funeral-pile millions of men; the Inquisition, which
disinterred the dead to burn them as heretics; which
declared the children of heretics infamous and incapable of any public honors, excepting only those who
shall have denounced their fathers; the Inquisition,

which, while I speak, still holds in the Papal library the manuscripts of Galileo, sealed under the Papal signet. These are your master-pieces. This fire which we call Italy you have extinguished. This Colossus that we call Spain you have undermined — the one in ashes, the other in ruins. This is what you have done for two great nations.

" What do you wish to do for France? Stop! You have just come from Rome. I congratulate you; you have had fine success there. You come from gagging the Roman people, and now you wish to gag the French people. I understand. This attempt is still more fine ; but take care, it is dangerous. France is a lion, and is alive."

This closing sentence I quoted to you last Sabbath. Freeman of America! here is the exchange which Rome would make for your public schools. The Constitution proscribed, the Bible banished, history made to speak falsely under the command of the Pope; multitudes of men that know not how to read, other multitudes made criminals for lack of instruction, other multitudes made paupers by the greed of the hierarchy. This is what Rome offers to America. O, men and brothers! if you be men, before you lose what your fathers bought with their blood, by your ballots, by your pulpits, by your newspapers, by your hope for America and your love of mankind, I charge you think, act and strike for your country's intelligence, prosperity and virtue.

Sermon IX.

THE MORALITY WHICH ROMANISM WOULD TEACH
AMERICAN YOUTH.

Our subject to-night is the morality which Romanism would teach American youth. The subject of
next Sunday evening will be a continuation of this,
in a somewhat different way. You will find the
texts, first in the 19th Psalm, the 7th verse: " The
law of the Lord is perfect, converting the soul."
The second passage, Matthew 5 : 17, is a confirmation and corroboration of this by our Lord Jesus
Christ: " Think not that I am come to destroy the
law or the prophets ; I am not come to destroy but to
fulfil." For the sake of condensation in preliminary
statements, and in order to reach most directly the
facts which bear on Romanism, I will beg you to
excuse me for five minutes while I read the propositions which lay the foundation of the discourse.

The perfection of God's law for the government of
physical nature in man, or elsewhere, is not greater
than its perfection as relates to the rules of conduct
which are commonly called morals. The law of
God, which is perfect in the eye of the Psalmist, is
not merely the law of physical creation, which needs
no amendment, but also the law of moral conduct,

which cannot be tampered with without doing great injury to man and to society. The system of perfect human conduct which is embodied in the Bible, is, in the Old Testament Scriptures, most concisely expressed in the moral law of the Ten Commandments, which code has frequently been the subject of our careful study and of our emphatic commendation. The law of the Ten Commandments is repeated in every particular in the Christian system as developed in the New Testament, since our Lord came not to destroy but to fulfil; and He expressly names and sanctions severally, nearly every one of the Ten Commandments, giving them a broader, a deeper, and stronger meaning.

Any system for human government must minister to and conserve morality; else, whatever its other good qualities, it is deserving only of denunciation on the part of good men. For example: a piratical colony might exhibit bravery, and display remarkable obedience to its chief, and might be enviably rich, as the result of an evil conspiracy against the property of other men. But such a band cannot be commended for their good qualities, because of the essential immorality of their purpose and of their society.

Especially, any system of religion, in order to substantiate a claim to divine origin, must be justified or condemned by what it exacts and produces in moral conduct. A good religion cannot produce, teach, nor sanction a bad morality; and I say this, in order that those who seek, and perhaps ·find, in other religions than the true Christian religion some excellence, may understand that such religion must be subjected to a moral test, and that if its morals are not consistent with the highest welfare of man, the religion is impeached at the outset as not being from God. This test is especially justified concerning any system professing to call itself Christianity. Any religion which theoretically and practically debases morality, would, by that, be proven false and unchristian, and should not be disseminated. If a religion calling itself Christianity violates domestic sanctity, blasphemes God, encourages invasion of property-rights, takes human life without sanction of the principles of justice, it is not and cannot be a Biblical or Christian system of faith.   Any religion which degrades man in this world, cannot guide him to the heavenly world, nor is there anything in the system of Christianity to suggest that, out of a bad morality in a present religion, a man shall be evolved into a pure character in the heavenly life.

Proposing to apply this test to Romanism, in order to clear your minds of uncertainty, let me state two or three preliminary propositions : 1. The immorality of a few members of any church cannot discredit it, nor can such evil-doing discredit their creed, provided it be shown that such immorality is contrary to their creed and theory, and in practice is discountenanced also by the church. This is a rule to apply widely and always. It is undoubtedly true, that there is no religion however good, no form of Christianity however pure, which has so purified all its

professed adherents that there shall be no hypocrites
among them; but if the creed and the system
denounced, opposed and resisted all immorality, it
cannot justly be held responsible for that immorality.
Even the fall of ministers into grievous sin, does
not discredit the system of religion which they teach,
provided that system of religion and that church suspend their function, discipline them, and forbid
them to exercise the calling which they have disgraced. I do not infer, if some Roman Catholic
priests, or bishops, or popes are bad, therefore the
whole system is bad; for such inference would
impeach Protestantism also, and would be manifestly
unfair and untruthful. 2. Moreover, there may be
portions of a church's history not consistent with its
highest and best understanding of divine truth. A
church may, under unfortunate conditions, have an
incorrect idea of what is right and wrong. I do not
think that the early Puritan church as such, can be
held responsible, as a-whole, for the persecution and
hanging of people called witches ; but, if you choose
to hold the entire church responsible, we are glad
that at the present time, and for a very long period
of time, all these barbarisms have been repudiated
and denounced. On the other hand, the Roman
Catholic Church, as a whole, should not perhaps be
discredited by the Inquisition of the Middle Ages, if
they had since and now repudiated it. But the
impeachment we bring against the Romish Church is,
that it has never, in the slightest degree, officially
denounced the Inquisition, and that it sanctions,

defends and recommends it to-day. So Romanism takes and deserves as a system the whole responsibility of the Inquisition.

The whole Ten Commandments are moral law, one as much as another. The first, second and third are principles more nearly relating to religion. The fourth is just as truly a principle toward God, while it relates also to the wants of man in the physical and visible world, because it seeks to give him a day of rest. The remaining six commandments relate to human society : the fifth to the family, as also the seventh ; the sixth to the sanctity of the person and life ; the eighth to the rights of property ; the ninth to truth in human intercourse ; the tenth to the disposition of the heart in regard to selfishness. Some of these commands are so related to God and to man, that while essential to morality, they cannot wisely be made the subjects of statutory legislation.

For instance, experience proves that it would not be wise for us to legislate that a man should not worship an idol, if he desired to ; because that would trench upon the province of his conscience and religion. Nor would it be exactly wise for us, in the case of every man who swears a profane oath, to shut him up in prison ; much as the wickedness of the act shows how unfit he is for human society.

But in relation to the commandments affecting the integrity of the family ; as, for instance, the seventh commandment, " Thou shalt not commit adultery ;" in relation to the commandments affecting property, rights," Thou shalt not steal ; " the protection of the

person, "Thou shalt not kill;" in matters of truth and
honesty, "Thou shalt not bear false witness;" in relation to these, society could not exist unless there
there was legislation against the violation of the law
of God in these special particulars.   The violation
of these last commandments we call immorality; the
keeping of these commandments we call morality.
In my next discourse, I shall speak of Rome in its
relation to the higher morality, that is, the first
four commandments; in this, of Rome in reference
to the common morality; that is, morality that
relates to the integrity of the family, the rights
of property, the protection of the person, and
to truth and honesty in the intercourse of man
with man.   What, then, is the relation of
Romanism to the law of property?   What is its relation to the law of family?   What is its relation to
the law for the protection of human life?   And what
its relation to each of the five commandments of the
second table of the law?

The theory in detail of Romanism is immoral.
Romanism, by her accredited theologians, teaches
the violation of several of these commandments of
the moral law.   Who are the authorized theologians of the Roman Catholic Church?   I answer,
foremost among them is Peter Dens, who was
born in the 17th century, and died about the
year 1775.   Peter Dens has received the sanction
of the Roman Catholic Church in Ireland as
a body; his works are put into the hands of the
young priests to be studied; the questions which he

says ought to be asked in the confessional are asked there. He is the theological tutor of the young Roman Catholic priests, a standard authority.   2. Liguori, an Italian, who is called a " saint,"and whose writings are similar to those of Dens, is also an authority.   The Congregation of Rites, in 1803, after an examination for twenty years of Liguori's works, decreed, that " in all the writings of St. Alphonsus Liguori, there is not a single word that can justly be found fault with." (Montagu's " Sower and Virgin.") His " Glories of Mary," in 1868, was heartily com- mended by Cardinal Manning.   3.   J. P. Gury, whose Moral Theology is on sale in a Boston book- store, (where I myself saw it), and who has written theological works similar to those of Dens and Liguori, is also an authority, and his work was published in Ratisbon, in 1874, and is a standard among Roman Catholics.   These, and many others who might be quoted, who stand in the same relations to Roman Catholic teaching, are accredited and standard theolo- gians.   Moreover, I call you to notice the remarkable fact in regard to every one of these books, that none of them can be printed in the English language ; because the laws of this country very properly forbid it.   I can give a very striking confirmation of that from a book which I hold in my hand : "The cele- brated work of Peter Dens contains several numbers, in Vol. IV, upon this subject (the confessional), with which I am unwilling to soil these pages, even by the insertion of the Latin.   Several years ago, in the city where I reside, a gentleman read and translated these before an audience where there were no ladies, and an honest young Roman Catholic layman present was so shocked that he caused him to be arrested and carried before the mayor upon a charge of public indecency." (That is the statement of R. W. Thompson, on page 192 of "The Papacy and the Civil Power.")

You will remember that, when a Roman Catholic finds the justification of his conduct in the writings of one of their theologians or fathers, he proceeds with good conscience to the performance of acts which they justify. The theological works by Protestant Christianity are not authoritative in any such sense. All the books of the Roman Catholic Church are issued by the authority of The Sacred Congregation. The Sacred Congregation gives its assent and seal to these writings. Every man, therefore, writing under the assent of The Sacred Congregation of the Index, stands as sanctioned by Rome, and Rome stands as sponsor for him.

Now, concerning all the above authorities, Dens, Liguori, Gury and others, I say, they sanction lying, deceit, perjury, the breaking of faith, theft, murder, and so present and excuse adultery as to make it common even among their ecclesiastics. The first of these propositions, which I shall demonstrate from their own words, is this : 1. That theologians of Rome, and therefore the Roman Catholic Church, sanction lying, deceit and perjury. Liguori, whom I have already named, says (I have before me the Latin text, and its translation also, in Chiniquy's "Fifty Years in the Church of Rome," chap. xiii) : "A culprit or a witness questioned by a judge, but in an illegal manner " (of which I suppose the culprit is to be the judge) "may swear that he knows nothing of the crime about which he is questioned, although he knows it well, meaning mentally, that he knows nothing in such a manner as to answer." When the crime is very secret and unknown to all, Liguori says, the culprit or the witness must deny it under oath. . Here are his own words : " He may swear that he knows nothing, when he knows that the person who committed the crime committed it without malice ; or again, if he knows the crime, but secretly, and there has been no scandal. When a crime is well concealed, the witness, and even the criminal, may, and even must, swear that the crime has never been committed. The guilty party may yet do likewise, when a half proof cannot be brought against him." Liguori asks himself : " If one accused, legally interrogated by a judge, may deny his crime under oath, when the confession of the crime might cause his condemnation, and be disadvantageous to him?" and he answers : " It is altogether probable that when the accused fears a sentence of death, or of being sent to prison, or exiled, he may deny his crime under oath, understanding that he has not committed this crime in such a manner as to be obliged to confess it." "He who has sworn to keep a secret is not obliged to keep his oath, if any consequential injury to him or to others is thereby caused. If anyone has sworn before a judge to keep the truth, he is not obliged to say secret things." Liguori asks whether a woman, accused of the crime of adultery, which she has really committed, may deny it under oath? He answers: " Yes: provided she has been to confess, and received the absolution ; for then," he says, " the sin has been pardoned, and has really ceased to exist." Liguori maintains that anyone may commit a minor crime in order to avoid a greater crime. He says: "It is right to advise any one to commit a robbery or a fornication, in order to avoid a murder."

These are but samples, and the authority which adduces these, being perfectly familiar with the theology and morality of the Church of Rome, says : " I could fill volumes with similar statements." But this is not all.

A Roman Catholic, according to this authority, may perjure himself to conceal his faith. And here again : " We may be allowed to conceal the truth, or disguise it under ambiguous or equivocal words or signs, for a just cause, and when there is no necessity to confess the truth. If by that means one can rid himself of dangerous pursuits, he is permitted to use it. When you are not questioned as to your faith, you are not only allowed to conceal it, but it is often more to the glory of God and the interest of your neighbor. If, for example, you are among a heretical people, you can do more good by concealing your faith: or if, by declaring it, you are to cause great trouble, or death, it is temerity to expose one's life." The Pope has the right to release from all oaths. " As for an oath, made for a good and legitimate object, it seems that there should be no power capable of annulling it. However, when it is for the good of the public, a matter which comes under the immediate jurisdiction of the Pope, who has the supreme power over the Church, the Pope has full power to release from that oath." Dens says (in "Papacy and Civil Power," note to p. 560 — I read you this verbatim, because I want you to know that the citations are exactly correct) : "It has undoubtedly become the settled law of the Roman Church that the Pope may dispense with any promissory oath, by withdrawing the promise or prohibiting its performance." The doctrine is thus laid down by an author greatly distinguished in the Church for his learning. In answering the objection that the obligation of an oath is of natural and divine right, and therefore that it cannot cease to be binding through dispensation, commutation or veto, he says : "The consequence is denied; because through dispensation, etc., it is brought about, that that which was included under the oath, by withdrawing, prohibiting, etc., is *not included* under the oath, and so there is nothing done contrary to the oath."

Further, the Lateran Council — and the Lateran Council was, like the Pope, infallible,— has said : "They are not to be called oaths, but rather perjury, which are in opposition to the welfare of the Church and the enactment of the Holy Fathers." Pope Innocent XI. sanctions perjury in the following words : "If any, either alone or before others, whether asked or of his own accord, or for the purpose of sport or for any other object, swears that he

has not done something which in reality he has done,
by understanding within himself something else
which he has not done, or a different way from that
in which he has done it, or any other truth that is
added, he does not really lie, nor is he perjured."
That these rules are part of the Jesuit system of
" mental reservation" is undoubted. Sanchez, one
the fathers, says : " A man may swear that he never
did such a thing (though he actually did it), meaning within himself that he did not do so on a certain
day, or before he was born, or understanding any
other such circumstances, while the words which he
employs have no such sense as would discover his
meaning." The reason given by him, and Filiutius,
another father, is, that " it is the intention that determines the quality of the action."   " After saying
aloud, ' I swear that I have not done that,' to add, in a
low voice, ' *to-day*': or after saying aloud, ' I swear,'
to interpose in a whisper, ' *that I say*,' and then to continue aloud, ' that I have done that.'"   In this, the
same : " No more is required of them to avoid lying
than simply to say that they have not done what they
have done ; provided they have in general the intention of giving to their language the sense which an
able man would give to it." And Escobar, another
and greater of the Jesuit fathers, lays down the
following demoralizing rule : " Promises are not
binding, when the person in making them had no
intention to bind himself." (" Papacy and Civil
Power," page 607.)

Do you wonder that Roman Catholics perjure

themselves in our courts? Do you wonder that Roman Catholic saloon-keepers, who constitute nine-tenths of all the saloon-keepers, will swear directly contrary to fact in the courts? That is the theology of their Fathers, of their Councils, of their Bishops and their Priests; and pray tell me, why it should not be the practice of the laity also? Do you wonder that they deny history? Do you wonder that now, on one hand, we have Bishops affirming their purpose to destroy our public schools; and on the other hand, Bishops affirming that they purpose no such thing? Do you wonder that Roman Catholics cannot endure the truth of history, and that they falsify everything which goes against their infallible Church? Do you wonder that the Pope and the Emperor broke faith with John Huss, who had come to the Council of Constance under promise of "safe conduct," and burned him to death? Do you wonder that the Councils of the Roman Catholic Church have accused Popes of perjury, and substantiated by proof their accusation? When I say to you that the Roman Catholic Church in theory favors falsehood; that its doctors, lawyers and chief theologians favor falsehood, lying, deceit and perjury; I only ask you, if you can, to believe what they themselves say; for Heaven knows they might have been lying when they said this.

For instance, to take the matter of indulgences. William Hogan, who was for many years a priest of the Roman Catholic Church, says, on the 172d page of his book, which he wrote after he became a dis-tinguished lawyer in the southern United States: "I pronounce all Roman Catholic Priests, Bishops, Popes, monks, friars and nuns to be the most deliberate and wilful set of liars that ever infested this or any other country, or disgraced the name of religion." So says a man who was a priest, who lived with them and knew them, and who abandoned them, and gave us the result of his observations. "I have asserted, and continue to assert, that there is not a Roman Catholic church, chapel or house of worship in any Catholic country where indulgences are not sold. I will go even farther, and say, that there is not a Roman Catholic priest or inquisitor who has denied the fact, that does not sell indulgences himself. And yet these Priests and these Bishops,— these men of sin, falsehood, impiety, barbarity and immorality,— talk of morals and preach morals; while in their lives and their practice they laugh at such ideas as morality.

"I would ask all or any of them, if they have ever heard mass in any Catholic Church in Dublin, or any other city in Ireland, without hearing published from the altar a notice, in the following words. 'Take notice, that there will be an Indulgence on —— day, in —— church. Confession will be heard on —— day. Prepare, those who wish to partake of the Indulgence.' I have published hundreds of such notices myself; and any American who may visit Ireland, or any other Catholic country, and has the curiosity, may enter the Roman Catholic chapel and hear these notices read; and when he returns to the United States he will hear the Roman Catholic priest say that there are no indulgences sold by the Romish Church. Beware, Americans! How long will you be the dupes of popish priests?" (Hogan's "Popery," p. 172.) And yet the twelve Protestant members of the school board of Boston, because of the mild statement in Swinton's History, were either so ignorant of the modes and wiles of Rome, or else were so culpably negligent, that they voted at Rome's bidding that the History should be taken out of the schools, because it stated mildly what every man knows to be true who knows anything about Rome.

But the indictment goes much farther. Only the lapse of time, which lapses so rapidly, prevents me from citing J. P. Gury, whom I have already spoken of as a standard theologian of the Roman Catholic Church; who in detail, on the same points, one after another, lays down rules of conduct precisely as damaging and as immoral as those that I have already mentioned.* There is no misunderstanding them; they directly inculcate lying, perjury, deceit and falsehood as a part of the practical morality of the Roman Catholic Church. Do not understand me as saying that every Roman Catholic is a liar. Not by any means! I do not believe it! I do say that every Roman Catholic may perjure himself and not come under the censure of his Church because in so doing he follows the rules of moralists, so-called, to whom the Church has given her sanction. No other rational inference can be drawn from their doctrines or practices.

I stated to you that stealing is encouraged; and I quote again from Liguori, the distinguished

authority of the Roman Catholic Church. Let me
read to you exactly what he says, as follows:
"A servant has the right to rob his master, a child
his father, and a poor man the rich." The Salmautes
say that a servant may, according to his own judgment, pay himself with his own hands, more than
was agreed upon as a salary for his own work, if he
finds that he deserves a larger salary; "and," says
Liguori, "this doctrine appears just to me." "The
poor man who has concealed the goods and effects of
which he is in need, may swear that he has nothing."
(Lying and stealing both.) "In like manner an
heir, who, without taking an inventory, conceals his
goods, when it is not the goods mortgaged for a debt,
may swear that he has concealed nothing, understanding the goods with which he was to pay." There
are many opinions about the amount which may be
stolen to constitute a mortal sin. "Nevar has said,
too scrupulously, that to steal a half piece of gold is
a mortal sin: while others, too lax, hold that to steal
less than ten pieces of gold cannot be a serious sin.
But Tol, Mech, Less, etc., have more wisely ruled,
that to steal two pieces of gold constitutes a mortal
sin." Is it a crime to steal a small piece of a relic?
(Liguori now): "There is no doubt of its being a sin
in the district of Rome; since Clement VII. and
Paul V. have excommunicated those who have committed such thefts.

"But this theft is not a serious thing when committed outside the district of Rome; unless it be a
very rare and precious relic; as the wood of the

Holy Cross, or some of the hair of the Virgin Mary."
Once more : " If any one steals small sums at different times, either from the same or from different
persons, not having the intention of stealing large
sums, nor of causing a great damage, his sin is not
mortal ; particularly if the thief is poor, and he has
the intention to give back what he has stolen. If
several persons steal from the same master, in small
quantities, each in such a manner as not to commit
a mortal sin, though each one knows that all these
little thefts together cause a considerable damage to
their master, yet no one of them commits a mortal
sin, even when they steal at the same time." (Still,
if there are enough of them, they could take about
all a man has, according to that. There is more of
this.) Liguori, in speaking of children who steal
from their parents, says : " Silas, cited by Croix,
maintains that a son does not commit a mortal sin
when he steals only twenty or thirty pieces of gold
from a father who has an income of 150 pieces of
gold,"— you must regulate it according to what your
father has, — " and Lugo approves of that doctrine.
Less, and other theologians say, that it is not a mortal
sin for a child to steal two or three pieces of gold
from a rich father." I wonder if they teach that in
their Sunday schools? " Bannez maintains, that to
commit a mortal sin a child must steal not less than
fifty piece of gold from a rich father ; but Lacroix
rejects that doctrine, except the father is a prince."
(Chiniquy " Fifty Years," chapter xiii). Great
advantage in having a prince for a father ; you can
steal all you have a mind to !

Now, when your Roman Catholic servant-girl takes out of your house sundry articles of food or clothing, for needy persons that are related to her, as cousins of one degree or another, you see that she is acting in harmony with the definitions and directions of the sanctioned theologians and saints of Rome. Moreover, the despoiling of heretics has been, in theory and in practice, the rule of that church. Always. Now, you understand me. I do not say that every Roman Catholic is dishonest: far from it. I do not say that every priest teaches this outrageous and thievish doctrine. But I do say, that the theologians of Rome, who have the sanction of the Roman Catholic Church herself, and who teach by that sanction infallible doctrine, do countenance and encourage and excuse theft and stealing. You may judge of the consequences of such teaching.

They also sanction and authorize murder, the murder of heretics. For example, let me quote you their exact language; for what they say is so much worse than anything that I could say if I tried to quote its substance, that I like to read it exactly as they state it. Dens says, in his "Theologica Moralis :" "A man who has been excommunicated by the Pope may be killed anywhere, as Escobar and Deaux teach ; because the Pope has an indirect jurisdiction over the whole world, even in temporal things, as all the Catholics maintain, and as Suarez proves against the King of England." An excommunicated man may be killed anywhere ; and we are all excommunicated, you understand. Only last week, I read you the Papal bull excommunicating all heretics.

Lord Acton, one of the Roman Catholic peers of England, reproaching the bloody and anti-social laws of his own church, wrote : "Pope Gregory VII. decided it was no murder to kill excommunicated persons." This is taken from the *London Times*, July 26, 1872, written by Lord Acton. Gregory says : " This rule was incorporated in the canon law. During the revision of the code, which took place in the sixteenth century, and which produced a whole volume of corrections, the passage was allowed to stand. It appears in every reprint ot the *Corpus Juris*. It has been for 700 years, and continues to be, part of the ecclesiastical law. Far from being a dead letter, it obtained a new application in the days of the Inquisition; and one of the later Popes has declared, that the murder of a Protestant is so good a deed that it atones, and more than atones, for the murder of a Catholic." That is to say, according to this infallible Pope, if a man has murdered a Roman Catholic, he may expiate the deed by murdering an excommunicated person ; and all Protestants are excommunicated. This is their own language.

In the last Council of the Vatican, has the Church of Rome expressed any regret for having promulgated and executed such bloody laws? No ! On the contrary, she has anathematized all those who think or say that she was wrong when she deluged the world with the blood of the millions she ordered to be slaughtered to quench her thirst for blood ; she positively said that she had a right to punish those heretics by torture and death. Further than that: They claim the right to murder all rulers whom they consider apostates; and has it ever been brought to your attention (I speak of it as a curiosity only), that every person who had anything to do with the assassination of Abraham Lincoln was a Roman Catholic? — that John Wilkes Booth was a Roman Catholic; Payne and Atseroth, also Dr. Nudd, who dressed his leg; Garrett, in whose premises he was killed; also, that Harold was a Roman Catholic; Mrs. Suratt and her son were Roman Catholics; their house was the head-quarters for Roman Catholics and for the Jesuit priests. All this was brought out before the military tribunal which condemned some of them to death. As early as 1861, certain political partisan papers of this country were filled with statements that Abraham Lincoln was an apostate, who had been born in the Roman Catholic Church and left it. This was false; but was evidently intended to arouse fanatical hate against Lincoln as an apostate. I do not say that Rome planned that murder; but remember, that when John Suratt fled from Washington he was taken charge of by Jesuits, and under a Jesuit convoy was carried to France. If they murdered Abraham Lincoln, they acted in harmony with the authority of their theologians.

Repentant heretics, we are told by this same standard of morality, cannot have their lives spared, although they have repented. Let me give you the words: " Though the heretics who repent must always be accepted to penance, as often as they have fallen, they must not in consequence of that always be permitted to enjoy the benefits of this life. When they fall again they are admitted to repent; but the sentence of death must not be removed." That is what they practised in the Inquisition. When heretics recanted Protestant doctrine, they were, in repeated instances, slain, by the orders of the Inquisitors. The Lateran Council has given us a declaration in favor of the extermination of heretics in language like this : " Catholics who shall assume the cross for the *extermination of* heretics, shall enjoy the same indulgences and be protected by the same privileges as are granted to those who go to the help of the Holy Land. We decree, further, that all who may have dealings with heretics, and especially such as receive, defend or encourage them, shall be excommunicated. He shall not be eligible to any public office. He shall not be admitted as a witness. He shall neither have the power to bequeath his property by will, nor to succeed to any inheritance."

The Roman Catholic Church, as we have shown, has been a bloody church. The Inquisition, whose history we have in the language of Llorente, himself secretary of the Inquisition,—the Inquisition has been recommended, and I have read the recommendation in your hearing, by Segur, whose books are on sale in Boston ; by LaMaistre, whose books have been on sale in Boston ; by Fredet, whose history bears the mark 1886, published in Baltimore by John Murphy.

This Church is a church that is red with the blood

of the saints; and as I have said to you here before, if one day the priests and bishops of Rome should say to you, We are your brothers, and will do nothing to your injury; and the next day they should strike you dead; they will do exactly what the Romish Church, and Charles IX., and Catherine de Medici, his mother, did to Admiral Coligny, and to seventy thousand Protestants, at the massacre of St. Bartholomew. They may profess the utmost friendship; but they violate neither their theology nor their principles when they take the lives of heretics.

It may be that it has not come to your attention that Roman Catholics are forming and drilling military companies here in America, composed entirely of their own adherents. I do not know what they mean by it, and I do not care. There are other men who can handle a gun in America, when necessary, to resist treason and tyranny. I touch now upon delicate ground, and shall be very brief, for I reserve a considerable part of this to another discourse, when I shall not have a mixed audience present.

The crime of adultery has the sanction of the Roman Catholic Church, in this wise. Now listen closely. They deny all civil and Christian marriage to be true and lawful marriage when not performed within the Roman Catholic Church, and Pope Pius IX. calls it "*filthy concubinage.*" They have divided between a husband and wife in England — I quote from Mr. Gladstone in his preface to " Vaticanism " — because they were not married by a Romish priest; this man having embraced the Romish faith for the

sake of getting rid of a noble and excellent wife.
Mr. Gladstone calls attention to the fact, and wonders
that the menace to human society contained in the
act had not been taken more account of in England.
The history of a celibate priesthood, which fills this
remarkable volume now in my hand, "History of
Sacerdotal Celibacy," by H. C. Lea, is written by one
of the most judicially minded historians that ever wrote
history. The work of six hundred and fifty pages
is full of facts, stated in the most judicial and impartial manner, by a man who has no case to make out,
but has simply gone to the fountain-heads of information and learned what the state of that celibate
clergy has been ever since it originated. And
though the book is most elevated in style and exalted
in motive; though it is not in any sense obscene;
though it might be read by any man, woman or
child without a blush; there is more recorded vileness
in that book, more history and record of abomination,
than I have ever found in any book; and the authorities for its statements are almost invariably Roman
Catholics. If the system makes necessary such a
record, alas for the seventh commandment; or rather,
alas for the system of Romanism. I have to limit
this to private discussion; but as I pass it, I confess
to you, my friends, that if I should tell you the tithe
of what I have read in that book, giving names,
dates and places, from the earliest times until now,
you would be inclined to drive me from this house;
and yet, you would know that my statements were
true.

I pass now from this portion of my subject, and call your attention to another portion that is equally interesting, and quite as conclusive. I have given you already their rules of conduct as stated in their theologians, and bring now a broader impeachment. As a system, Romanism leads directly to immorality. The framers of the system favored the violation of the moral law. I propose to demonstrate that in brief words. Among the doctrines and dogmas of the Roman Catholic Church is this, that the Pope may be never so vicious, and still the infallible head of the Church as vicar of Christ, deserving the most exalted names and titles. On the 511th page of Fredet's History — I quoted that last week — it is explicitly stated that, whatever the character of a Pope, whether he be a Eugenius, a Gregory, a Benedict VIII., or an Alexander VI., or whatever monster of crime he may be, he is equally infallible in his legislation and leadership as head of the Church. You remember that fact was read to you from their standard history. Now, notice further, that the same rule applies to bishops and priests. Every Archbishop, Cardinal, Bishop, or Priest in the Church of Rome, according to the law of that church, may be a vile, immoral and criminal man, and still exercise all his functions. No matter what he has done, it does not vitiate the sacraments which he performs.

I will read it to you in the exact phraseology of the Roman Catholics themselves, and show you their position. On the 173d page of this work of R. W.

Thompson, there is a quotation from the Catechism of the Council of Trent. (The Council of Trent is probably the most esteemed of all the councils of the Roman Catholic Church.) Listen to the language. Referring to such as are excluded from the pale of the Church, it is here said (Ibid., pp. 73-4) : " Were even the lives of her ministers debased by crime, they are still within her pale, and, therefore, *lose none of the powers with which her ministry invests them.*" That is to say, a man may be never so bad a man, and may be a good Pope, giving infallible doctrine and law to the Church ; a good bishop, a good priest, confessing and absolving men, women and children, although, as they say, he be a vile man, and guilty of crime.

Now, if a cleric may be a good pope, bishop, or priest, and be a bad man, *why should not a layman be a good Catholic and still be a bad man ?* For a layman may be made a priest to-morrow ; it is in the power of the church to do so. And I know the intelligence of Roman Catholics well enough to know that when they understand that the priest may be a good priest and a bad man, they have sense enough to infer that a Roman Catholic may be a good Catholic and a bad man ; and their reasoning is just as good and their conclusion is just as sound as that of the Council of Trent in reference to the priests. I ask you, if such doctrine does not naturally lead to all manner of immorality ? If a man may be a good Catholic and a bad Christian, may be a good priest and a villain, where is the limit that the church sets to immorality as excluding men from her sacraments ?

Moreover, this system of casuistry, by which the words and commandments of men are exalted, equal to or above the word of God, creates confusion, and immorality results. I cannot cite to you all the demonstrations of this. Here is one. Pope Sixtus V. brought out a translation of the Vulgate Bible that abounded in errors. There was neither scholarship nor sense in it. It was so scandalously bad that, although he pronounced an infallible anathema on all who did not receive it, Bellarmine, the famous Jesuit undertook to set it right, and when Bellarmine undertook to set it right by the help of another Pope, he went on to say that it had not been published, that Pope Sixtus had not intended to make it public, and that those slight recensions were a part of the intention of Sixtus V. — every statement of which was a downright falsehood, as proven by facts. (Barnum, p. 171.) When they have thus deceived concerning the Sacred Scriptures (for a Pope can lie easily, and by the casuistry of the Church be excused), do you not see how they confound all moral definitions?

The Church makes a mortal sin of very little things, and at the same time sanctions great enormities, the result of which is to produce the utmost confusion in the minds of her people. For illustration of that, on page 519 of this book, Dr. Barnum gives the following quotation about mortal sins (I will first read to you from page 518 from the Catechism sanctioned by the most reverend Dr. Hughes, Archbishop of New York, that you may know what is a mortal sin) : "Q. What is a mortal sin? A. A mortal sin is that which kills the soul and deserves hell. Q. How does mortal sin kill the soul? A. Mortal sin kills the soul by destroying the life of the soul, which is the grace of God." Passing from this, I want to tell you what the Rt. Rev. Armand Francis Mary de Charbonnel, who was the Bishop of Toronto in Canada, declared were mortal sins. He says: " Catholic electors in this country who do not use their electoral power in behalf of separate schools, *are guilty of mortal sin.* Likewise parents not making the sacrifices necessary to secure such schools, or sending their children to mixed schools. Moreover, the Confessor who would give absolution to such parents, electors, or legislators as support mixed schools, to the prejudice of separate schools, would be guilty of a mortal sin." " It is a gross and very common error to believe that to drink in violation of one's pledge is a sin in itself. To drink beyond measure, is a mortal or venial sin of intemperance, according to the degree of drunkenness; but to drink with moderation, though in violation of one's pledge, is not a sin, unless the pledge has been taken with an obligatory intention, or by way of vow or oath; which should never be done without a spiritual father's advice."

There you have as a sample the confusion that they create. They say a man will go to hell if he does not vote against mixed schools; that a parent will go to hell if he permits his children to go to them. They say that a priest will go to hell who absolves the people who do these things; and turn right round and say that when a man has vowed that he will not drink, he commits no sin in breaking his oath, although he commits a sin if he gets too drunk. By means of such confusion all moral definitions are confounded, and the confounding of those definitions inevitably leads to immorality. While in this way monstrous evils and sins are made almost virtues, what can you expect in the field of morality?

They teach as doctrines that some very just acts are exceedingly wicked; for instance, that it is a sacrilege for any man to strike a priest; and yet if some of the outraged husbands and sons should follow the dictates of their natural indignation, there would be a great deal of that kind of sacrilege committed. Many a priest would get a blow from the hand of outraged virtue, that now, by reason of his arrogance and assumed power, he escapes.

Moreover, they declare that the marriage of priests is incest, and what can be a viler crime? And yet the Church has licensed and collected taxes, not once but many times, of priests who keep in their houses not wives but other women, by permission and sanction of ecclesiastical authority, provided they paid the tax to the Church. Out of similar sin the Church has gained great revenue. How all moral definitions are thus confounded, and how inevitably immorality follows!

Father Chiniquy says, they teach that the duty of obedience lays the entire responsibility of the act, whatever that act may be, upon the Superior, and not on the person who has done the deed. Now I am very near the close, although I have not finished all that I have to say on this topic.   Permit me to read to you as follows, from St. Liguori once more : "The principal and most efficacious means of practising obedience due to superiors, and of rendering it meritorious before God, is to consider that, in obeying them, we obey God himself, and that by despising their commands, we despise the authority of the Divine Master."   Notice very closely now   (I am reading to you from Saint Liguori, in a volume addressed to the nuns) : " When thus a nun receives a precept from her prelate, superior or confessor, she should immediately execute it, not only to please them, but principally to please God, whose will is known by their command.   If, then, you receive a command from one who holds the place of God, you should observe it as if it came from God himself.   It may be added, that there is more certainty of doing the will of God by obedience to our superiors than by obedience to Jesus Christ," (God forgive us for reading such blasphemy !) "should He appear in person and give His command.   St. Philip used to say, that the nun or monk shall be *most certain of not having to render an account of the actions performed through obedience ; for these, the superiors only, who commands them, shall be accountable.*"   (Chiniquy chap. xiii.)

Let me comment in a word.   Here is a nun and a monk sworn to absolute obedience ; as the priest is to the Bishop and the Bishop is to the Pope.   To her the Superior gives a command ; any kind of a

command. What shall the person do who receives
that command? Obey it as if God spoke! Obey it
more than if God spoke!! That is clearly what is
stated. Whatever the deed which that person is
commanded to do, and shall do, the doer has no
moral responsibility for the deed; but the responsibility rests solely on the person who directs her
to perform the deed, and he will be absolved by
another man who has done the very same thing.
Thus the very foundations of all society are imperilled; all moral obligation is destroyed; all proper
definition of what is right and wrong is set aside, by
such a theory and doctrine as this.

But I must not weary you. I have given you as
much as you can think of and remember; although
much remains to be said upon this topic, which I will
bring forward on the next occasion. I just now
stated that a priest may absolve from sin, whatever
his character.

The superstitions of the Roman Catholic Church
aver this: that the priest, of whom I have spoken,
in the mass, makes out of the wafer God. Then he
falls down and worships it; the people all about
him fall down and worship it: and although it might
be poisoned by chemistry, or might be eaten by rats,
or might perish from moisture or drought, they say
that that wafer is God, the body, soul, and divinity
of God, and that all of God is there present. At
once you infer that the creature who can create God
is greater than God. The man who can manufac-
ture Deity is greater than the Deity that he manu-

factures.   If the priests can make God out of wheat
and flour bread, then they are more divine than God
himself.   But this priest who is held in such superstitious veneration, of course, has power to absolve
from sin.   Why not?

And what does he do with that power?   He
absolves his own companions in guilt; he absolves
his own paramours in lust; and when it is done, those
persons can say, under oath, that they have never
done it; because the sin absolved is as though it had
not been done.   Where is the chance for morality
here?   The priests have done this so often, that
Father Chiniquy says a very great number of them
are atheists and unbelievers, because the natural
conscience, given by the universal diffusion of the
spirit of God, makes it impossible for a man to believe
such things to be right, and do them.

I cannot speak of their alleged miracles; you know
how many there are.   They claim to have the thorns
that came from the brow of the bleeding Son of
Man; and say that these thorns bleed on certain
occasions!   There are two cities that have the holy
coat woven without seam, Treves in Prussia and
Argenteuil in France, and they have often contended
over their rights in the matter!   During the present
century, the exposure of that alleged coat has
brought hundreds of thousands of dollars into the
Papal treasury.   They liquefy, on certain occasions,
in Naples, the blood of St. Januarius, and the superstitious crowd supposes the Church is working a great
miracle.   The priests, the Bishops and the Pope

know better; but they permit it. We remember when the time came round in Naples once for the miracle to occur, the French were in possession of of the city, and the priests were so enraged that they would not let the blood liquefy. The crowd was furious and frantic, and a riot was imminent. Their fury was against the French troops. The blood would not liquefy, and some great calamity was going to fall upon them. Whereupon the French commander planted cannon before the church and at the corners of the streets, and sent word to the priests that, unless the blood liquefied in ten minutes, he should open fire. In about five minutes the miracle (?) was done, the people were satisfied, and order was restored !

Now, my friends, I close with these words. Our papers here, as I have already said, are not protesting, as leaders of public opinion should, against parochial schools. They are rather helping them. We are treated to two columns of an address by a priest at the laying of the corner-stone of a parochial school in honor of Leo. XIII. called after him, and not one word of warning or remonstrance against Rome's avowed policy. Public opinion in this city and throughout the country is awakening, but our papers have no word to say. Now when Rome teaches our youth what I have read you, as an essential part of Romanism, when Rome has taught that and made the people receive it, she will make of us what she has made of other nations. And Rome has always taught and practiced such immorality. Our immoral and

godless schools of which they talk, are worth more
to-day for the purification of morals than all the
Papacy. I would give more for the diffusion of
American public schools throughout all Europe
and the world, as a moral force, with the American
spirit in them, than for all that corrupted Romanism
is doing to-day; and I am giving my strength
to this work, sanctioned by your splendid support,
which I know will not fail, that we may conserve the
interest of a morality as strong as Plymouth Rock,
and may build up the colossal empire which God has
given us to up-build, on the foundations, not of Romish casuistry or Papal superstition, but on foundations of pure morality, sound learning, free education,
the ten commandments, and the true religion out of
which all these blessings spring.

Sermon X.

SHALL ROMANISM TEACH A PAGAN MORALITY TO AMERICAN YOUTH?

You will find my text to-night in the Ten Commandments, the first and second. I might also include the third; for they are all germane to what I shall say. In the 20th chapter of the Book of Exodus we read: "Thou shalt have no other gods before me: Thou shalt not make unto thee any graven image, or any likeness of any thing that is in heaven above, or that is in the earth beneath, or that is in the water under the earth. Thou shalt not bow down thyself to them nor serve them: for I, the Lord, thy God, am a jealous God, visiting the iniquity of the fathers upon the children unto the third and fourth generation of them that hate me, and showing mercy unto thousands of them that love me, and keep my commandments. Thou shalt not take the name of the Lord thy God in vain: for the Lord will not hold him guiltless that taketh his name in vain."

As the base of a great pyramid, so are these first commandments of the ten to all that follow; for all the Second Table, as it is called, that command man in his relations to his fellows, and on which we spoke on last Sabbath evening, are founded on those views

of God and relations to God which we are taught to
cherish. It is therefore particularly appropriate that
the Ten Commandments should be based on God and
true worship, inasmuch as morality must find its
only sure foundation in religion. These commandments, given in an idolatrous age, pointed directly at
and against all Polytheism, the worship of many gods;
and all Paganism which forgot God; all Atheism,
which denied God; and all Idolatry, which substitutes
some other thing for the God who alone is worthy of
worship. The Commandments so solemnly announced
at Sinai and recorded in the book of Exodus, are
still further elaborated throughout all the Sacred
Word, in which no sin is more frequently spoken of
or more strongly denounced than the sin of idolatry.

Through all the Old Testament Scriptures, from
almost the first words to the last, you find the holy
prophets and the sacred historians teaching us of
the ruin that is wrought by idolatry; how contrary it
is to the divine word, how sinful it is in the sight of
God, and how hurtful to all mankind. We think ourselves so far away from such gross and false worship,
that, as we turn our thoughts to paganism and idolatry, we are ready to say: Where in all the world do
these things now exist? and can it be that there is any
place so benighted as that men there fall down to
worship stocks and stones? And we congratulate
ourselves that a better faith prevails over the land
where we live; and that we are removed, as we
fondly suppose, by thousands of miles, from any people that so violates the plain precepts of God, of

reason and of morality. But let us inquire a little
concerning paganism and idolatry, and we may be
compelled to confess that we are not so far removed
from it as we supposed.

Paganism, by thoughtful and philosophical writers,
is divided for discussion into three parts. You know
that the word Paganism means, originally, the people
who live outside cities ; for as the true faith of God
came to be known first in the great centers of population, while the people outside of those centers still
adhered to their ancient superstitions, it came to pass
that those who dwelt outside were denominated
pagans, on account of their false worship. Paganism,
as false religion, is divided into three divisions.

First, we speak of *fabulous* paganism, or paganism
founded on story, and legend, and myth ; such as you
find scattered all through the early Roman, and Greek,
and Assyrian mythologies, and through all the nations
of the north.   Strange, weird and marvellous stories
are made the object of the credulous faith of the
people.   The second type of paganism is spoken of
as *physical* paganism ; that is seen among people who
have an idea of the great Ruler of the world, and yet
who think it impossible to approach the sovereign
God, and so imagine a great number of inferior gods
or demi-gods, who are characterized sometimes as
demons and spirits, and sometimes as mighty
men and heroes. This kind of paganism has
also prevailed in many quarters of the world at various periods of history.   The third type of paganism
is known to thinkers as *political* paganism ; that is to

say, a form or system of idol worship, with elaborate ceremonial liturgies and formulas, favored by the rulers, and used to suppress the freedom of the people, to attract their attention and to make them at rest under various forms of tyranny. You know that Cicero and Seneca did not believe in the gods of their time; but they thought it a good thing for the people that they should so believe; and so they cultivated all the elaborate ritual of the early Roman paganism, in order that the people might have some sort of religion satisfying to their minds, closely linked to the state, and under state control.

All history illustrates these various types of pagan worship. And myths, mediators and ceremonials are strikingly suggestive of the practices of a corrupt and paganized Christianity. By idolatry we mean, that exhibition or form of paganism in which the object of worship is a graven image of some sort, or a man, or a hero, or some animal, or something else than the great and true God. The Egyptians were idolators when they worshipped a great variety of living creatures; the Romans were idolators when they sacrificed to the emperors; the Greeks were idolators when they adored the beautiful statues of the Parthenon; the African and the American Indian are idolators when they roll up a little hair in a wad, called a fetich, and bow down to that as giving them good luck and favorable fortunes.

In contrast with all these types of paganism, how sharp the distinction is when compared with true religion. The elements of the true Christian religion seems to me to be these : first, a belief in the one only true God, the father and creator of all things ; second, a belief in the general sinfulness of mankind in their relations to God as the result of the violation of His law ; third, a belief in the Mediator between God and man, Jesus Christ, very God and very man, who in the fulness of time was manifested for human salvation ; fourth, repentance, and faith in the Lord Jesus Christ, by which men come to be partakers of His merit and grace ; and finally, to sum up as compactly as possible our relations to man, the spirit of love, of generosity and of humanity, with Christ as that type of manhood which we are all to seek after and imitate.

When you contrast this system of true religion with paganism, how marked the antagonism. For, instead of one God, the pagan believes in many gods ; instead of one mediator, he believes in a great variety and number of mediators, who variously affect the supernal Power, and obtain favors for men. Paganism not only believes in a variety of spiritual mediators, but also believes in the mission of priests ; who, as the priests of paganism, always had an extraordinary power over the people, because those people supposed that all the favors which they could possibly obtain from Deity must be obtained through the intervention of these priests. Moreover, paganism always tends to a very elaborate and sensuous ceremonial ritual, with a great variety of sacrifice, show, form and splendor. It burns incense ; clothes its images in gorgeous apparel ; and supposes that from those images, on certain festivals, special favors can be obtained. Not only so, but paganism has shrines which are counted especially holy, where favors can be obtained for men. To these, pilgrimages are made, when thousands of people move to the sacred shrine, to get from it, as from the Delphic oracle, some enlargement of knowledge concerning divine things. Paganism, moreover, is always intolerant, fiercely so. The spirit of paganism cannot tolerate any other gods than the gods which they themselves worship; and therefore there have always been religious wars between pagan nations on account of their mutual hatred of each other's religion. Not only is paganism fiercely intolerant and inhuman in its relations to mankind, but it is grossly immoral, and always so. There is not an idolatrous worship in the world, nor has there ever been one, that has maintained a high standard of pure morality. And this fact is a demonstration that the moral law is a unit, inasmuch as those who are violators of the first commandments are always disobedient to those that follow. Not only is paganism grossly immoral, but the ideals of manhood which are entertained by pagan nations are invariably false. Sometimes their ideal man is a cruel conqueror; sometimes he is a hidden ascetic; sometimes he is a filthy fakir; sometimes he is one who subjects himself to self-immolation, and who is able to endure torture like the American Indian, stoically, and without a cry of suffering.

These are some of the features that mark paganism and systems of idolatry. Now we suppose when we think of Romanism that it is a form of Christianity.

Before fully considering it, we naturally say that Romanism is a part of the Christian Church. We suppose that they accept the same God whom we accept; they worship the same Saviour in whom we believe; they cultivate the same morality that we cultivate; they advance the kingdom of Christ which we seek to advance; and they undertake to further the same doctrines which we profess. To a degree, it is true that a portion of the doctrines of the Roman Catholic Church are Christian doctrines; and it is also true, that if we look at a few Biblical doctrines Romanism may justly be called a Christian Church: but is just as true that in Romanism error has been so mingled with truth that while Rome does adhere to some of the fundamental doctrines of Christianity, it adheres *to all the doctrines of paganism;* and while Rome on the one hand holds as truth not a few of those things that are held by Protestant Christians, on the other hand it exhibits and developes every feature that characterizes idolatrous systems and pagan theologies.

Observe, if you please, that Romanism receives as the word of God, equal to the Gospels, the word of the Pope, the canon law, the decrees of councils. Besides the true God, they worship other beings, paying them divine honors. They worship the Pope, the mass; they have their sacred shrines; they burn their incense; they have their elaborate and sensuous ceremonials; they clothe their images with splendid apparel. They have pilgrimages to special shrines, exactly as idolators have always had. Moreover, among their mediators they glorify the Virgin Mary, as much or more than Christ. They depend for their salvation not on Christ alone, but as truly on martyrs, whom they petition, and to whom they appeal. They worship images; they worship them all the world over, and believe that in the image itself there resides some supernal power. A large number of their images have been supposed to be able to work miracles, as I shall hereafter show you. Not only this, but their priests exercise the same extraordinary sway over the people that was exercised by the pagan priests in former times, and that is exercised to-day. Those priests are mediators between God and man. Men are dependent on them for forgiveness and heaven! They with the martyrs and saints, the Virgin, the images and the mass, stand between God and man, and hold the superstitious veneration of millions of their deluded followers as being almost more than human. But moreover: Romanism, like Paganism, is fiercely intolerant. It visits all other religions with anathema, with excommunication and with curse, and has visited them from time to time with the sword, with the Inquisition, and with the vengeance of torture and death. Moreover, as I showed you on last Sunday night, Romanism is grossly immoral. It teaches immorality by its theologians. It practices immorality by its Priests, Bishops, Popes and laymen. It justifies immorality by false reasoning; and throughout all the world where its teachings prevail, exhibits a standard of moral teaching which is closely allied to that of paganism. Not only is Romanism immoral, but it is inhuman in its conception of the ideal man. Popes, Councils and Bishops have lauded what they call virginity or the unmarried state as far superior to holy marriage, while **they have founded their innum-erable** houses of monks and nuns which have needed to be reformed very many times by the laws of the Church, on account of the vile immorality into which they have plunged their votaries; and while they have done this, they have multiplied immorality in practical life throughout all nations which they have controlled; so that to read the history of Roman Catholic countries to-day is to read a history of viciousness which brings a blush to every Christian's cheek.

While, therefore, Romanism, on one hand, has some attributes of Christianity; on the other hand it has *all* the attributes of idolatry and paganism; and I shall show this evening, and on next Sunday even-ing, if God spares us until that time, first, that the Roman Catholic Church worships and indorses the worship of images; second, that they worship the mass, which is no more nor less in fact than an object of adoration, as God: third, that they worship the Pope, and call him God: again, that they worship saints and martyrs, and entreat their interest at the Throne of heavenly grace: in addition to this, they believe in charms, and attribute to them supernatu-ral powers. Relics, also, are objects of their wor-ship. The idols of Rome are scarcely fewer than the idols of India.

Do you ask me why I bring this impeachment against them? I answer, for the following reasons: They demand the allegiance of us all. They denounce against us the direst excommunication. They remand all of us to perdition (their Popes do, some of their liberal clergy do not); for I have read you from this pulpit the excommunication of all heretics by the Pope. They denounce our schools as godless, saying that they will make them godly by teaching Romanism; which in itself is a falsehood of vast magnitude. And they are putting forth all their energies to substitute on this continent, in the last part of the 19th century, a system of religion as foreign to the intelligence and piety of our people as the system that prevails in India, or which prevailed in Egypt, or in the Roman Empire at the beginning of the Christian era. Therefore I resent their claims; therefore I call your attention to them; therefore I impeach their Christianity; and therefore I pray, that the day may never come when we shall have idolatry substituted for the pure word of God and the fellowship of saints.

The Roman Catholic Church is idolatrous, worshipping images and sanctioning their worship. That is a startling charge, but listen to the proof.

In the first place, the Roman Catholic Church, in many of its standard works, takes out of the Ten Commandments the Second Commandment; and in order to make ten, divides up the tenth into ninth and tenth. Here is their first attempt for the justification of their idolatry, the suppression of the word of God, so that the plain command, "Thou shalt not make unto thee any graven image, nor any likeness of anything that is in heaven above, or that is in the earth beneath, or that is in the water under the earth ; thou shalt not bow down thyself to them, nor serve them,"— this commandment is bodily rejected from the ten. I have here in my hand a list of five of their catechisms in which this has been done. Let me read. From Dr. Barnum's "Romanism," p. 630, I read : "The Roman Catholic Church sometimes suppresses the second commandment of the decalogue in its catechisms," etc. Of works published in this country, "The Catechism of the Council of Trent," "'The General Catechism of Christian Doctrine," prepared by order of the National Council, "St. John's Manual," etc., bring the first and second commandment into the first, and divide the tenth into the ninth and tenth. "Butler's Catechism," as published in New York, gives the Ten Commandments thus, word for word : "(1) I am the Lord thy God : thou shalt not have strange gods before me, etc. (2) Thou shalt not take the name of the Lord thy God in vain. [Here I omit what intervenes between the 2nd and 9th.] (9) Thou shalt not covet thy neighbor's wife. (10) Thou shalt not covet thy neighbor's goods." "Collet's Doctrinal and Scriptural Catechism" abridges the commandments still more : giving the first, on page 277, as : "Thou shalt not have strange gods before me," and then devoting more than thirty pages to this command as thus given. Yet on pp. 274 and 277, the copy of the commandments as they are recorded in the Holy Scriptures, Book of Exodus, chapter 20, gives the first as above, with this in addition : " Thou shalt not make to thee a graven thing : thou shalt not adore them nor serve them." The Catechisms published in this country are thus inconsistent in their citations of this commandment. Those published in thoroughly Roman Catholic countries probably omit more uniformly that part of the First Commandment which we properly call the Second Commandment. The Roman Catholic Church thus rends the Ten Commandments, the basis of all moral law, in order that they may not, with all their affrontery, stand up defiantly and face the moral law as God gave it.

Pagans were wont to set up images in nearly all places, as well as in all their temples. The Roman Catholics also set up images in all places : from the great fane of St. Peter's in Rome, down to the crossroads in Switzerland and Italy, you find everywhere the images placed there by the Roman Catholic Church. Images form a part of the stock-in-trade of the religious furnishing-houses of that church. Images made of zinc, of the Virgin and the Child, are offered for sale at prices varying from $5 to $350. As concerning these images, the pagans formerly supposed that images (in some way, they knew not how,) contained the disembodied spirits of those whose image was worshipped. Romanism teaches exactly the same doctrine. I have a book here which I have not introduced to you before, written by the Right Hon. Lord Robert Montagu, who was a member of

the Church of England, and who afterwards joined
the Roman Catholic Church. He remained in that
Church for a number of years, and at length left it
on account of its utter inadequacy to satisfy his soul,
and has given us the benefit of his great learning and
of his careful observation, in a work which is called
"The Sower and the Virgin;" a work that is published in England, but which I am so fortunate as to
have obtained. From this I will read (p. 162), to
prove to you that Romanists believe that spiritual
powers reside in their images : " Particular localities,
churches, or shrines, were held to be more frequented
by the saints than all other parts of the world, and
those places were therefore visited by thousands, who
came from vast distances to pray to those omniscient
and omnipresent saints. Moreover, images of those
saints, in accordance with the teachings of the Neo-
platonists, were supposed to contain their disembodied spirits in some way, which rendered prayers
to images an efficacious way of obtaining the fulfil-
ment of one's desires. This was exactly the doctrine of the pagan priests of antiquity. It was this
doctrine which gave sanctity and power to the images
of Jupiter, of Mercury and of Apollo. It was this
doctrine which lay at the root of the practice of
ignorant heathen, from the time of the primeval
Chamites of Africa to the Turanians of India in their
fetich worship. The bones of supposed martyrs, the
bits of the real cross, the blessed crucifixes that had
taken the place of the barsam, the amulets and talis-
mans and charms, which were supposed, in old times,

to foretell the future, to repel evil spirits, and to heal the diseases of body and mind."

The Eighth General Council commands the adoration of images. The fatuous superstition of that age is perhaps more fitly illustrated by the third canon of the Eighth General Council, which was held in Constantinople, in 870 A. D.: "We decree that the holy image of our Lord Jesus Christ, the liberator and saviour of all men, shall be adored equally with the Book of the Holy Gospels" (Remember, this was the infallible Council laying down dogmas that are just as much believed in the Roman Catholic Church as we believe the Bible); "for as by uttering the syllables which are found written in that book we all attain our eternal salvation, so also, by the operation of the imagination on the colors of the image, we all, learned and unlearned, derive an equal advantage. Every one, therefore, who does not adore an image of our Saviour, shall not behold Himself when he comes in his glory, to be glorified with and to glorify all his saints : but such an one shall be debarred from all communion with him in his glory. The same rule applies to the image of Mary, his pure mother, and the mother of God : so it does also to the images of the holy angels, and also to images of the most praiseworthy apostles and prophets and martyrs and holy men, and to the images of all the saints. We must honor and adore all those images also. And if any one should omit to adore them all, let him be anathema from the Father, the Son, and the Holy Spirit." (Montagu, p. 224.)

Here you have the verbatim declaration of a General Council, which makes the salvation of every Romanist, and every other person, to depend on his adoration, not only of images of Christ, but images of the Virgin, and the apostles, and martyrs, and all other images that are set up in their churches to be worshipped.

St. Thomas Aquinas is one of the great saints of the Roman Catholic Church; and perhaps he deserves his saintship quite as well as any of them, for it must be said in truth, that many of the saints of the Roman Catholic Church were chiefly distinguished as sinners. St. Thomas Aquinas tells us that the service rendered to the person ought to be also paid to the image. I read on the 268th page of this book: " Thomas Aquinas declares that the same service or worship has to be paid both to the person and to the image of the person; the same to an image of Christ as to Christ himself; the same to Mary and to an image of Mary; the same to a saint and to an image of the saint. As Christ must be worshipped with supreme devotion, therefore an image of him must always be adored with supreme devotion." Further, Thomas Aquinas says, mentioning the cross on which Christ was crucified: " We say that a cross is to be worshipped with the worship due to God; and for this reason we supplicate a cross, and we pray to a cross, as if Christ himself, hanging on the cross, were before us!"

Many and many a time, in foreign lands, have I seen the poor people drop down in the presence of a cross by the road-side, or in a chapel, and embrace it as though they held the feet of Christ himself; and you remember, that in so doing, they are simply following out the teaching of their most revered theologians and their canonized saints.

They claim further, that images have the power to work a variety of miracles. I might read passages to you affirming this, and should be glad to, if I had time. There is in Auvergne, in France, an image called The Black Virgin, which is reverenced by the superstitious people as the very Mother of God. This image is said to have performed a variety of miracles. Moreover, there are images that are said to roll their eyes, and other images sweat blood on given occasions; while other images are able to heal the sick, and others to give personal benefits of great value to such as frequent their shrines. Some of these images have passed under my own eye, among them the famous Bambino.

In the Church of the Aracoeli at Rome, at the Capitoline hill, there was formerly a bronze image of a she-wolf that was worshipped by the old Roman pagans. They have taken away the bronze image of the she-wolf, and have put in its stead one of the most hideous-looking wooden dolls that one ever beheld. That Bambino (the word means baby) as an object of worship, I have looked at, while hundreds were thronging in and prostrating themselves before it. It is most carefully guarded by the priests of that Church, as containing miraculous power. More deference is paid to the gem-crusted, swathed, ugly, modern image of Bambino Jesu, kept by the friars of the church of Aracoeli, than to any other image of Christ in Rome. It is supposed to work miracles, and gems are offered from the sick whom it has healed. It is taken in a splendid carriage, with servants in livery, to the sick person, and if when laid upon the body it remains red in the face a cure will be effected; if it becomes pallid, the sick person will inevitably die. Not only so, but they adorn their deities with splendid dresses; the Bambino is clothed royally, and decorated with glittering gems. I have seen images of the Virgin clothed in almost royal robes. On her head crowns are placed sparkling with jewels, and these robes and these crowns are to make more life-like the images before which the superstitious people bend in fervent and devout adoration. If the day shall ever come when the shrines of Rome shall be spoiled for the sake of getting back into the hands of the impoverished people a part of the ill-gotten wealth which has been lavished thereon, it will be found that there will be an abundance of treasures which now adorn images that are supposed to be invested with supernatural power.

Charms are said to be wrought by little images, and those charms are believed in exactly as the pagans believed in theirs. "Just as Scylla, the dictator, consulted a little Apollo hung around his neck, (B. C. 68), so Pope Gregory XIV. (A. D. 1590) put his trust in a figure of St. Philip Neri, by which image he believed that his life was saved in an earthquake at Beneventum." (Hare's "Rome," vol. 2, page 168.)

And so that man, the head of the Roman Catholic Church, arrogating to himself to be the vicar of Christ, worshipped as a demigod, and even a god, by his people, believed in charms : exactly as the savage, roaming the Western plains, believes in the little bunch of hair that he carries about his neck !

Among the images that I must mention, in order to give you a just idea of their prominence, let me remark on that in St. Peter's, the image of Peter himself. Under that grandest dome in the world, in a church the splendor of which exceeds anything your eyes ever rested on, unless you have seen that itself, on a high pedestal, higher than my breast, stands this bronze statue, larger than life, cast from the bronze that was formerly in an old Roman statue, now made to represent the apostle Peter. This also is clothed with the Pope's robes, once in a year ; on its head is placed the triple crown, and on its finger the ring of the Pope ; and every day when that church is open, (I think it is open every day in the year), the thronging multitudes crowd about the image and bow themselves down before it as if it were God. The bronze statue of Peter is worshipped devoutly by the peasants and lower population, who kneel long on the marble floor before it ; then reverently approach to kiss the worn toe, that records the millions of kisses it has received. I saw a noble-looking priest, robed in white, his head as white as his dress, reverently approach this statue, carefully wipe the worn toe, kiss it, and press his forehead against it ; kiss it a second time with tokens of awe and reverence, and then retire as from the presence of a royal ruler. In the Cathedral at Pisa is an old image of Mars, now called St. Ephesus, and held in great veneration.

" At St. Paul's Church, in Rome, is venerated a crucifix saved from the great fire of 1824, which spoke to St. Bridget. These are but a few instances from thousands of images worshipped."

What farther proof is needed that the Roman Catholics are idolators by command of their councils ; by the command and toleration of their popes ; by the examples of their priests, and by the word of their greatest theologians? Do you say that they only use these images for the sake of assisting devotion, and that they really do not worship them? I answer, that a friend of mine, who was a missionary in India, conversing with the better class of natives, asked : " Can it be that you worship these grotesque images?" And they answered : " Oh, no ; we do not worship the image. The image assists our devotion ; but we worship the great being that is suggested by it." So said they, and we call them idolators ; but as a matter of fact, we know that while the more intelligent Hindoo or Roman Catholic may think of diviner things than the statue, most of them pay their devotion to the statue itself, and suppose that the image has in it God ; just as much as the old Greek supposed that Zeus, or Minerva, or Aprodite, or any other of their gods was present in the marble statues with which they decorated Athens, and to which they paid their vows. When these images are alleged to work miracles, to laugh and cry, to

roll their eyes upward and downward, to sweat drops
of blood ; and when sometimes their perspiration is
is said to be so holy that the people almost trample
on each other to get closer in order that they may
apply their finger to the sacred moisture ; when these
things are occurring every day, how can we hesitate
to affirm that the Romish adorers of images are violating the fundamental law of God, and that they are
idolators, just as much as any who ever lived on the
face of the earth.

I have not time, nor do I know as I have the disposition, to tell you how these images are made to
appear to work. Every intelligent person here
present knows that by various devices all this could
be done. However, for example, there was found
an image in South America which had great fame as
a sweating image. It was made of papier mache,
and a pipe connected the interior of it with a hot
water tank, from which the convenient liquid was
passed into the statue, to the wonder of the awe-
inspired crowd of worshippers.

And they worship also the "mass." You know
that Christian churches celebrate the Lord's supper
by the use of bread and wine. The Roman Catholics,
in celebrating the Lord's supper with very great ceremony, get out of the bread, or the wafer, which they
use at the mass (as they say in their catechism and
their theological works), the body and blood, the
spirit and divinity of Jesus Christ ; and when the
priest has performed over this piece of bread the
ceremonial of the mass, he bows down and worships

it, as being truly and all divine ; and then lifts it up as a sacrifice to God. Father Chiniquy says, that when he was made a priest he believed that the making of the bread of the mass into the body of Christ was a greater miracle than that performed by Joshua when he commanded the sun and moon to stand still ; and he tells of the devout feelings with which he bowed himself when, for the first time, this divine thing was in his hands. Pope Urban II. tells us, and I will read his own words, that this bread is truly God and to be, worshipped. (Montagu, page 231.) Pope Urban II. who had sanctioned the indiscriminate murder of all excommunicated persons, came to the Papal throne in 1088. While presiding over a council, he made the following declaration, and all the members of the council shouted "Amen" : "The hands of all priests are exalted to an eminence denied to all angels ; for priests create God, the Creator of the universe ; then with their hands they offer him up for the sins of the whole world." There is more similar to this that I could read you, but this is sufficient.

Father Chiniquy tells us, that when he was in the seminary of Nicolet in Canada, the Father-Superior was wont to tell them the following story, to illustrate the power of the priest : that once a French priest, condemned to death, while passing along the street, performed the ceremony of the mass on every loaf of bread that there was in the street ; so that, according to the Father-Superior, every particle of that bread was the very body and blood, spirit and divinity of Christ. And he also told his students, that one priest had the power, if he chose, to turn every loaf of bread in the universe into that same Divinity !

A friend of mine told me, ten years ago, that in the city of Montreal he could remember the time when a procession was passing, with the Host (that is, with the sacred bread made into the body of God), elevated in the midst of the procession ; and he said, the people were expected to fall on their knees all along that street as it passed. And when a Protestant gentleman declined to fall down, he was struck on the head a violent blow by one of the passers-by, and was compelled by force to kneel. That was in Canada within the past twenty years ; and it shows how great their reverence is for this mass-worship.

In order to give you a clearer idea of this whole matter, allow me to read from an author who quotes Roman Catholics so fully that his words are more emphatic and convincing than my own. I read from Edgar's "Variations of Popery," p. 418 : "Transubstantiation varies from our ideas of matter and the evidence of the senses, while it presents the absurdity of creating the Creator, and the horror of cannibalism in eating the Incarnate God ! This dogma contradicts all our ideas of material substances. Matter it represents as divested of dimension, figure, parts, impenetrability, motion, divisibility, extension, locality, or quantity. Length, breadth and thickness, according to this theology, exist without anything long, broad or thick. Substance remains without accidents, and accidents without substance. The same body is in many places at the same time.

Jesus, at the same instant, is entire in heaven, on earth, and on thousands of altars ; while millions of bodies are but one body. The whole is equal to a part, and a part equal to the whole. A whole human body is compressed into the wafer, and remains entire and undivided in each of ten thousand wafers.

"The person who can digest all these contradictions must have an extraordinary capacity of faith—or credulity.

"The Popish dogma also contradicts the information conveyed by our senses.

"Sight, touch, taste, and smell declare flesh and blood, if this theory be true, to be bread and wine. No man can see, feel, taste or smell any difference between a consecrated and an unconsecrated wafer. The senses, not merely of one, but of all men, even when either the organ or medium is indisposed, are, according to this theory, deceived, without any possibility of detecting the fallacy. Many subjects, such as the Trinity and the Incarnation, are beyond the grasp of our bodily senses, and, indeed, of human reason ; these are to be judged by the testimony of revelation : but bread and wine are material, and level with the view of our organs of perception. The sacramental elements can be seen, smelled, touched or tasted. Our external organs, say the friends of transubstantiation, are in this institution deceived in all men, at all times, and on all occasions.

"Cardinal Biel extends this power to all priests. 'He that created me,' says the Cardinal, 'gave me, if it be lawful to tell, to create Himself !' His Holiness

not only manufactures his own God, but transfers,
with the utmost freedom and facility, the same prerogative to the whole priesthood. 'This power,' Biel
says, 'exalts the clergy not only above emperors and
angels; but, which is a higher elevation, above Lady
Mary herself. Her ladyship,' says the Cardinal,
'once conceived the Son of God and the Redeemer of
the world; while the priest daily calls into existence
the same Deity. These creators of God, therefore,
excel the Mother of God.' The Popish clergy, as
they make, so they eat their God, and transfer him to
be devoured by others. The Papist adores the God
whom he eats, and eats the God whom he adores.
This divinity is tasted, masticated and swallowed,
and, accidents excepted, digested. The eating of the
sacramental elements, if transubstantiation be true,
makes the communicant the rankest cannibal. He
rivals the polite Indian, who eats the quivering limbs
and drinks the flowing blood of the enemy. The
Papist even exceeds the Indian in grossness. The
cannibals of America and New Zealand swallow only
the mangled remains of an enemy, and would shudder at the idea of devouring any other human flesh;
but the partizans of Romanism glut themselves with
the flesh and blood of a friend. The Indian only eats
the dead; while the papist, with more shocking fero-
city, devours the living. The Indian eats man of
mortal mould on earth; the Papist eats God-man as
he exists exalted, immortal and glorious in the heavens. The Egyptians worshipped sheep, oxen, garlic,
onions; but even these deluded votaries of idolatry

and superstition abstained from eating the objects of their adoration. The believer in the corporeal presence, at once worships and swallows, adores and devours his deity. Saturn, according to pagan mythology, devoured his own offspring. Jesus, according to the Popish theology, swallowed his own flesh. He ate the sacred bread and drank the hallowed wine which he administered to the Apostles. Such are the horrors which follow in the train of this absurdity.

"This is the light in which the corporeal presence has been held, not only by Protestants, but also by Jews, Mahometans and heathens. ' Christians,' said Crotus the Jew, 'eat their God.' 'I have travelled over the world,' said Averoes, the Arabian philosopher, 'and seen many people; but none so sottish and ridiculous as Christians, who devour the God whom they worship.' Cicero entertained a similar opinion. 'Whom,' says the Roman orator, 'do you think so demented as to believe what he eats to be God?' Roman philosophy shames Romish theology; transubstantiation accepts the Popish deity to be devoured not only by man, but also by the irrational animals. This divinity may yield a rich repast to mice, rats, vermin, worms, and every reptile that crawls on the earth. ' The smallest mouse,' says Bernard, 'sometimes gnaws the species of the bread.'"

Did you ever hear anything more absurd? I think not. Would it not be a more reasonable and sensible kind of idolatry for one to carve a little image with his own hands, as was so felicitously and so ridiculously described by Isaiah the prophet in onr Scripture lesson : burn a part of it to get one's dinner, and save the little image as the object of one's worship? And yet this idolatry of the "mass" is performed every Lord's Day once, twice, or thrice, in every Roman Catholic Church in this city, and the people are all taught just exactly this !

I have one more point to sustain, just before I close, and as you have heard me so kindly heretofore, I will now bring that to your attention.

Not only do the Roman Catholics worship the "mass," but they worship the Pope as God ; they call him God. "The sainted Bernard affirms, that no one, except God, is like the Pope, either in heaven or on earth. The name and the works of God have been appropriated to the Pope by theologians, canonists, popes and councils. Gratian, Pithou, Duram, Jacobatius, Musso, Gibert, Gregory, Nicholas, Innocent, the Canon Law, and the Lateran Council have complimented His Holiness with the name of Deity, or bestowed on him the Vicegerency of Heaven. On the authority of the Canon Law, they style the pontiff the Almighty's vicegerent, who occupies the place not of a mere man, but of the true God. According to Gregory II., 'the whole Western nations reckoned Peter a terrestrial God,' and the Roman pontiff of course succeeds to the title and estate. 'The Emperor Constantine,' says Nicholas I., 'conferred the title of God on the Pope. He, therefore, being God, cannot be judged by man.' According to Pope Innocent III., the Pope holds the place of the true God. The Canon Law, in the gloss, denominates the Roman hierarch 'Our Lord God.' Marcellus, in the Lateran Council and with its full approbation, called Julius, 'God on earth.' This was the act of the General Council, and therefore, in the Papacy, counted as the decision of infallibility." (Edgar, p. 157.)

Pope Sixtus IV. placed on a triumphal arch, erected on the bridge of St. Angelo, an inscription in which he calls himself God. On page 331 of this book of Montagu I find the following statement of that fact: After having given us some Latin concerning what the Pope did that I dare not translate in this presence, he says: "He set himself up as a god. On the triumphal arch, erected to his honor by his creatures, on the bridge of St. Angelo in Rome, these lines were inscribed:—

'Thy words an oracle which all obey :
That thou art God on earth we truly say.'

This horrible man hired assassins to kill the Prince de Medici while at mass, and the elevation of the host was the preconcerted signal for the murderers to strike with their poniards. He, moreover, enriched himself by imposing a tax on the inhabitants of brothels; and to increase his exchequer he encouraged their multiplication; so that, at last, Rome was said to be one vast brothel — a veritable mother of harlots." And yet, at this day, not one of all the Romish theologians, priests, bishops or Popes, dares to deny infallibility to this man; and he is canonized as infallible, like God himself.

If you have never heard of blasphemy, if you have never heard of idolatry, of paganism, in its lowest, most abominable and accursed form before, you have heard it to-night, from Romish Popes and theologians. The works and attributes of God are attributed to the Pope. "The works as well as the name of God have been ascribed to the Pope, by Innocent, Jacobatius, Durand, Detius, Lanier, the Canon Law and the Lateran Council. 'The Pope and the Lord,' in the statement of Innocent, Jacobatius and Detius, 'form the same tribunal; so that, sin excepted, the Pope can do nearly all that God can do.' Jacobatius, in his modesty, uses the qualifying expression 'nearly,' which Detius, with more effrontery, rejects as unnecessary. 'The pontiff,' says Jacobatius and Durand, 'possesses a plenitude of power, and none dare say to him, any more than to God, 'Lord, what doest thou?' He can change the nature of things, and make nothing out of something, and something out of nothing.' The same is found, in all its absurdity, in the Canon Law, which attributes to the Pope the irresponsibility of the Creator, 'the divine power of performing the works of God, and making something out of nothing.' The Pope, according to Lanier, at the Council of Trent, has 'the power of dispensing with all laws, and the same authority as the Lord.' An Archbishop, in the Lateran Synod, called Julius, 'Prince of the world;' and another orator styled Leo, 'The possessor of all power in heaven and on earth, to preside over all countries of the globe.' This blasphemy, the holy, unerring

Roman Council heard without any disapprobation, and the pontiff with unmingled complacency. Some of the Popes,' says Coquille, 'have allowed themselves to be called omnipotent.' Others make the Pope superior to God. According to Cardinal Zabarella, 'The pontiffs, in their arrogance, assume the accomplishment of all they please, even unlawful things; and thus raise their power above the Lord God.' The Canon Law declares that 'The Pope, in the plenitude of his power, is above God, can change the substantial nature of things, and transfer unlawful into lawful.' Bellarmine's statement is of a similar kind. The Cardinal affirms that the Pope can transubstantiate sin into duty, and duty into sin. 'He can,' says the Canon Law, 'dispense with right.' Stephen, Archbishop of Petraca, declared in the Council of the Lateran, that Leo 'possessed power above all powers, both in heaven and in earth.' This brazen blasphemy passed in a General Council, and is, therefore, stamped with the seal of Roman infallibility." (Edgar's "Variations," Chap. IV.)

I am going to close my sermon to-night with a little revelation made by a Roman Catholic saint. This Romish saint was a woman, and her name was Bridget. There are a great many Roman Catholic saints of that name, I suppose; but not all of them are deserving of the canonization which this Saint Bridget got. She was said to be an inspired woman. She said a great many things, about the year 1360, that caused her to be consecrated a saint in the Roman Catholic Church. Some of the things she said I cannot agree with ; but the following I think I can agree with fully. Saint Bridget says : " The Pope is a murderer of souls. He destroys the flock of Christ, and fleeces it. More savage is he than Judas, and more unjust than Pilate, and worse and more wicked than Lucifer. He has exchanged all the ten commandments of God for this single one of his own : 'Give me money, money, money !' "(I think St. Bridget had it right.) "The Pope, with his clergy, are the forerunners of anti-Christ, rather than the servants of Christ. The Pope's court on earth plunders the heavenly court of Christ. The clergy never read the Book of God ; but they are ever studying the book of the world. For them the wisdom of God is reputed to be but folly, and the salvation of souls a mere fable." She adds : " I once loved priests more than men and even angels, but now they disgust me more than all the Jews and Gentiles, and all the devils, too. The kiss of peace of those fornicating priests is the kiss of Judas when he betrayed our Lord." (Those were awkward words for a saint and prophetess to have used.) Cardinal Cajetan tried to escape from it, by observing that Bridget was canonized during the great schism of the West, when there was no undoubted Pope, that is, no Pope at all, according to the maxim, 'A doubtful Pope is no Pope.' The Jesuit Cardinal Bellarmine tells us, that the Pope's canonizations are doubtful and subject to error. Perhaps that was the reason why Pius V., who bribed Ridolfi to assassinate Queen Elizabeth, was canonized. But here again we get into difficulty. The Pope's canonizations are subject to error; but Cardinal Manning, in his "True Story of the Vatican Council," p. 89, positively asserts that the canonization of saints comes under the head of "faith and morals;" in all which cases the Pope's judgment is infallible, they say. Putting the two Cardinals together, we get this result: The Pope's infallibility is fallible and subject to error. To make matters worse, Cardinal Newman, in his preface of 1887 to his "Via Media," p. 84, says of canonization, ' The infallibility of the Church must certainly extend to this solemn and public act, canonization; and that because on so serious a matter, affecting the worship of the faithful, . . . the Church, that is, the Pope, must be infallible.'

"So then, the canonization of Bridget was infallible, and her revelations were authentic and true; and, therefore, it follows, that the Pope is a murderer, and more savage than Judas, and more unjust than Pilate, and that he has exchanged all God's Ten Commandments for this one of his own—'Give me money, money, money.'" (Montagu, pp. 305-6.)

I am glad St. Bridget was canonized. There are some Romish saints in whom I believe, and St. Bridget in just so far, is one of them. Thus by Rome, truth is mingled with contradictions, follies, irrationalities, absurdities, things ridiculous, contemptible, disgusting and disgraceful. And this is the religion that is to be taught in " godly " schools! and this is what we are to have substituted for the " godlessness " of New England education ! !

Sermon XI.

SHALL ROMANISM TEACH A PAGAN MORALITY TO AMERICAN YOUTH?

You will find our text exactly where you found it last Sabbath evening, the first three of the Ten Commandments, in the Book of Exodus, the tenth chapter:

" Thou shalt have no other gods before me.

" Thou shalt not make unto thee any graven image, or any likeness of any thing that is in heaven above, or that is in the earth beneath, or that is in the water under the earth. Thou shalt not bow down thyself to them, nor serve them; for I, the Lord, thy God, am a jealous God, visiting the iniquities of the fathers upon the children unto the third and fourth generation of them that hate me, and showing mercy unto thousands of them that love me and keep my commandments.

" Thou shalt not take the name of the Lord thy God in vain; for the Lord will not hold him guiltless that taketh his name in vain."

The pagan idolators, of whom we spoke on last Sabbath evening, added to the list of their gods who represented men, goddesses also, or women gods; so that every idolatrous cult in the world has female divinities, as well as male. The Egyptians had Isis, as well as Osiris; the Phœnicians Astarte, or Ashtaroth, as well as Baal; the Greeks, Hera, as well as Zeus; the Romans, Juno, as well as Jupiter. They had many other female gods besides these chiefest ones that I have named, too many to mention. The Romans, who in the great city of Rome had the seat of their empire and their most splendid temples, worshipped not only Juno, but Venus, Fortuna, Ceres and many others, who received almost equal adoration with the first named. The descriptive names by which these goddesses were called, were almost the same in all lands. The various peoples spoke of them as " Queen of Heaven," " the mother of gods," or " mother of God," " the mediatrix between God and man." They characterized them as " defenders," " protector," " solicitor" or " pleaders" for human welfare.

On the very ground where the goddesses were worshipped, and before the people had forgotten the forms of idolatry that were so persistent in their national history, there sprang up a corrupt form of Christianity, that put in place of these goddesses, especially the chiefest of them, a wholly imaginary being, suggested by a historical character, unlike all the creatures of her sex, and having the idolatrous names that were applied to the old heathen goddesses, under the primary name of The Virgin Mary. She, too, is called by her worshippers the " Queen of heaven," as was the Phœnician Astarte; she is called the " mother of God," as was the Egyptian

Isis ; she is known as the mediatrix between God, the great God, and men, as was Fortuna, the god dess of fortune ; she is addressed as the mother of love, as was Venus of the Romans, and the Aphrodite of the Greeks. The ordinary Protestant, little informed of the worship of the Virgin Mary, who is known by all these names, can hardly conceive of the prominence that she has in the Romish ritual. To her they offer prayer, adoration and devotion ; to her they erect the most splendid of their churches and temples of worship ; to her they consecrate their most sacred shrines ; to her they raise the most costly and splendid images, which images they adorn with richest and almost royal apparel ; the prayers to her are the most popular in the Romish Church ; the " Rosary of Mary," as it is called, is their favorite act of devotion. And they so fill the horizon of the Romish mind with Mary, that after you have travelled in Roman Catholic countries, as I have done, you come to the inevitable conclusion that Mary has a very much larger place in the thought of a Roman Catholic than is given to Jesus Christ.

The Protestant mind, accustomed to a generous sentiment toward all religions, (for tolerance is the law of Protestantism), is accustomed to regard the worship of The Virgin Mary in a somewhat esthetic and sentimental light. We are wont to say, that to bring into the barbarous times of the early ages the idea of a woman, pure, good and elevated, who should take the place of the cruel gods, the thoughts of whom debased the minds of the people, was a very happy idea, and must have exerted a softening, genial, and gracious influence upon the minds of those who were taught thus to reverence and adore her.

This kindly sentiment toward Romish idolatry is not warranted by the facts of history. For the worship of the goddesses of the pagans was always attended with the worst obscenity, the utmost vice, and the most abominable rites. There is nothing in the worship of the man-gods of the Egyptian, Phœnician, Grecian or Roman that can be compared for abominableness with the worship of their woman gods : and while sentiment may suggest to you that the elevation of a woman to the high platform which The Virgin Mary is occupying in the Roman Catholic Church, may have a happy and tender effect upon the popular mind, you must remember that history is against you ; and while Protestantism teaches us to cherish the most elevated sentiment toward noble and pure womanhood, *woman worship* has always been the fruitful source of the greatest abominations that ever afflicted the world. Montague says, that Mariolatry, in the Roman Church, has always flourished most in times of the greatest immorality and wickedness. When, therefore, The Virgin Mary (not the real virgin of the Holy Scriptures, not the maid of Nazareth who welcomed the message of her Lord, and who, with human infirmity and frailty, herself doubted the Messiahship of her Son, and afterward finished her life in quiet with John, (the beloved apostle as we suppose)—

when the Virgin Mary of Roman Catholic worship, who is made up of myth and legend, imagination and superstition unwarranted by history, is elevated to divinity in the minds of Roman Catholics, there are very many things expressed and implied connected with her worship that have the flavor of idolatry in its worst forms.

Among the nameable things, they say of her that she was immaculate in her conception; that is to say, that she had no taint of original sin when she was born of her mother. They say also, that she was perpetually a virgin; that she had no other children than Jesus Christ; although the Bible says differently. They say, that she was carried up to heaven without going through the process of death and decay as we go through it, and glorify in art this alleged "Assumption of the Virgin." The immaculate conception of the Virgin Mary, which takes her out of the ranks of those tainted with original sin, is a dogma of the Roman Catholic Church, which they must believe under penalty of loss of salvation.

On the eighth day of December, 1854, Pope Pius IX. sat under the dome of St. Peter's, with a triple crown, blazing with jewels, on his head, and with the splendid apparel of the Pope upon his shoulders. Around him knelt five hundred prelates and dignitaries of the church; before him were ten thousand of the faithful; and in the great square outside fully forty thousand more. As they solemnly waited in this presence, a cardinal arose, and advancing toward the Pope, said slowly : " Father, tell us if we shall believe and teach that The Virgin Mary was immaculate in her conception;" and the Pope solemnly answered, "We do not know. Let us inquire of the Holy Spirit." And all joined to sing, "Come, Holy Spirit." Then the cardinal again arose, and advancing as before, asked the same question, and the Pope answered: "We do not know now. Let us ask the Holy Spirit." And once more the assembled thousands sang, "Come, Holy Spirit." When for the third time, in all the pomp and magnificence of ceremony, the cardinal advanced, the Pope answered to the question, "Shall we believe and teach that The Virgin Mary was immaculate in her conception?" "Yes, Yes. The Virgin Mary was immaculate in her conception. So believe and teach. There is no salvation to those who deny this teaching." And it was then proclaimed a dogma of the Church.

So, in contradiction of the opinions of many of the most distinguished fathers of the Church, after long years of effort on the part of the most superstitious wing, contrary to sound reason, contrary to truth, and in contradiction of the claim of the Church which says it never changes, in the year 1854 was made a new dogma, which thousands of Roman Catholics do not believe, but which they were told they must believe on pain of the displeasure of the Church and the penalties which are inflicted on heresy.

I proceed now to show you that The Virgin Mary is a veritable idol goddess, in the worship of the Roman Catholic Church; but as I pass, I wish to vindicate in a few words the authorities that I shall quote. The only embarrassment which I meet, is the abundance* of authorities and the fulness of their testimony. Every night when I have spoken to you, the time has expired before I could give you all that I had selected bearing on the subject under discussion. But some have said to me, That certain Roman Catholics deny that the authorities which you bring forward are truthful in their statements. For instance, when you bring forward St. Liguori, they say, either that he did not say this; or else, that St. Liguori has no authority. You remember that this distinguished saint is the one from whom I read so freely in regard to theft, lying, and sundry other things, a few nights since. I think I fully vindicate his right to speak for the Roman Catholic Church, by the fact that the Sacred Congregation of Rites, of Rome, after twenty years' examination of the works of St. Liguori, said, that there was " not one word in all his writings that could justly be found fault with." In 1852, an edition of the " Glories of Mary," by St. Liguori, appeared with the sanction of Cardinal Wiseman of England, and the eminent Cardinal Manning, in 1868, spoke in the highest terms of approval of this authority.

The kind of testimony that I bring to you here is the kind of testimony that I think would stand before a jury; and if Roman Catholics, or any others, deny or seriously doubt it, I will meet them with the following proposition: Let us enlarge this jury until it numbers two thousand people. The Roman Catholics shall select one thousand, and I will select one thousand, under mutually fair conditions. I will meet any priest of Rome of the city of Worcester, or from any other part of the country, on the public platform, in Mechanics Hall. I will present the authorities for sustaining every proposition which I have made here. If they can refute them, or show that they are unreliable, I will withdraw them, provided that they on their part agree, that if I can substantiate my statements by full proof, they will accept them, and confess error.

I have stated on this platform at least a hundred propositions. I began by stating, concerning the Jesuits, what they were, and what they do. I am prepared to make good all that I have stated. In my third discourse, I said that the Pope was the enemy of civil and religious freedom, and substantiated that by various testimonies. I am prepared to bring forward those theses and stand by them until they are refuted. I then set forth in at least twenty particulars that Romanism was contrary to the Constitution and the laws of the United States. I do not retract one word of that argument, and am willing to have any representative of the Roman Catholic Church take up these statements before a selected audience for the purpose of fairly refuting the argument. I then, in three sermons, set forth that the purpose of Romanism was to destroy our public schools. Those sermons stand unimpeached, until they can be contradicted by something more than the round assertion that my statements are not true.

And what I say about the paganism of Rome I am prepared also to vindicate, by adducing still more copious proofs, in any presence, whether before a congregation of Worcester, or the just bar of the eternal God. Let no man therefore say that the authorities which I quote are not reliable, unless he knows it; and if he knows it, let him so say it that I may have the benefit of his proofs. For I say to you, my friends, here to-night, that mere victory in an intellectual struggle has never been dear to me. Truth is more precious than rubies; the triumph of truth is all that I seek. If I have it not, let me have it; and if I have it, let no man wrest it from me. Truth, truth I want! Not arrogance, not presumption, not pretence, not false history, not round denial! Truth let us have; and if that truth cuts away the foundation of Protestantism, let us thereby get nearer to the Rock of Ages; if it demolishes the pretences of Romanism and sinks the system, let us man the life-boat to save every man of them, by holding out the truth of God.

And now, in harmony with this purpose, I proceed to show that the worship of the Virgin Mary in the Romish Church is idolatrous; that she is really worshipped as a divine being with divine attributes, according to the consent and statements of Popes, of cardinals, of saints, and of doctors of theology.

I. My first proposition is, that they consider and call The Virgin Mary divine, giving her the attributes of Jehovah. Pardon me if I read the proofs. I wish I were a better reader, but you are such good

listeners that it takes away the half of my embarrassment.

1. Divine powers, and powers above divine, are
accorded to Mary. St. Bernardinus Senensis offers
to us the following, in one of his sermons, (and a
saint becomes a saint because he receives the sanction of the Roman Catholic Church) : " In order to
become the mother of God, the blessed Virgin Mary
had to be raised *to an equality with the Trinity*, so to
speak, *by being made infinite in perfections and
graces*, an equality which no creature ever obtained.
He who was himself God, served, and was subject to
His mother on earth. Yes, this is true. All things
are subject to the empire of the Virgin ; even God
Himself is subject to her." Proceeding further, he
says : " The blessed Virgin, all alone, did more for
God, or at least as much, so to speak, as God did for
the whole human race. Rendering, then, to each their
due, (that is to say, what God did for man, and
what the blessed Virgin Mary did for God,) *you will
perceive that Mary did more for God than God did
for man*." Again he says : " There is no grace comes
from heaven to us, unless The Virgin Mary dis-
penses it to us. For this office she, and she alone,
obtained of God from all eternity ; as is testified by
Proverbs 8 : 23 : ' I was set up from everlasting ; '
that is, as the dispenser of all heavenly gifts."

2. It is also distinctly stated by authorities of
the Church that The Virgin Mary *is omnipotent* ;
where it is said : " The most blessed Virgin is the
Empress, because she is the wife of the eternal

Emperor, of whom it was said 'He that hath the Bride is the Bridegroom.'" Further: "Since the blessed Virgin is the mother of God, and God is her son ; and since every son is by nature inferior to his mother, and is her subject, and the mother has the pre-eminence and is superior to and above her son ; it follows that *the blessed Virgin is superior to and above God*, and God is her subject, because of the humanity which He derived from her." This was Bernardinus de Bustis, who flourished about the year 1480, and who was a Franciscan monk.

3. The Virgin Mary is said to be possessed of *infinite power*. It certainly was a great privilege and most singular grace that was conferred upon her, they say ; while Laurentius Chrysogonus and a modern saint and doctor of the Roman Church (the places in their works are given) say the following : "To the most holy Virgin all things are possible, because of the most high dignity of her Divine maternity, which brought *her an infinite power and empire* in the things of all the world." This is continued and amplified ; but the expression " infinite power " fully vindicates my statement that they accredit her with infinite power.

4. They, in so many words, declare that she is eternal ; as, for instance, when it is said by St. Sabas the abbot : " O, virgin-mother of God ; of thee alone it has been proved to the world that thou wast pure *from all eternity*." And this is very much like an Orphic ode from the heathen poets to heathen divinities, and reminds the classical scholar of such.

They pay to her divine honors, and think her worthy of those honors. This I shall also so amply prove in further quotations, that several quotations I had intended here to employ I will omit.

5. She is called the "lamb of God," as I will read to you now. Georgius, the Archbishop of Nicomedia, is quoted by Zoller, a Roman Catholic historian of the whole doctrine of the Immaculate Conception, as saying, in the passage which the Archbishop addresses to the Virgin Mary : " *O immaculate Lamb*, who wast taken up to the feast of angels, and fed with angels' food : O immaculate Lamb, victim acceptable to God, who wast offered in God's temple, and from whom was born that Lamb of God who takes away the sins of the world : O Lamb verily immaculate, more pleasing than every sacrifice, who wast sacrificed to the Creator, not as an offering rendered acceptable by God, but as acceptable through the excellence of her purity."

6. She is also called the wife of Christ. This passage I will read from one of the saints already quoted, St. Sabas, the abbot, and this is only one of many passages teaching us the same : " From thee, Mary, Christ's only parent, *did thy husband come forth* — thou most pure lily, growing amid thorns and thistles."

7. She is said to *be married to God the Father*. You will see in a moment that all these are only reproductions of the old heathen fables. A Cardinal of the Roman Catholic Church, Cardinal Hostiensis says : " There is a state of marriage existing between God

and the blessed Virgin Mary," (and the Latin phrase is given here that he uses) ; "wherefore it is said : Lo ! thou art fair, my love ; behold thou art fair ; thou hast dove's eyes ! " As though the Father God ever said this to the Virgin Mary ! " The Angel Gabriel was sent," says Cardinal Hostiensis ; " then the contract was made between the parties by the words : ' Thou hast found favor with the Lord,' " and so on.

Now if you compare this with ancient myths you will find in it a very remarkable likeness to them. The Egyptian God Khem, was called Kuh-mut, the husband of his mother. That is identical with what is said about Christ and the Virgin Mary. The youngest Horus was the son of Osiris and Isis (brother and sister), and he too was husband of his mother. In Rome, it was Fortuna and Jupiter. So concerning Janus, he was both the son and husband of Cybele. In Asia, it was Cybele and Deioius. In Greece, Cybele was called Ceres, the great mother ; also Domina, or Our Lady ; and she was represented holding a babe. In India, we find the mother and child as Isi or Parvati and Iswara. We also find that Astarte, the Phœnician goddess, was said to be the wife of her son. Yet again, the same strange and awful blasphemous statement is made, that Mary is the wife of God the Father !

8. She is also called the sole mediatrix ; that is, the one standing between God and man, by whom all favors can come to this world. Let me read to you the exact language. In St. Bonaventura's writings it

is said : " O, our Empress" (this is in a work called the " Crown of the Virgin Mary "), " and Lady most benign, by thy maternal rights, command thy most beloved Son, our Lord Jesus Christ, to vouchsafe to turn our minds from the love of earthly things, and direct them to heavenly thoughts. Since the blessed Virgin is the *advocate for sinners*, the glory and crown of the righteous, the wife of God, and the couch of the whole Trinity to lie upon, and the most beautiful bed for the Son to prostrate himself upon, therefore sin had no place in her."

Then St. Bonaventura, in order to carry out this idea of the divineness of the Virgin, made a paraphrase on the Psalms of David, in which he puts her name in place of the Divine name in every case, and thus lauds and magnifies her as God, travestying the Holy Scriptures in order to express the same. It will sound strange to you to hear the Sacred Word so read ; but let us hear it. The language was used in the " Psalter of The Virgin Mary," and received the sanction of the Pope. In Psalm 109, for instance : " The Lord said to our Lady : Come and sit, My mother, on My right hand, until I make thy foes thy footstool." Psalm I : " Blessed is the man who loveth thy name, Virgin Mary." Psalm II : " Come unto her, all ye who labor and are heavy laden, and she will give rest and comfort unto your souls. Come unto her, when in tribulation, and the light of her countenance will establish you." Psalm III : " Our Lady ! how are they increased that trouble me. But thou art a shield for me ;

with thy power thou shalt pursue and scatter them. Have mercy upon me, O our Lady, and heal thou my sickness." Psalm XXX: "Into thy hands, O our Lady, do I commend my spirit."

Reading thus from this blasphemous perversion of God's word, I might go on and give passage after passage, taken from that Psalmody, by which the Virgin Mary is elevated by this Roman Catholic saint to the place of the Lord God. They even corrupt the wonderful *Te Deum* which we sometimes sing. In the Paris edition of 1852, you find the following as standing for the *Te Deum*, in place of the familiar beginning : "We praise Thee, O God ; we acknowledge Thee to be the Lord ; " " We praise thee, O Mary, we acknowledge thee to be the Virgin. All the earth doth worship thee, the wife of the Eternal. To thee all creatures continually do cry : Holy, holy, holy, Mary, mother of God, mother and virgin. The glorious company of the apostles praise thee, as the mother of their Creator." The Litany also is adapted in the same way.

Did you know that these were the sentiments of saints, popes and divines of the Roman Catholic Church ? Have you thought that we were surrounded by idolatry identical with the worship of the ancient heathen goddesses? Had you supposed that these unfortunate worshipers were so under the bondage of Papal superstition that they were standing 1900 years behind this age, in the dark of superstition, and calling on a human creature, deified as the ancient pagans deified their heroes and heroines,

as though she were God, attributing to her divine
names and functions, making her the equal of the
whole Trinity ; saying that her power is infinite, that
she is eternal, and that she is the sole sacrifice for
human sin, and the veritable lamb of God? And
yet, this is all taken from Roman Catholic authorities,
and has been indorsed, and never protested against,
by this infallible church !

II. *Mary is worshipped as God;* not only called
divine, but worshipped as God ; having not only the
name of God, but the adoration due to God. Now
we know that there is a magical charm, to the Eng-
lish-speaking peoples, in the name of John Henry
Newman — the Cardinal Newman who left the English Church, and was honored for his apostacy by
the Roman Catholic Church with the cardinalate.

1.   Cardinal Newman, unfortunately plunging himself into this abyss of superstition, uses the following language concerning the Virgin Mary : "There
was a wonder in heaven." "A throne was seen, far
above all created powers, mediatory, intercessory ; a
title archetypal ; a crown bright as the morning star ;
a glory issuing from the eternal Throne ; robes pure
as the heavens ; and a sceptre over all. And who
was the predestined heir of that majesty? Who was
that wisdom, and what was her name? 'The mother
of fair love, and fear, and holy hope,' 'exalted like a
palm tree in Engaddi, and a rose plant in Jericho ;'
'created from the beginning,' in God's counsel ; and
'in Jerusalem was her power?' The vision is found
in the Apocalypse : a woman clothed with the sun,

and the moon under her feet, and upon her head a crown of twelve stars. The votaries of Mary do not exceed the true faith, unless the blasphemers of her Son come up to it. The Church of Rome is not idolatrous, unless Arianism is Orthodoxy ! ! "

Thus speaks the chief dignitary of the Romish Church in Great Britain, in his " Essay on Development." And this he says after such a panegyric upon the Maid of Nazareth, who, if she were alive and here in our midst, would deprecate his idolatry as much as any one of us can.

There was an attempt made by some of the Romish writers to assume that the worship paid to the Virgin Mary was different from the worship paid to God ; and they had two or three Greek words by which they described the shade of difference between the worship of the Virgin and the martyrs and the worship of God. They said that the worship of the martyrs was "*dulia*," that the worship of the Virgin was "*hyperdulia*," that the worship of God was "*Latria*." Confusion only follows these words, which have hardly a shadow of difference in their meaning, and they were pronounced by Cardinal Bellarmine totally unequal to the work of preventing the same worship being paid to the images and to the Virgin as was paid to God Himself.

2. They worship the Virgin Mary as a goddess. In the city of Lisbon, Portugal, there is a church dedicated to Mary as a goddess, in the following words : "To the Virgin, goddess of Loretto, the Italian race, devoted to her divinity, have dedicated

this temple." I have seen kindred inscriptions to that on old Roman temples, where some object of their idolatry had received the dedication from their votaries of the palaces in which they were worshipped. Here they have spoken in no uncertain tones, and the Virgin of Loretto, a divinity and a goddess, has a modern temple dedicated to her, in one of the most Roman Catholic countries of the world !

III. Mary is repeatedly praised as Saviour. This praise runs through nearly all that is said of her, and is so generously given that it does not seem as though there is any necessity for any other God, since she fulfills all the functions of the same. It is said, for instance, in one of the standard writers of the Roman Catholic Church : " I and my Father are one," parodying the same and applying it to the Virgin Mary. Again, there is a plate of the crucifixion with Mary at the foot of the Cross, having a sword in her breast, and the inscription : " Thy beloved Son did offer in sacrifice His flesh for us ; but thou didst offer in sacrifice thy soul,—yea, both thy body and thy soul." You see pictures of the bleeding heart of Mary in Roman Catholic book and picture stores, and the sword thrust through her heart indicates, as above stated, that she suffered more than Jesus ; while He gave His body to suffer, she gave the sufferings of her soul. She is idolatrously worshipped : worshipped as any one would worship the supreme Deity.

Liguori had occasion to express himself on the Divine powers of Mary in the following words (I do not think I will take time to read it all, but his

"Glories of Mary" contains an extended portrayal of her powers, some portions of which are not fit to be repeated. Suppose I tell the substance, without reading it, to save time) : Liguori tells a story, and the incident is also narrated by Father Chiniquy and Hallam as a sample of Romish fable, displaying the divine power of Mary. He says, that a certain nun, becoming tired of her vows, forsaking the nunnery in which she lived, plunged into a life of sin ; after a period of ten years, she came back and inquired if sister Beatrice (meaning herself) was missed from the nunnery, and they answered : Oh, no ; she had never gone away or been missed ; she was there, and was one of their most devoted nuns. And then it came to pass, says Liguori, that Beatrice found out that the Virgin Mary, out of love for her, had taken her place and performed her duties for the space of ten years or more ; whereupon, of course, she penitently enters the nunnery again, and becomes a most devoted nun.

There is a similar fable told of a young girl who was beloved of two men, and these men contending about her, in the conflict her head was accidentally cut off and thrown into a well. (Now it is a great misfortune to lose your head under such circumstances.) But presently the head appeared on the well-curb and remained there for two days. It desired to confess, saying : " I was in mortal sin when my life was taken. I have come to confess." And after she had confessed, and variously exhorted the people, I suppose the head went back into the well. But St.

Liguori, telling this as a sample of Mary's power, says that the reason why the murdered girl had this opportunity to get out of perdition by confession was, because she had been very faithful in her use of the rosary of Mary ; and Mary, out of her marvellous love for her, undertook to save her in this astonishing manner.

There are stories that are not so fit to be repeated, in which Mary is represented with very remarkable power over her special votaries, and the wonders that she works are as marvellous as they are fabulous.

And these narrations are taught as history to Roman Catholic youth. I prefer Swinton's History.

Pope Sixtus IV., of whom I told you on last Sunday night, who erected a triumphal arch on the bridge of St. Angelo, on which he called himself God, granted to those who prayed to the Virgin Mary an indulgence of one hundred thousand years. I should say that if an indulgence of one hundred thousand years is so easily obtained, the believers in Mary had better bestir themselves and get as many indulgences as they can. It must be very convenient for some of them to have a little surplus of indulgence to keep them out of purgatorial fire.

In the prayer-books of this time, there is a prayer to the Virgin Mary to which Pope Sixtus IV. had attached an indulgence of 11,000 years for all who should devoutly recite it. In a Dutch prayer-book of the beginning of the next century, there is a prayer to Mary which carries an indulgence of 100,000 years, together with many other such graces of shorter periods. Some of these indulgences of 20,000 years are given to every one who shall say five Paternosters before such and such an image, and are full of superstition. There is one of the Popes who granted an indulgence, Pope John XXII., (he was the man who cursed the Council of Constance and got as good as he gave,) that any one who should kiss the measurement of the Virgin Mary's shoe (I have not learned how they got that), was granted an indulgence of 700 years. I suppose in some place they have what they allege to be the measurement of this sacred foot, and whoever should go to that place and kiss the proper spot should have an indulgence of 700 years.

The rosary of Mary, says Dr. Barnum, in his book, is the most popular of all the forms of Roman Catholic devotion. That rosary has on it 15 beads, and every one of these has associated with it a special thought of prayer. These prayers are offered variously, with certain changes of form and manner, to the Holy Virgin Mary.

But returning now to Liguori. I wish to read to you what he says in his "Glories of Mary" concerning the excellence of this divinity that he worships. I can only read a part of his praises and ascriptions. On the fourth page of this book, which is put into the hands of the people as a manual of devotion in the Roman Catholic Church, and which Father Chiniquy says he studied when he was a student in Canada, it is said: "It is the will of God that all graces should come to us by the hand of Mary."

Page 5 : "To reverence the Queen of Angels is to gain eternal life." Page 8 : "All graces are dispensed by Mary ; and all who are saved, are saved only by means of this Divine Mother." Page 14 : "The Eternal Father gave the office of Judge and Avenger to the Son ; and that of showing mercy, and relieving the necessitous, to the Mother." Page 16 : "We believe that she opens the abyss of God's mercy to whomsoever she will, when she will, and in the way she will ; so that there is no sinner, however great a sinner, who is lost, if Mary protects him." Again, on page 21 : "I am thine, O Mary : save me." Page 34 : "We can say of Mary, that she gave her only begotten Son to die for us, when she granted Him permission to deliver Himself up to death."

On page 53 : " Neither on earth, nor in heaven, can I find any one who has more compassion for the miserable, and who is better able to assist me, than thou canst, O Mary." She is "the only hope for sinners," it is said, on page 67, "for by her help alone can we hope for the remission of sins." Page 67 : "He falls, and is lost, who has not recourse to Mary. (Where are we all going to?)" Page 84 : "Hail, O certain salvation of Christians, . . . and salvation of the world." Page 85 : "God has placed the whole price of redemption in the hands of Mary, that she may dispense it as she will. Thou, O Mary, art the propitiation for the whole world." Pages 90, 85 : "Our only city of refuge : the only Advocate for sinners : the only hope of sinners.' And later : 'O, our Lady in heaven, we have but one Advocate, and that is thyself." Page 98 : "Before Mary, there was none who could thus dare to restrain the arm of God. But now, if God is angry with a sinner, and Mary takes him under her protection, she withholds the avenging arm of her Son, and saves him." Page 105 : "I worship thy holy heart: through thee do I hope for salvation." And so on : who knows when it will end? Page 129 : "The intercession of Mary is ever necessary to salvation." Page 128 : "Mary was made the mediatrix of our salvation." Page 132 : "In Mary we shall find life and eternal salvation." (I think not.) Page 136 : "All gifts, all virtues, and all graces are dispensed by Mary, to whomsoever, whensoever, and howsoever she pleases. Page 143 : "The way of salvation is open to no one, otherwise than through Mary. No one is saved, except through thee." Page 144 : "Our salvation is in the hands of Mary : . . our salvation depends upon thee." Page 251 : "Thou art omnipotent to save sinners." Page 230 : "Let us, therefore, go with boldness to the Throne of grace, that we may obtain mercy, and find grace to help in time of need. The throne of grace is the blessed Virgin Mary. If, then, we wish for graces, let us go the throne of grace, which is Mary." Then, on page 479, the following : " Jesus Himself said : 'Were it not for the prayers of my mother, there would be no hope of mercy.'"

That is a lie; and so is the whole of it. Now, concerning the alleged powers of the Virgin Mary, just a little further. You read that she is made to

be about all there is in heaven for the hope of sinners. The Carmelite monks are her special favor-
ites. Do you want to know why? There is a small
square piece of cloth devised by the Carmelite monks,
which is called a scapular. They put one on each
end of a string, or ribbon, and wear it on their
shoulders. That is called the scapular of the Carmelites. Now the Virgin Mary has special favor
toward the Carmelite monks; and it is said that the
Saturday after a monk dies, she goes down into purgatory and takes him out. She spends her Saturday
afternoons that way, according to this declaration.
Have you seen these Carmelites? I saw some Carmelite monks in Venice and Rome. I remember
them very well: the vision rises before me now. I
think they were among the dirtiest of all the monks
that I ever saw; and that is saying much. I do not
see why The Virgin Mary should go to purgatory for
them: positively, I think that, in the case of those
whom I saw, a little purgatory would have done
them good!

Now, to close, you remember that I brought
before you, some time since, the book called
"Judges of Faith," purchased in a Roman Catholic
bookstore, sanctioned by three hundred and eighty,
or more, distinguished dignitaries of the Roman
Catholic Church; in which book we found a large
share of our information about their intentions towards our public schools. On the 132d page of that
book it is said, that piety toward the Virgin Mary is
one of the things that is to be especially taught in

tho parochial schools. If I remember correctly, that quotation is from the words of the Baltimore Plenary Council. Piety to the Virgin Mary is especially to be taught in tho parochial schools ; I suppose, in the one just started in Worcester, and those in Brookfield, and in Waltham, and in Boston. What is piety to the Virgin Mary? We have heard Roman Catholic answers to that question. I suppose they may take Liguori's "Glories of Mary" as one of their reading-books, possibly ; and may get not only what we read, but a very great deal more of the same tenor. Is that education?

The Virgin Mary, as you may not know, has been made the patroness of America, as St. George is of England, St. Andrew of Scotland, St. Patrick of Ireland, St. Denis of France, and St. James of Spain. The Virgin Mary is to be the patron saint of Americans ; and I suppose, therefore, they would teach American youth more about her than they would teach youth in any other part of the world. When this teaching has been taught, what will be the condition of tho mind of those who are so instructed? I confess, this whole thing staggers me, as I come to see what Rome purposes to teach.

Some years ago, I read of a company of people, in New York, who proposed to revive the old Greek idol-worship. We were told that they had secured a beautiful marble statue for a divinity, and a little band of them had gathered together to worship tho statue. It was a very strange story, and very highly interesting to me ; yet it caused a shudder,

as I thus learned that, even at this late age of
Gospel civilization, there were yet people in our
midst who had so forsaken truth and dishonored God
that they were worshipping idols. And yet, my
friends, the power that is threatening to dominate
this country, is a power which does that very thing.

Last night, a friend, who is very familiar with
French literature, told me that Victor Hugo once
wrote a very impressive poem satirizing Romish
idolatry, developing the following ideas: The poet
imagines, in this work, that the Lord Jesus Christ,
in heaven, finds that he is receiving neither prayer
nor praise. When the Lord observes that neither
prayer nor praise is sent up to him, he has a feeling
of loneliness from being neglected, and he says:
"Why is this, that I do not hear from earth, either in
the way of prayer or praise? I must inquire about
it. I have a vicegerent down there, whom I have
appointed, and to whom I have given the power of
the keys; and yet I get no words or messages from
the earth." And so the Lord resolved to descend
from heaven, and see what was the reason of this
neglect; and he said: "Because I have been on
earth in the form of a peasant, I shall be best known
to my church in that form; and I will thus descend,
to see why it is." So he came down from the
heavens, in form as he was in Nazareth and Galilee;
and he went to the great city where the Pope, his
vicegerent, lives; and beheld the splendor of the prelates, and the poverty, and vice, and superstition of
the people; and when he came to the door of the

palace there were the Swiss soldiers, in their yellow
and black uniforms, who denied him admittance.
They repulsed him rudely.   At length he, by some
means, found his way in, and finally obtained an
audience with the Pope.   No sooner did this humble
peasant come into the presence of the Pope, who was
seated on a throne in all the paraphernalia and splendor of his exalted office, than He was frowned down
by His own vicar, spoken to in a contemptuous and
bitter manner, and bidden begone.   Upon this, throwing off His disguise, and assuming the majestic form
at which all classes of beings tremble, the mighty
Saviour began to address deserved reproof to this
usurper, who had taken the place of the true Bishop
of souls.   In terrific   words of truth, he told the
trembling sinner that he was without the spirit of
the Master ; that he was the plunderer and destroyer
of souls ; that he was extorting from men a superstitious and undeserved veneration ; that the prayers
which should ascend to God in heaven, were stopped
by saints, and images, and relics, and popes, and
bishops, on earth ; and that, instead of the ends of
the great plan of salvation being served, by leading
men to God, there had been built up a hierarchy as
selfish as it was hateful, which barred the way to
heaven.

The poet-satirist was wholly right in his dream.
When the Lord Jesus shall be revealed from heaven
with flaming fire, to take vengeance on those who
know not the Lord, and who have abolished and
degraded His truth, I believe that His vengeful

lightnings will first strike that usurping power, which, in the name of the lowly Jesus, has vaulted to the very heights of blasphemy, and has sunk to the very depths of superstition. And I hope that the American people will see that certain purpose of eternal justice soon enough to save themselves from the desolation which this curse, this pagan curse, has wrought in other lands.

Sermon XIX.

SOME FURTHER ASPECTS OF PAROCHIAL SCHOOLS.

If you turn to the 60th Psalm, the third and the fourth verses, you will find the following words: "Thou hast shewed thy people hard things; thou hast made us to drink the wine of astonishment. Thou hast given a banner to them that fear thee, that it may be displayed because of the truth."

It must be confessed that the stupendous scheme of political tyranny which we have been compelled to describe from this pulpit in the last three months, is an astonishing thing for the Protestant Christian to hear, and a hard thing for the American people to comprehend. If we may trust their own statements and rely on their own utterances, the Pope and the hierarchs of the Roman Catholic Church not only claim the absolute political allegiance of every person throughout the world, but they define themselves as irreconcilable enemies of all that our fathers gave their lives to purchase, and all that our brothers died to preserve. No less true is it that against the great institutions of the country, through which is diffused the large intelligence necessary for the preservation of a republic, have they put forth their

utmost strength, and have resolved that Romanism,
not Americanism, shall be taught to little children in
schools. When they have swept away our public
system of education, they are resolved to teach that
creed and its practices which I described to you in
the last three discourses.

There were many, no doubt, who, listening, said :
" It is a hard thing, and who can believe that Roman
Catholic doctors of theology sanction the grossest
violations of the moral law ; that they teach the people absolute paganism and idolatry ; that they are at
least nineteen hundred years behind the spirit and
doctrine of Protestant New England, in the type of
religion which they teach ? "   It *is* a hard thing ; and
we have " drunk the wine of astonishment " while
we have considered these discourses which have
brought it to our attention.   But in the face of such
facts, is anything truer than the second verse of this
text, that if God has committed any trust to intelligent men, He has intrusted us with a banner by
which to represent His truth, an uplifted symbol of
our antagonism to all that enslaves the human mind,
and corrupts the morals of society.   Can there be any
doubt as to whether God has given us a banner to
display in the face of such an assailant?   Is it doubtful whether it is a Christian minister's duty, or a
Christian patriot's obligation, to confront this organized tyranny which is threatening to subvert our
liberties and our laws?   I think there can be no
doubt.

What, then, is the banner that we have been

entrusted to hold up? what is the symbol that
we display in the face of a foe who always displays
the black flag of intolerance? what banner do we
advance in the face of the Roman Catholic Church, as
it marches from out the centuries where it has trodden down the nations in blood, to add another to its
list of prostrate peoples? I answer, that we elevate a
double symbol : the banner that we rear in the name
of patriotism, is the flag of a free Republic ; the standard which we present to them in the name of truth
and religion, is the open Word of God. No hatred
soils that flag ; no malignity disfigures that page.
And while they blaze with excommunications and
avowed hate ; while their instruments of torture are
red with the best blood of all nations ; we challenge
them with a flag which forbids slavery, and a book
that has never sanctioned superstition !

It seems a necessity at this time, as we move forward in the line of argumentative conflict under such
standards, that we should gather up some of those
truths which are likely to have been dropped out and
forgotten in a discussion so protracted and one
involving so many particulars ; and because I do not
wish to leave the subject of parochial schools without
saying some things that I have not yet said, I propose
to-night to recur to that, a little out of the general
progress of the discourses, rather than to neglect
some really important phases of the subject. While
it is true that everything that I have said in the last
three months bears directly upon their effort to subvert public education, what I shall say to-night is
specially upon that design.

In a connection that will, I hope, make these practical suggestions of value, I beg you to attend first to the fact, that the agitation against American schools, which we are now forced to consider, is solely the work of the priests, and not of the laity of the Roman Catholic Church.   From first to last it is the attack of ecclesiastics and not of laymen. The authorities which I have cited to you, so adverse to our public schools, are popes, cardinals, bishops and priests; but I have not cited to you from the Roman Catholic Church, one lawyer, one physician, one man of business, one merchant, one teacher.   It is therefore obvious to you, that the authorities, at least those we have presented for the assault on public education in the form that we have it, are priestly authorities, not lay authorities.   Indeed, it is evident that the laity of the Roman Catholic Church have not been consulted about this matter.   When were they ever consulted about any matter that had been resolved upon by priestly power?

The Roman Catholic people, many of them, object to being dragged into a position of hostility to our schools; they insist on keeping their children in the common schools, for a time at least; occasionally also, there is even a priest who favors public schools. But whether or not they insist on keeping their children in our schools, they are being driven, under the lash of priestly despotism, to take them out of those schools.   I regard this as a very significant impression to be left on the mind of every intelligent American hearer, that this is not an attack of the

people, who are deriving benefits from our public
schools, upon them ; it is not a revolt against our system of public education by those who have enjoyed
the benefits of that system ; but it is an onslaught of
solely clerical tyrants upon the freedom of the people, and upon the freedom of America ; and those
tyrants wear the priestly gown, the bishop's mitre,
and the papal tiara.

There have recently appeared in the New York
Independent a series of very remarkable articles,
written by a Roman Catholic layman. The editors
of the New York *Independent* are known to me, as no
doubt they are to many of you ; and while the paper
has a very high character, the editors have an even
higher character, if that were possible. These
gentlemen have vouched for the fact that this writer
is a layman of the Roman Catholic Church ; and he, in
speaking of the relation of the laity to the Church,
uses, in the issue of October 11, the following words :
" One cause, and I believe the principal cause, of the
failure of the Roman Catholic Church to maintain a
continued hold of the love and devotion of the people
of any country, has been the complete isolation of the
interests of the laity. The Roman Catholic papers
are full of complaints of the indifference of the laity
to Roman Catholic interests. If these papers are
to be taken as true witnesses in their own case, this
indifference exists to an extraordinary extent even in
this country, and it is not a ' note ' of ecclesiastical
advancement. Now, there must be a cause for this
indifference, and we have some personal knowledge

of this cause." He goes on and discusses at length
the reason why the laity of the Roman Catholic
Church are in a condition of bewilderment and indifference, scarcely knowing what to do, and in course of
that discussion uses the following language : " Now
what is true of the general public and the influence
of the Pope on national politics, is true of the power
and influence of every bishop and priest in local politics. As members of an infallible body, they are
practically infallible ; as members of the most powerful combination on earth, their power to control the
Catholic laity is unlimited. If the commands of the
Pope must be obeyed by all nations and rulers at the
risk of eternal loss, the commands of the priests are
practically, if not equally, binding; or to all purposes quite as effectually binding. Hence if the Pope
can change the policy of a king or emperor, the
bishop can change the policies and purposes of the
mayor or aldermen." And then he adds : "The Roman
Catholic laity have come to know this very well ;
hence their marked unwillingness to interfere in any
affair whatever which is in any way under ecclesiastical control ; and what is there that is not so controlled? Nor are they willing to place themselves
in any position where they may be made to feel the
weight of the ecclesiastical arm. A priest, consciously
or unconsciously, uses his spiritual powers to attain
his temporal ends ; if he did not, he would be more
than human."

He then proceeds to speak of the fact that the
Polish Roman Catholics in the city of Chicago have

revolted against their priests because of the priests'
attempted dominance over them in all minute affairs.
This is what they say in their declaration addressed
to the Pope: "The priests want to control the private, as well as the religious, affairs of their parish-
ioners, and render them virtually slaves to do their
bidding, and failing in this, the priests have maligned
members of the Alliance, and sought to create prejudice against them.   The petitioners represent that
they are true Catholics; do not belong to any
socialistic, nihilistic or anarchistic organization;
and in everything have deported themselves as true
sons of the Church."   The spirit of Sobieski, who
labored to achieve universal liberty, has not wholly
died out of Polish Roman Catholics; and it
seems that they, in the city of Chicago, have lifted
up their voices in protest against having the priesthood push them on to a position which they deprecate,
denounce and reject.   Furthermore, we have here a
statement from a Roman Catholic layman in the
South, as follows: "A Southern gentleman, whose
opinion would command extraordinary respect if I
could give his name, said, not long since: "We (the
laity) have given up all interest in church affairs.
We do whatever we believe to be necessary
to save our souls, and we attend to our own
business.   Several times when we have tried to
interest the Bishop in plans which we believed would
greatly benefit the Church and advance the interests
of religion, we found our suggestions were not taken
in good part, and were, in fact, considered as imper-

tinent intrusion : and we heard so much of humility and obedience that we determined for the future to withdraw altogether from Church affairs. The Roman Catholic Church in the South," continues this representative Roman Catholic, " is dying of dry rot : we have indifferent bishops, who are scarcely ever seen by their people, and who do not care in the least to consider any plan which they have not suggested themselves ; and who only express an interest in the laity when they want to get money." If this is a representative utterance of the intelligent laity of the Roman Catholic Church (and it comes certainly from that source), then we have additional proof that the laity, the main body of the Church, are not interested in the overthrow of our system of public education.

It simplifies matters somewhat, if we find that we are only fighting gowned priests in this matter. If the Roman Catholic people are being bullied and driven into a position of hostility that they do not desire to take, then, O my brothers, let us try with all our might, to give them that moral sympathy, that enlightenment and that help, which will make a clear division between them and their oppressors, and will save to America and to patriotism the warm-hearted Irishmen and Frenchmen who are now being forced, by priestly and foreign power, into antagonism to their own best interests and the nation's welfare.

Now, although the laity are not consulted, the vast cost of those schools is to be borne by the laity, not by the priesthood. The founding of parochial schools involves a very large expense : that expense is to be met by the people, not by the priests. The priests have no interests particularly in popular education. I mean they have no families ; they have no recognized children that are to attend these schools. Many of them live in luxury, and have few cares, except their churchly cares. You very rarely hear of their giving large subscriptions for the promotion of parochial education. While I was visiting a little town in Connecticut, a man told me that, on a recent occasion, there came ten priests to a funeral, (I suppose of a priest) ; and he said, after the funeral the ten priests went to a hotel and had a dinner ; that the proprietor of the hotel said he never had a company in his house who made such epicurean demands as these. They called for all the best liquors in his cellar ; they drank most freely ; and they were exceedingly hilarious. They sang indecent songs and told immodest stories, until he was glad to have them leave his house ; but they made a very large bill, which they paid ; and I suppose the publican who would sell rum, would not much object to the circumstances under which the sale was effected.

The priests are not all used to luxury. Many of them are noble, self-denying men ; but the priests who control the great parishes of cities where the parochial schools are being founded, are not denying themselves for the sake of getting adequate funds to build up these schools. The people have to furnish the money.

We have pictures of extortion by priests drawn by

their own laymen. I have been told in this very city, by a man who knew the facts, in whose word I can have only confidence, and a Roman Catholic, of the priest's habit of going up and down the aisle himself and taking the collection ; not because there was no one else able to take it, but because, in the arrogance of his priestly power, he compelled men to give who otherwise would have refused. We have a case not long ago, in a Massachusetts' town, where, when a man declined to give as the priest presented the box, the priest took off his priestly robe, and proposed to throw the man out of doors, and actually forced him out of the church, because he declined to contribute.

This is the position of the priests ; but what is the condition of the people? We have the same authority in the New York *Independent* of Sept. 27, giving us an idea of what is being done to oppress the people in the matter of acquiring funds. It is an article entitled : " Is the Roman Catholic Church Advancing?" He says : " Its numerical strength is the great point made by Catholics, when they wish to impress on their own minds, or on the minds of others, the great power of the Church in this country. And so far, the numerical strength of the Roman Catholics in America has told, beyond all doubt, in politics. But what is the real, rather we should say, what is the spiritual value of this preponderating influence? Is it to lessen crime? Is it to lessen suffering? Has it elevated the moral or intellectual condition of the masses in New York? He

would be a bold man who dared to say, in the face
of facts, that the Roman Catholic Church has been
a powerful influence for good in that city."

If I should talk so about Congregationalism in this
city, and if I had justifiable occasion so to talk, you
would think that there was certainly need of a great
reform in that body. Thank God! it can never be
said of any Protestant denomination of which I know,
that its presence is a moral curse. "But what solid
foundation lies underneath?" he asks. "The
Churches are magnificent, and costly, and heavily
burdened with debt; but few are consecrated, though
they are built for many years. Is this creditable to
ecclesiastical management, or to religion? The poor
are heavily, I might almost say cruelly taxed to pay
these debts, or rather to pay the heavy mortgages on
these churches, and with little hope of reprieve."
And then he goes on to state, that Father Colton, the
successor of Dr. McGlynn, at the Church of St.
Stephen, where there is now a debt of $140,000,
proposes to add $60,000 to the debt, in order that he
may erect a parochial school, and adds, that Father
Colton is being very much praised for so doing;
while he continues: "As in the case of Dr.
McGlynn's successor, each new priest must do some
new work to get credit for his zeal. But all this is
done at the expense of the poor of his parish. The
priest gets all the honor and the poor get all the burden." He then quotes the *Freeman's Journal* as
declaring "that Father Colton is quite cheerful about
it, and he well may be, considering that not one

penny of the expense will come out of his pocket, and that he will get all sorts of ecclesiastical and episcopal honor and glory for using other people's money."

There is another little fragment here that he introduces from the *Freeman's Journal,* a bit of superstitious fraud, which is so good a morsel you must have the benefit of it. The statement of the editor of the *Freeman's Journal* is amusing in more ways than one, and we give it here. He says: " St. Joseph is a rich and powerful friend " (that is, the husband of The Virgin Mary), " who has often proved himself a benefactor to others, even in darker hours than now, frequently causing magnificent churches, convents, and other institutions to rise seemingly out of nothing, as in the case of the splendid building erected by the late Rev. Father Dromgoole, in this city (known as the Mission of the Immaculate Virgin, but erected by the St. Joseph's Union through the medium of twenty-five-cent subscriptions), at a cost of over $300,000, not including the property on Staten Island; which, with other expenditures, would bring the total cost up to about half a million of dollars. Would it not be well to try some special devotion to St. Joseph with the above intention; such, for instance, as keeping a light burning constantly before his statue until the debt is paid?" And the Roman Catholic layman comments as follows: " Well, if burning candles to St. Joseph will pay the debt, by all means let them be burned. But we fear the poor Irish servant girls of the parish will have a good deal more to do with the payment than St. Joseph, and that it will remain for another pastor to increase."

This, from an inside standpoint, shows us where the money is coming from that is demanded in such vast sums for the purpose of creating parochial schools. The people have to find that. There are many in this congregation who have had their servant girls come home and say they must have another fifty cents or another dollar a week. Now you are not unwilling that wages should be raised in proportion to service rendered, but if you happen to overhear the arrangement being made between the Sister of Charity soliciting, and the servant girl, by which the additional wages are to go into the treasury of the Church, you may naturally object; not but what you want your servant to have adequate wages, but you do not particularly feel under obligations to build the palaces of bishops and parochial schools.

This question of the wages of the Roman Catholic is an interesting question. You might raise the wages of the Roman Catholic people as high as it were possible, and they would be just as poor as they are now. Why? Because their surplus is grasped by the rapacity of priests, for the purpose of erecting splendid churches and parochial schools, and for increasing the luxury of the priests. Sometimes our Protestant Christian people say: "Oh, how Romanists raise money. I wish that we could raise money as they do." God forbid! God forbid! If we raised money as they do, we would be no more a Christian Church. They raise money by all sorts of oppression and threats. Aye, some of them frighten even you, when they threaten. There came into the store of a friend of mine the other day solicitors for a Roman Catholic fair. They insisted that he should give something. He said : " Gentlemen, I have nothing to give for that purpose ;" whereupon the representatives of the Papacy said : " Well, if you do not give, we will boycott your store ;" and he said, in effect : " Go and do it ; *go now !*" He emphasized the *now*, and they went. There is a merchant in this city who, under similar circumstances, being asked to give to a Roman Catholic fair, was told if he did not give to their Church they would not trade with him. He said : " I do not do business in that way : I shall give nothing !" I am thankful to say that this store-keeper is prosperous yet. Within the last week I have been told that if I were a merchant I should not dare to say what I am saying, because the Romanists would boycott me. Thank Heaven ! I am not in any position to fear the threats of Rome. My support depends on Christians and freemen ; not on slaves, or creatures of Romish priests.

There is a great amount of Protestant money put into these schools and into these churches that ought not to go there. Father O'Connor said to me, in New York, the other day : " You are reaping in New England what you have sown. You have made the Roman Catholic Church what it is. You have given the money to build their churches ; you have given the money to build their schools; and now they turn and try to destroy you. You have warmed the viper in your bosom," said he, " that now is trying to sting you to death." He spoke the truth. We know that he spoke the truth. Business men have stopped me on the street in this city, and said: "What is our duty in regard to this matter of giving money so that it goes into the treasury of the Roman Catholic Church?" I say: " It is your duty not to give a dollar; any more than you would have bought the bonds of the Southern Confederacy, when Jefferson Davis, at its head, was trying to ruin the country. Not a dollar, not a penny, for Romanism in America, from Protestant hands and pockets! If that policy were adopted, it would make a vast difference to the strength of this enemy of freedom. Thus the people have to furnish the money, and I have already intimated that the Protestant people are furnishing too large a part of it. This brings me to another very interesting aspect of this matter of parochial schools.

There is a very large amount of Protestant money invested in Roman Catholic Churches and in Roman Catholic schools. You know that they have erected magnificent churches in almost every city. These churches cannot be consecrated until they are free from debt. The Roman Catholic layman from whom I have just read, says, that there are almost no Roman Catholic churches in New York that are consecrated. I was told by a Roman Catholic gentleman in this city, that probably not one of the Roman Catholic churches in this city had been consecrated.

That is, because there are heavy mortgages on this property. But who has mortgaged this property? who holds it, and owns it? Here is an interesting question. If any Protestant church desires to secure money on mortgage, it has a perfectly legal way of proceeding, by which the corporate body, that is the entire society, or its representative legal corporation, incurs and becomes responsible for the debt. Sometimes money is obtained for a Protestant church by means of an individual becoming responsible; and it is the law in some States, that trustees who are on the paper of a church when the debt is incurred, cannot take their names off that paper so long as the debt stands, because they are held personally responsible. Now who holds the property of Roman Catholic churches? and who mortgages that property?

Not Roman Catholic laymen, whose labor and money must pay the mortgage. All the property of the Roman Catholic Church in a diocese is held by the bishop, and in the bishop's name. I think that is so in the State of Massachusetts. I was looking up the law; and, as nearly as I can see, that is the universal law of Roman Catholics, and the law in this State. Very good. Who is the person that owns the Roman Catholic churches of Worcester? The men who built them? the men who worship in them? the men whose wages and whose money have gone into them? No; but a stranger, whom they call "My Lord," and who lives somewhere else.

Is he responsible, financially, to such an extent

that it is wise for banks to loan vast sums of money on Roman Catholic property? Whose money is this which is loaned? Suppose the bishop should say, as he might say; "We default on these mortgages," and the property were thrown on the market, who would buy it? Those whose money was there, would lose almost every dollar of it. And suppose that the bishop was an honest man, but that the Pope should send out word to America, where these mortgages are so plentiful, "I protest against your paying the heretics their money;" every bishop would obey his command, on penalty of perdition. We may be exceedingly capable in the management of our business, and our banks may be shrewd and wise; but when I mark the conspiracy of Romanism against property, and against nationality, and against intelligence, and against everything non-Romanist, then, I say, Gentlemen, in managing your business, it seems to me it would be well to understand who is going to pay the mortgages that are on these vast properties, and by which parochial schools are being created. Do you say, The Roman Catholic people are going to pay them? If I were in their place, I would not pay a dollar; and I shall do all I can to create a revolt among them against this lavish and wicked expense, which they did not create nor consent to, and which they ought not to pay. But you say : The bishops are honest, and they will pay. Well, their moral theologians, St. Liguori, Peter Dens, J. P. Gury and others, concerning whom and from whose works I have read to you here, are the teachers of bishops; and if the bishops choose to follow their moral standards, they can repudiate every dollar, and not feel one qualm of conscience. Suppose they should follow their moral theologians, and do it. I do not say that they will; but I say, that if I had money to lend I would not lend it to them, with the risks that are involved, and the moral principles that they teach.

Now, while thus impoverishing the people, they do not take care of those whom they rob; that is certain. I find here a statement, in this same article, by the Roman Catholic layman, that the Roman Catholic Irish in this country embrace "a few millionaires, a host of politicians, and a vast population of thriftless, shiftless, ill-cared-for people. Better, a thousand times better, that these people should be back in the bogs of Connemara, with their pure, fresh air, and their pure, fresh life, than in the crime-haunted liquor saloons of New York and Boston. Millions of Irish Catholics have fled to America; and when one thinks of their miserable state in this country, it is hard to feel that the Head of the Church, whom they support so loyally, has not one word to say to stop this bleeding of the nation—this destroying of a people, who have loved him, one might dare to say, 'not wisely, but too well.'"

While they furnish hosts of pauperized people, and apply the moneys that they extort to building up their ecclesiastical institutions, they do not take care of the poor whom they make.

Go to the Roman Catholics countries of the world,

and you are beset by myriads of beggars. Of those who live at the public expense in this country, we know that a very considerable proportion are Roman Catholics. Why do they not take care of the poor whom they make poor? I will tell you why. Because they expect you to do it; and you do it. No matter how much they may plunder them, you support the plundered masses of the Roman Catholic Church. Did you ever have a beggar come to your door, who impressed you as being altogether worthy of help, and whom you found to be a Roman Catholic? Did you ever say to such, " Go to your priest! Why do you come to me, a Protestant minister? Go ask your priest for help!" I have done so; and did they ever go to their priest? Never. Why not? Because they knew they would not get anything from him, if they did go. I do not say that some of the priests of the Roman Catholic Church are not generous, self-denying men. I believe they are. I speak now of the generality—of the class—and I say, that I have never been able, in dealing with the poor of great cities,—I have never been able, when I visited them in their garrets and cellars, to get them to go and apply for charity to their own priests. Why not? The priests are spending their money in building up the hierarchy, and we are caring for their poor. Nothwithstanding all this—and all this is true and well known — the plundered people still give to these schools, and yield to priests their money to put into them.

You say, Why do they not revolt? Why do

they not come out and deny the right of the priests
to rob them? We cannot hope that they will do that
at present.   I do not see any signs of general revolt.
There is great unrest; and Father O'Connor said to
me, he knew a thousand priests that would gladly
break away from Rome to-day.   They are full of
unrest; but the likelihood of a present revolt from
the demands of Rome is not great.   And why do I
so conclude?   It is because, although they resist and
curse, they yield?   Did not a gentleman say to me,
in this city, that his servant girl came home, swearing and cursing?   (Of course, that is according to
the practice of the Roman Catholic Church: the
Popes are distinguished for cursing.)   And the lady
of the house said, "What is the matter?"   And the
girl, swearing at the priest, calling him bad names,
said he had demanded of her so much a week, and
she swore she would not pay it.   A month from that
time she was still swearing; but she had paid it.
That is the way they do.
   As an illustration of the manner in which they
yield to the Papal power, ultimately,—yield under
pressure—yield by force of education and training—
we have a most graphic illustration in the present
paralysis of Irishmen concerning Home Rule in Ireland. We cannot recall that too often.   A little
while ago, this city was full of agitation concerning
Ireland : the air was full of it ; the papers were full
of it.   Home Rule was the great cry : it was almost
as prominent as the Tariff is now.   Then came the
rescript from the Pope, who has been the enemy of

Ireland from the first. I have in my possession a book, given me by an ex-priest, written by a man trained a Roman Catholic, a judge of the Supreme Court of California. He sets forth the fact, from Romish sources, that since the day when the Pope of Rome gave up Ireland to be ruled and plundered by the King of England,—from that day to this, at least five or six times, the Pope has interfered when Ireland was on the verge of gaining liberty, taking sides with her tyrants ; and prevented her progress into a better national life. Irishmen ought to know that, and some of them do know it.

Full of burning enthusiasm and energy, the Irishmen were talking and giving, when, all of a sudden, the man whom they call the " vicar of Christ," in Rome, spoke. Their hands dropped powerless and paralyzed. My friends, if my heart is not touched, and I cannot say that it is, there is a little corner of my mind which is partly filled with anxiety to know what will happen to those agile American politicians who, a little while ago, so carried Ireland on their hearts, that in their agonized interests over " Home Rule," you would have supposed, from great senators down to ward politicians, that the dearest interest of their lives was the state of Ireland. Since the Pope has spoken, they, with their dupes, have been in the condition that the farmer's boys put the young turkeys in at Thanksgiving time ; when they seize them by the neck, and hold them so tight that, though their mouths are open, they can make no sound. So the Pope has seized our politicians, senators and all, by the neck. I listen to hear that cry of "Home Rule for Ireland." I listen to hear a peep, if I cannot hear a cry; but silence reigns around. I should think they would burst in their agony, because they cannot speak. No; all are silent. The Roman Catholic editors are silent. The Roman Catholic priests are silent. Even the Roman Catholic bummers are silent. And down under them, in a lower grade, the American politician is silent. So when you ask me why it is that the Romanists do not break away from the power of Rome, when they know that they are being plundered for measures they have not sanctioned, I ask you, why New England men here in Worcester have been muzzled by the Pope, and speak or keep silent at his command? I can pity the Irish Roman Catholic; but I can only despise the American politician.

There are those who, at this great juncture of public affairs, do precisely what such men have done in all exigencies of public affairs, who say that "all this agitation is premature; the time has not come for it. Better not say it." Did I hear any pulpit in Worcester say that, when speaking of us? I think I did. "It is true; but better not say it." So they said when Patrick Henry, in the House of Burgesses, in Virginia, while George III. was oppressing the colonies, cried: "Cæsar had his Brutus, Charles I. his Cromwell, and George the Third" (then they cried "Treason, Treason" all about the house: it was premature, this agitation; but that man of thunder hurled out his final word) "and George III. should profit by such examples." The

men that dare to be called "premature" in agitating
great interests, are the men that we must look to for
leadership. Were not Samuel Adams and James
Otis called premature in their agitation in the Revo-
lutionary days? Were not Garrison and Phillips a
little premature in forcing the barbarism of slavery
on an unwilling country? Were they not? Are
those who deprecate agitation to consent to have
the millions plundered and the nation threatened?

Nor can we trust for leadership those who say out
of their sentiment and kind feeling: " I dislike very
much to make an attack on anybody, because I have
friends who are Roman Catholics, and it disturbs
me exceedingly to think that anything should be said
detrimental to them." My friends, I have never said
a word from this pulpit against Roman Catholics as
men, and never shall; but if I should cease to speak
against the machinations of the Romish hierarchy, I
pray that God may let me die before my shame
becomes known to freemen.

I know men who sell liquor who are gentlemen in
their manner, beneficent in their gifts, in their social
life are delightful, and educated intellectually.
Because of my friendship for those men, am I to be
silent about the curse of the saloon? We knew
men years ago who were slave-holders, who said that
they deprecated all the dreadful things of slave holding as much as we did. Because I shake hands with
the lily-fingered slave holder, should I lose by that
grip all the muscle which should break a shackle and
free a man? I look on the Roman Catholic people

of this city and of the world with kindness. Even
their priests are not the objects of my dislike in any
degree. But because I have a priest a friend, or a
layman a friend, shall I therefore permit them and
the nation to be trampled down for lack of a brave
word?

My friends, we cannot look to timid sentimental-
ists or begging politicians to lead us. We want
leaders: whom shall we look to? Let us do as men
have always had to do, who had heard God's call to
duty. Let us look to our God and to ourselves, and
do our duty without any other leadership, rather
than wait to follow blind leaders of the blind.

As an illustration of the want of leadership in
this matter, let me call your attention to a very interesting fact. There is a law in this country forbidding
the importation of contract labor. There is great
zeal in enforcing that law, on the part of officials
generally. This law was made, I suppose, in the
interests(?) of the voter, and I suppose very largely
in the interests of the foreign voter: they who rose
up and said, You have imported enough, now wait
and give us a chance. And our subservient legislatures said, No more contract labor imported. How
is that law applied? Not long since, the Rev. Mr.
Berry was called to Plymouth church, Brooklyn.
If he had come, he would have been compelled to
pay a fine of $1,000 to the United States government,
because he came under contract. The Rev. Dr.
Warren was called to Trinity Church, New York,
the richest Episcopalian Church in America: he was

sued because he came over under contract and was adjudged to pay a fine of $1,000. What have we seen here in Worcester? We have a parochial school formed here, and as far as the chain of testimony is known to me, we have the following facts: We have four Irish Brothers imported from across the sea to teach us — what? To teach us how to be like Ireland? I hope not. How did they come? I am told by those who read the Roman Catholic papers, that it was announced at a certain time, that a priest in this city was going to Ireland to get such men. It was afterwards announced that he had gone to Ireland to get such men. Then it was reported that he had secured such men; and the next thing we knew, the men were in our midst. Now the law of the United States says, that whether contract be expressed or implied, if these men come for their board, or come for ten thousand a year, it makes no difference. If they are engaged for service beforehand, then it is violation of the law of contract labor. Why does not some lawyer in this assembly rise up and test the law? Why does not the District Attorney find out whether the occupation of the teachers of this city has been put in jeopardy by having teachers imported in violation of the law of contract labor? Why do not the teachers combine to press the case, and learn their rights under the law? Surely, it is much better to have honest and competent workmen brought here under contract, than men sworn to a foreign allegiance, to teach hatred of American liberty and free institutions.

A gardener coming, not long ago, I think, for a gentleman in Massachusetts, a nice Scotchman, a clean, fine man, was sent back because he came under contract. Why not an emissary of the Italian prince-pope? It might not be best for a minister to prosecute this matter personally, perhaps; for he does not wish to be too much entangled with the affairs of the world; but if any man here is a lawyer, or a teacher, or a business-man, and interested in the law of contract labor, why, gentlemen, you have my permission, you have my sanction and my benediction, if you will find out whether that law has been violated by having those men imported hither; and we would be very glad to have you take up an evening on this platform in reporting the results of your investigations, if it seemed best. But I am compelled to draw to a close.

There are two or three remarks, however, that ought to be made, before we part with this subject of parochial schools. They have a practical bearing on the matter, and I think that they will so impress you. Suppose all the Roman Catholic children are taken out of our schools and put in parochial schools, to be taught according to the standards and purposes of the Roman Catholic Church. They are not going to get the same kind of education that is received outside those schools. If they were to receive the same kind of education afforded by our schools, then they would not be taken from our schools. We are to have, then, on the one hand, American education,—for the public schools are not sectarian, in any sense—and, on the other hand, Roman Catholic education. All denominations of Christians, and people not Christians, send their children to the public schools; and they are taught according to the general standards of truth on which this nation exists. In this camp, then, you have American education: in that, you have Roman Catholic education. Now, do you not see that, from their earliest childhood, the children are to be brought into hostility and antagonism to one another? For, while the children of the public schools may cherish a magnanimous feeling toward those of the Roman Catholic schools, you know that Romish education is never magnanimous—never. You remember the charming talk we had the other Sunday morning from the Rev. Mr. Beaudry, who said to me (speaking of his early education): "My mother, who was a saint, told me the following, when I was a child: She said, 'Martin Luther was so bad a man that, before he died, the fires of hell burned within him. They burned so fiercely that he would shriek and scream with anguish because of their flame and heat. He used to be put,' said my mother, 'in a tub of cold water, and the water, in a few moments, would boil around him, because of the fires of hell that were in him.'" And he said: "I believed that, and was trained up in that belief; and Luther and Lucifer were interchangeable terms in my early thought." Now, he told this, as being a matter of education in his early life and experience.

This gentlemanly man who stood here, who was converted after nearly three years' study of the Holy Scriptures, said that was what he was taught. Do you not see that, if any approximation to that is taught, — if the history which Rome teaches and tolerates is taught,—we are to have hostile camps of American citizens growing up; or rather, American citizens on the one side, and devotees of Rome on the other? What does that promise for the future of the nation? I see in it only threatenings of evil. But in Roman Catholic schools, it is possible that the study of history may be forbidden.

An ex-Roman Catholic, writing in the *Congregationalist* of September 27, states the following: "In Ireland, where priestly power is supreme, no history is allowed to be taught. The children may be taught anything—Greek and Latin roots, algebra, chemistry —everything, in fact, except history: but history and the Bible are forbidden. Are the rising generations of the American children to be forbidden the knowledge of history as it is, or of the Bible? The Bible is forbidden: is history to be forbidden also?" I am told that the History substituted for Swinton's in Boston, leaves out the mention of Indulgences as one of the causes of the Reformation. Is that history which suppresses fact? Is that history which leaves out truth? Is that what children are to be taught? Are facts to be left out, until only so much remains as will indorse Romanism? If so, all will be left out; for there is no history that indorses

Romanism, so far as I have ever been able to find or read.

Finally, we are told that some of our schoolhouses in this State are almost empty now; and we are confronted with the practical fact, that so largely have the parochial schools drawn on the attendance at these schools, that now there is no need of those buildings for school purposes. They stand empty. Confronted with such a problem, what are we to do with those buildings? I have a little plan in my mind, which I think would work well. There is a good deal said now about industrial education; and in those buildings, by means of the lathe, the chisel and the brush, I would teach the young to earn their living by cunning handicraft and skill. And, my friends, I would turn some of those empty school-buildings into reformatories and penal institutions; and I would see that they were provided with proper guardians and overseers; and that truth, morality, and righteousness were taught in them. And if we should turn these empty school-buildings into reformatory institutions, and put over them proper persons, I think it is pretty certain that we should have a very considerable per centage of the attendants at parochial schools back in them after a very short time.

THE ROMISH CONFESSIONAL: WHAT IT IS, AND WHAT IT DOES.

"And forgive us our debts, as we forgive our debtors. For if ye forgive men their trespasses, your heavenly Father will also forgive you. But if ye forgive not men their trespasses, neither will your Father forgive your trespasses." Gospel according to St. Matthew, 6th chapter, 12, 14 and 15 verses. Also in the Epistle of St. James, 5th chapter, 16th verse: "Confess your faults one to another, and pray one for another, that ye may be healed."

In the presence of the great God against whom we have all sinned, and in whose sight we have all done evil, we solemnly undertake to-night, not merely the ungrateful task of pointing out the errors and crimes of the ecclesiastical confessional; but, in contrast thereto, of inquiring, What is the true confession which every soul should make to a holy and righteous God? As there is no creed, no system, no form of faith which does not recognize the fact of sin against God and his law; so there is no creed or system which must not, of necessity, recognize the desirability and necessity of our becoming so adjusted to the God against whom we have sinned that we can live in peace with Him. All systems of religion, nearly, embrace the principle of sacrifice ; and sacrifice is always an attempt on the part of the sinner to placate the God against whom he has offended. Whatever may be our association with men, and whatever may be our harmony, or want of harmony, with the laws and statutes of the State, the relations which we sustain to God, and those alone, can properly be designated as sinful or righteous. Against the laws of the State we can say that we commit crime, but we do not say we commit sin ; for sin is a transgression of the law of God ; and he who commits sin offends directly the Majesty of heaven. Therefore, the sinner must come to God ; or hear from God concerning a way of forgiveness, in order that he may be saved.

Confession is necessary in order to pardon. "Whoso covereth his sin, shall not prosper ; but whoso confesseth and forsaketh them, shall find mercy." On the deep principles of that philosophy which understands thoroughly human nature, is based the duty of confession. No one is in a condition to be pardoned for the guilt that he has acquired, while he covers and denies his fault ; but in that moment when he honestly confesses the same, he has put himself in a condition whereby, other arrangements being made on the part of the just God, he, on his part, can be relieved from the burden of guilt and sin.

In that wonderful prayer from which the first of
our texts is taken, our blessed Lord tells us where
to go, and how, in order that we may be forgiven
our trespasses and discharged.of our debts. No suggestion of any other interposition than His own is
implied; no intimation that any other person than
God need be approached. Here, the child who addresses his Father-God, and who asks with the faith
of the little sparrows, assisted by the majestic reason
of the man, for daily bread; and who, in his love of
righteousness, prays for the coming of that kingdom
which is the greatest blessing to all mankind,—the
child, recollecting his own sin, humbly entreats the
divine Father: "Forgive: forgive' us our debts, as
we forgive our debtors."

Where is there any suggestion that any person
other than God need be present with this humble
and penitent soul when he prays, in order that he
may be relieved of his debt, and forgiven his trespasses? Or if we turn to the text in St. James,
which has been made much of by those who distort
the Scriptures to favor auricular confession, we hear
it said: "Confess your faults one to another, and
pray one for another, that ye may be healed." In
this Apostolic declaration, it is evident that one man
is under just as much obligation to confess his fault
as is another; and that if there is any law by which
a man is to confess his sins to a priest, by that same
law the priest is to confess his sins to that man; and
if it be necessary that the priest should pray for a
man in order that the man should be forgiven, it is

equally necessary that the man should pray for the priest in order that the priest may be forgiven. "Confess your faults *one to another, and pray one for another*, that ye may be healed." "The effectual fervent prayer of a righteous man availeth much;" but if the man who offers the prayer is not a righteous man, whether he be priest, bishop, or pope, his prayer availeth nothing.

The divine mystery of forgiveness has a deeper signification than appears on the surface, with which you who have heard the Gospel all your lives are entirely familiar. The provision for human forgiveness and salvation is by one great sacrifice, that of Jesus Christ,—by one great mediator, Jesus Christ, —by one great high priest, Jesus Christ; and by Him alone.

Now, on the evidence of perverted Scriptural texts—of casuistry, which is unreasonable—of superstitions, which cannot stand the light of truth—in the interests of priestly tyranny and ecclesiastical emolument, the Roman Catholic Church has built up, in the face of Heaven, the tower of auricular confession, far more injurious to mankind than the tower of Babel ever was, and producing more confusion in the minds of their devotees than ever that Babylonian tower produced in the tongues of its builders. Auricular confession is one with the boundless corruptions of an immoral theology—of Pope worship, image worship, mass worship, saint worship,—is a part of paganism, from first to last; creates a thousand times more sin than ever it rid the world of;

puts an iron collar around the neck of every Roman Catholic, and drags him, heart-broken and unhelped, behind the car of ecclesiastical espionage and of papal power. Confession is necessary, according to the reasoning of the Roman Catholic Church, in order to absolution; absolution is necessary in order to the communion; the communion, or the mass, is necessary in order to salvation; and, therefore, the confessional must precede salvation, and every man must be drawn through it to be saved.

I am reminded of those fires of Moloch through which the children of the heathen were drawn in order to be saved; and I truly think that they got as near to God when they were drawn through the fires of Pagan idolatry, as the Roman Catholic can get by being dragged through the slums of auricular confession.

A very distinguished and learned priest, in New York, only a few days ago, stated to me, that it was just here the light dawned upon his mind with reference to the falsities of the church in which he found himself. This very distinguished priest said: "I found myself five hundred miles from any other priest in Dakota. The nearest priest to me was an illiterate man—a man, so far as I know, of no elevation of character. I remembered while there, that if I were dying, it would be necessary for me to confess and receive absolution and extreme unction; and I knew that it was impossible for me to get the priest there, so that I might confess and receive his absolution; therefore," he said, "it dawned upon my mind that the

church had exacted of me an impossibility; that I
could not pass through the ceremonial of confession
and absolution and extreme unction, because I was a
missionary, and five hundred miles from any other
priest; therefore I was sure to be lost." And he
said: "As I walked the hills of Dakota and medi-
tated on that, it so opened my mind to the falsehoods
of the theology to which I was bound, that at length,
having fully considered it and made up my mind that
it was all wrong, I sat down and wrote a letter to my
bishop, saying that I resigned my charge. I packed
up what little effects I had (I left three or four hundred dollars of salary that I suppose I had a right to),
and directed my steps to New York, where I might
meet men who would tell me more plainly the way
of life." And I said: "I wonder why it is, Doctor,
(he held his doctorate of divinity from the Roman
University,) that you were so many years finding
this out." He said: "I cannot tell you, sir. It is
a strange fatuity that holds us; but how plain it is
when once we turn our reason upon it."

It is in the confessional that Rome has its strongest hold upon its devotees. It is here that you find
the reason why the men who are ashamed of the
falsehoods of their faith cannot break with it; because the spies of the confessional are continually on
their tracks, searching their inmost thoughts and
daily actions; and there is not an hour in which
they are free from the oversight of their tyrants, who
watch them with the purpose of holding them still
captives.

It is my purpose on this and on subsequent occasions, to open the door of the confessional, and to reveal, as it is, this sacrament, so-called, of the Roman Catholic Church, which, more than any other power, restrains the liberties of her people, mental and spiritual; and in order that in our consideration of it you may know that what I state will bear the scrutiny of the most careful eye,

1. I propose to state who are the witnesses whom I summon in order to tell you about the confessional. It is necessary, of course, that those witnesses should be unimpeachable. I have heard no answer yet to the suggestion which I made, that if the Roman Catholic priests or people were disposed to controvert my views publicly, they should have the opportunity; but, none the less, I am resolved that every word that I speak shall be so established that there can be no successful contradiction of it. One of the authors from whom I shall quote most freely to-night, says: "In contending with Rome, be sure you give your authorities; because it is the fashion and usage of that Church to deny what is not incontestably proven against it."

The first authority that I shall quote is De Sanctis, concerning whom we have the following facts, which will interest this audience. "Dr. De Sanctis was thoroughly versed in the mysteries of the confessional, as may be inferred from the fact that for fourteen years he exercised the office of confessor, and that for seven he held the highly responsible post of parish priest at Rome — being thus, in con-

formity with Papal usage, brought into intimate
relation with the secret police ; while for ten years
he fulfilled, though reluctantly, the office of consult-
er to the Roman Inquisition, and would hence be
introduced behind the scenes of the religious and
political drama enacted at the Papal See." It is
said further concerning him, that " fully aware of the
extent of the loss he was about to undergo ; knowing
that he exchanged honor for disgrace, wealth for
poverty, fame and distinction for obscurity and dis-
repute ; he heeded not the amount of the sacrifice,
but forsaking country, family and friends, he counted
all things but dross, so that he might enjoy the clear
sunshine of an untroubled conscience, and proclaim
with untrammelled freedom the rich mercies of the
Gospel, in all their purity and fulness. It is curious
that for his emancipation he was indebted to one of
the many honors heaped on him, till they almost
equalled in number the years he had been in Holy
Orders. Being appointed to deliver a course of
lectures against heretics, he received a license to
read their works. Gradually, the light of Divine
truth dawned more and more clearly on his mind ;
and the more earnestly he strove and prayed to be
led into the right way, the more did his growing
persuasion of the errors of the Church of Rome
deepen in intensity. To maintain a struggle against
conviction was inconsistent with the candor and
the integrity conspicuous in the character of De
Sanctis ; and henceforth he resolved to preach the

faith which he lately studied to destroy." (Preface to De Sanctis on The Confessional.)

There is no more reason for discrediting De Sanctis than there is St. Paul: he followed that illustrious apostle of the Gentiles in an almost similar course. Pius IX. (at that time Cardinal Feretti,) went to Malta, to which place De Sanctis was exiled; and, falling on his neck, entreated him with all the art of which he was capable, to return to the bosom of the Roman Catholic Church; but he preferred poverty and exile for the sake of the Lord Jesus Christ. From him, as an authority, I shall freely quote, holding in my hand a book of his writing, entitled: "Confession: a Doctrinal and Historical Essay."

2.   I shall also quote Pierre Hyacinthe, whom we know as Father Hyacinthe, the distinguished preacher at the Church of Notre Dame in Paris. Notre Dame is one of the grandest cathedrals under whose arches man ever stood. In that vast church thousands sat to listen to the rare eloquence of this man; who, finding himself at variance with the Pope and the theologians of Rome, abandoned the highest honors, and took an obsure position as preacher of Jesus Christ.

3.   I shall also quote Charles Chiniquy, known as Father Chiniquy, of Canada, who was fifty years a member of the Roman Catholic Church, and twenty-three years a priest. Concerning Father Chiniquy, the following facts may interest you, as showing that he was fully accredited by the Roman Catholic

Church, and that it is impossible to break down his testimony.

It is said here by his biographer (Father Chiniquy is still living; he spoke in Boston two weeks ago), that " the great city of Montreal, moved to gratitude by his service to the cause of temperance, presented him with a gold medal, on one side of which was: "To Father Chiniquy, Apostle of Temperance, Canada," and on the other, " Honor to his Virtues, Zeal and Patriotism." Moreover, the Pope extended to him his blessing. On the tenth of August, 1850, a letter, of which the following is a translation, and of which I will read a part, was sent to Canada by Charles T. Baillargeon : " I have taken the opportunity to present to him (the Pope) your book, with the letter, which he has received—I do not say, with that goodness which is so eminently characteristic— but with all special marks of satisfaction and of approbation, while charging me to state to you that he accords his Apostolic Benediction to you and to the holy work of temperance which you preach." Signed, after much more of the same import, " Charles T. Baillargeon, Priest."

Moreover, the Bishop of Montreal, when Father Chiniquy, in 1851, left his old field for a new one, wrote him a letter that says, among other things : " You ask me the permission to leave the diocese to offer your services to the Monseigneur of Chicago. As you belong to the diocese of Quebec, I believe that it appertains to Monseigneur the Archbishop to give you the excat which you ask. For me, I cannot but thank you for your labors among us. You shall ever be in my remembrance and in my heart, and I hope the Divine Providence will permit me at a future time to testify to you all the gratitude that I feel within me. Meanwhile, I remain, dear sir, Your very humble and obedient servant,

IGNATIUS,

M. CHINIQUY, Priest.   *Bishop of Montreal.*

Many times since then, Roman Catholic mobs have tried to kill this man, and still he lives to bear witness against the evils of Romanism and the wickedness of priests.

4. I shall also quote the Rev. Mr. Aubin, of this city, a Baptist minister, brought up a Roman Catholic, and a highly reputable man among us, who has told me some things concerning the confesssional. I shall quote also from the Rev. L. N. Beaudry, who stood in this pulpit not long since and addressed this congregation, and who is an esteemed minister of the Methodist Episcopal Church.

5. I shall quote also from J. Blanco White, who for many years was a priest in the city of Seville in Spain. He had a most excellent reputation among all men, and was a member of the Protestant Church for the space of fifteen years, after renouncing Rome.

6. I shall quote also from Henrietta Carracciolo, who was the daughter of Marshal Carracciolo. She gives us the result of her observations and experience in a work entitled "Twenty Years in a Neopolitan Convent." The high character of this lady, not excelled

by that of any woman in the world, guarantees, as does the corroboration of her testimony, the reliability of her words. But more than this. These are but a few of the many on whose testimony I shall rely. I shall read a letter in one of these books, signed by forty-nine Roman Catholic women, testifying to the abominableness of the confessional. These fortynine are only a part of hundreds and thousands that in Canada have renounced the Roman Catholic Church and have become Protestant Christians. I shall quote also from numerous priests.

In order that you may know that what I state cannot be controverted, even from the Roman Catholic standpoint, I shall quote the theologians of Rome in their confessions and their questions to priests.

7. For example, I shall quote from Kenrick's "Theology," which devotes seventeen pages to a consideration of the dangers resulting to priests in the confessional, from the character of questions which they are compelled to ask. I can give you the assertions of Roman Catholic authorities almost without number.

When I come to the final testimony, that is to be relied upon as beyond all controversy, I shall have in my possession the questions which the young priests are taught that they must ask in the confessional. I was given by a priest, the other day, the book which he studied in the college of St. Mary in Baltimore, where he prepared to be a priest, the work of Bishop Bouvier, also the work of Peter Dens, also of Liguori and of Debreyne,—all of these containing exactly what these priests are compelled to study and to ask of their penitents in the confessional.

Now my friends, something is to follow our consideration of this matter; something is to be done when we have learned the horrors of the confessional. When I have given you testimony that cannot be controverted, I want you to have so examined it, to so listen and to so satisfy yourselves, that if you are called upon to vote in this city as to whether Romanism shall dominate our schools and ourselves, you will not cringe and cower as so many times our American municipalities have done; but will know enough, and have courage enough, and heart and manhood sufficient to say to Rome, "Hands off! You are not fit to take control of any municipality in the nineteenth century." In other words, I want you, my friends, to have the truth, so as to act right; to act with that vigor, that assurance, that honor and that fearlessness with which our heroes acted in times gone by, when their convictions had to change for a time to defensive blows to save the nation from its enemies.

What, then, is auricular confession? The word "auricular" means, confession in the ear; and of course it means confession in the ear of a priest.

1. Most copious authorities prove that Roman Catholicism has borrowed this, as it has borrowed many other things, from paganism. I have here a list of a dozen authorities who agree in the following facts: "Auricular confession was enjoined in the Elusinian Mysteries, by Zoroaster in Persia, Buddha

in India, and was practiced by the ancient Babylonians and Egyptians, the Mexicans before Cortez, the Peruvians before Pizarro, by the Japanese, the Siamese, and others." In the list of those historians, not to read them all, we have Wilkinson in his "Ancient Egypt," Bancroft in his "Native Races," and other equally reliable authorities. We have also direct testimony that the priests of Bacchus, who was the God of wine, listened to auricular confession; and I beg you to notice what is said by a distinguished priest, confirming the truth of this statement: "Nobody can be surprised that the priests, the bishops and the Popes of Rome are sunk into such a bottomless abyss of infamy, when we remember that they are nothing else than the successors of the priests of Bacchus and Jupiter. For not only have they inherited their powers; but they have even kept their very robes and mantles on their shoulders, and their caps on their heads. Like the priests of Bacchus, the priests of the Pope are bound never to marry, by the impious and godless laws of celibacy. For every one knows that the priests of Bacchus were, as the priests of Rome, celibates. But, like the priests of the Pope, the priests of Bacchus, to console themselves for the restraints of celibacy, had invented auricular confession. Through the secret confidences of the confessional, the priests of the old idols, as well as those of the newly invented wafer-gods, knew who were strong and weak among their fair penitents; and under the veil "of the sacred mysteries," during the night celebration of their diabolical rites, they knew to whom they could address themselves, and make their vows of celibacy an easy yoke." "Let those who want more information on that subject read the poems of Juvenal, Propertius, and Tibbellus. Let them peruse all the historians of old Rome, and they will see the perfect resemblance which exists between priests of the Pope and those of Bacchus, in reference to the vows of celibacy, the secrets of auricular confession, celebration of the so-called "sacred mysteries," and the unmentionable moral corruption of the two systems of religion. In fact, when one reads the poems of Juvenal, he thinks he has before him the books of Dens, Liguori, Debreyne, and Kenrick."

It was not until the year 1215 that auricular confession became a dogma of the Roman Catholic Church. Prior to that time, confession was voluntary. At that time Innocent III. issued to the Lateran Council the edict by which, from that time, confession became compulsory; so, evidently, it is one of the later dogmas of the Roman Catholic Church. As Roman Catholics are compelled to believe, since 1850, in the Immaculate Conception, and, since 1870, in the Infallibility of the Pope; so, since 1215, they have been compelled to believe in Auricular Confession, under penalty of mortal sin.

2. Where is this confession heard? If you go into a Roman Catholic Church, you are likely to see what are called confessional boxes. They are little houses, large enough on the inside for one or two persons to sit. There is a grated window, at which the penitent kneels, on the outside. You find these in

all the great Roman Catholic Churches of the Old World; and, I suppose, in this country, although I have visited fewer Roman Catholic Churches here. The priest, sitting in the inside of this confessional-box, as it is called, receives the confession of the kneeling penitent on the outside. But not only there: the confession can be taken in a private house or private room, as we have known in this city of a priest taking the confession from his penitent in his parlor. It may also be received in the sick room, on the dying bed; but is always, I believe, conducted in private, only the priest and the penitent being present. Now, who are compelled to confess?

3. The answer to that question is, that *everybody* is compelled to confess; and that everybody is compelled to confess everything. For instance: I find here, from "Butler's Catechism"—a standard authority — the following statement, approved by several bishops of Quebec. On page 62 it reads: "That all penitents should examine themselves on the capital sins, and confess them all, without exception, under penalty of eternal damnation." We find in this book of De Sanctis, on page 21, that confession is absolutely necessary for forgiveness and salvation. In Bishop Hay's "Sincere Christian," the following question and answer occur: "Is this [auricular] confession of our sins necessary for obtaining absolution? It is ordained by Jesus Christ as absolutely necessary for this purpose." We have, on the 118th page, this statement: "In Rome, all religious instruction consists in teaching the people

to confess. Confession and Roman Christianity are their convertible terms. Do you wish to know a so-called good Christian? It is he who confesses frequently. Do you wish to carry a certificate of Christianity? Carry a certificate of confession. The servants of the Cardinals cannot touch their wages at the beginning of the month, unless they present the certificate of confession. Meanwhile, religious ignorance is such, that they do not even know that there is a book called the Bible, containing the Word of God. The people's article of faith is: 'I believe all that the Holy Church believes.' Such religious ignorance engenders superstitions, infidelity, immorality, and the loss of souls. But what signifies it? Such ignorance maintains confession?" That is by De Sanctis, who himself heard confessions in Rome for many years.

4. Now, as to the frequency of confession: the more frequent the confession, the more pious the person who confesses is supposed to be. When Martin Luther was in the bondage of Rome, he was accustomed to confess every day, and sometimes more than once a day. Other priests of the Roman Catholic Church are reported to confess once a day, and once a week; and sometimes the nuns, it is said, remain for two and three hours in the confessional, two or three times a day! But it is absolutely necessary, in order that a person shall have any standing in the Roman Catholic Church, that he shall take the communion at least once a year, and he cannot take the communion without confessing prior to it, and

receiving the absolution of the priest. Therefore, the Roman Catholic must confess once a year, and is commended for confessing as frequently as once a day.

5. What must be confessed? I already have read you one authority, "Butler's Catechism," with reference to that. But, further, I answer, the person who confesses to the priest, must confess every deed, every word, every thought, every dream. He must confess everything that has passed in his mind, or passed in his words, or in his acts, concerning which he is doubtful, and concerning which he is not in doubt. Let me give you an authority for that statement: "When the Council of Lateran decide? that every adult, of either sex, should confess all their sins to a priest at least once a year, there was no exception made for any special class of sins, not even those committed against modesty or purity. And when the Council of Trent ratified or renewed the previous decision, no exception was made, either, of the sins in question. They were expected and ordered to be confessed as all other sins. The law of both Councils is still unrepealed, and binding for all sins, without any exception." It is imperative, absolute; and every good Catholic, man or woman, must submit to it, by confessing all his or her sins, at least once a year. The celebrated controversial catechism of Rev. Stephen Keenan, approved by the bishops of Ireland, positively says (page 186): "The penitent must confess all his sins." And anything left out of the

confession so vitiates it, that it is not a good confession. If a person goes to the confessional and confesses ninety-nine out of a hundred sins, and leaves
out that one sin, the confession is of nothing worth.
I want you to notice this ; because of the tortures that
it inflicts on conscientious people who go to the confession. They are requested and desired to recall
every sin, every thought, word, dream, imagination
that they have had which may be considered a sin,
mortal or venial. If they try to do it, they may fail.
If they fail, they cannot be absolved for the sin ; and
if they fail in confessing everything, they are lost.
They struggle to find the sins—all of them,—and in
their struggle reveal a thousand things which should
never be on human lips ; at least, which should never
pass between any man or woman and the celibate
priest in the privacy of the confessional. But Father
Chiniquy says, that the fear and anguish which many
conscientious Roman Catholics have, lest their confession is not a good one, is a source of continual
distress to them.

Moreover, these fears as to the quality of the confession not only work exceeding grief to a soul, but
they afford an opportunity for the diabolical ingenuity of the bad priests to question and search and
probe and discover the deepest, the minutest, and
the most sacred secrets of the soul. "Though the
penitent is told that he must confess his thoughts
only according to his best recollection, he will never,
never know if he has done his best to remember
everything ; he will constantly fear lest he has not

done his best to count and confess them correctly."
"Every honest priest, if he speak the truth, will at
once admit that his most intelligent and pious penitents, particularly among women, are constantly
tortured by the fear of having omitted to confess
some sinful deeds or thoughts. Many of them, after
having already made several general confessions " (a
general confession is of all one's sins from the beginning of one's life,) " are constantly urged, by the
pricking of their conscience, to begin afresh, in the
fear that their first confessions had some serious
defects. Those past confessions, instead of being a
source of spiritual joy and peace, are, on the contrary, like so many Damocles' swords, day and night
suspended over their heads, filling their souls with
the terrors of an eternal death. Sometimes the
terror-stricken consciences of those honest and pious
women tell them that they were not sufficiently contrite ; at another time, they reproach them for not
having spoken sufficiently plain on some things fitter
to make them blush."

But there is a deeper dread than this which makes
the confession an engine of torture. It is this :
Every sacrament may be vitiated and made of none
account by what is called *the intention of the priest.*
Now the Doctrine of Intention in the Roman Catholic
Church is this : suppose that a priest is about to perform
the mass, and he has not the intention of really performing it, then the bread over which he has said the
mummery of the mass, is not, as they suppose, the
real body of Christ, but only bread ; and therefore,

for them, all its character is vitiated. Suppose that a priest stands up to marry a man and a woman, and in his intention he resolves that the ceremony shall not be what it seems to be, then these people are not married, according to the Roman Catholic Church. Suppose that the priest hears a confession in the confessional, and it is in his intention that the words of absolution which he speaks shall not really absolve the penitent, then the penitent is not absolved. So a vicious priest, who has not the intention of carrying out the sacraments as they appear on the surface, may jeopardize the eternal salvation of every soul who confesses to him. Do you see in what torture the Roman Catholic is?

Sometimes people are inclined to go over to the Roman Catholic Church, because they are so unspeakably lazy that they want somebody to attend to their religion for them, while they attend to the world, the flesh and the devil; but remember, that if you go over to the Roman Catholic Church, and if you leave the intention demanded by your sins to a priest, it may be that he will simply make an inclined plane for you, through the confessional box, to that ruin which you are trying to escape.

The probing questions of the priests enter deep into the soul of the penitent. Back of every word I say now, there is a revelation that I must not make to you about the questions that the priests, from the time they begin to take confession, are permitted, commanded, and compelled to ask.

I remember hearing the story told by Father Chiniquy of a beautiful woman in the house of whose father he had frequently been a visitor, coming one day to his confessional box, when he was a young priest. She knelt down beside the box at the little grated window, and her deep sobs and ejaculated prayers wrung his heart, for he knew not their cause. When he gently spoke to her, she answered, and besought him in the name of all that was good, for the sake of her soul, that he would not ask her the questions that her former two confessors had asked. She said to him : " When I went to the first, I was a spotless, stainless woman. He asked me those questions that poisoned and degraded my soul and blackened my life. The sin which followed was only the natural consequence. I left him in the bitterness of my spirit, and went, after a year of sin, to another confessor, an old man. The same thing followed again ; and now," said she, " I come to you, and I say to you, if you will promise not to ask me those soul-damning questions, I will confess to what a woman ought to confess ; but unless you promise I will not confess." He said to her : " I am compelled to ask counsel as to whether you must confess or not. I shall be obliged to go to my own confessor, to consult the authorities of the Church." He went. They told him that it was not in his province to decide what he would ask in the confessional ; that he must ask what the theologians and fathers of the Holy Church had prescribed. He came back to the confessional on another day. The broken-hearted and beautiful woman was there. Once more she proffered her request; and when he said to her: " I am compelled by the law of the Church to ask you those questions," she fell fainting on the cushions where she knelt. He rushed out, lifted her up, and and carried her to her home. The shock was too great for her. She steadily declined, and was on her dying bed. He went to visit her, in order to give her the last rites of the Church. It was necessary, before she could have extreme unction, that she should be prepared for death by confession; and he said to her, " I have no alternative; I must ask you these questions." She said: " I will not listen to them. You preached from the story of the Prodigal Son; it was that which awakened me when I was living in sin with the priest who had ruined me. Now I will not listen to those questions. I will throw myself into the arms of my Saviour, and die as I may." The last words she uttered were: " I shall not be lost." Her mother heard that last word "lost," and rushed into the room to find her daughter dead; and lived in the belief, from which Father Chiniquy could not deliver her, because of the secrecy of the confessional, that her child had refused to receive the last rites of the Church, and was lost.

One such fact as that will damn forever auricular confession : and when I say to you that facts like that are numbered by thousands and millions; that the witnesses to them are priests without number and authorities uncounted ; then I give you an idea of the kind of questioning, of the subtle inquiry, of the degrading methods for probing the conscience and searching the soul, that are adopted in the Roman Catholic confessional.

I believe there are priests who break the laws of the Church; that are too manly to ask those questions; that evade them and avoid them: but if they do, they do it at their peril, for the law of the Church is against them.

6. What follows confession? Absolution. What is that? Let me read the words, or part of them, in which the absolution is given. When the penitent has confessed, the priest uses the following language: "The passion of our Lord Jesus Christ, the merits of the blessed Mary always Virgin, and of all the saints, and whatever good you have done, and whatever evil you have suffered, be unto you for the remission of sins, the increase of grace, and the reward of eternal life. Amen." This is a part, an illustrative part, of the absolution which follows confession; and if the penitent believes that the priest has that power, and can believe with easy conscience that he has answered all the questions and confessed all the sins, he goes forth fondly believing that he is forgiven before God.

What follows? Why is it that the priest stands up in the presence of his congregation with that haughty air of arrogant pride? Why is it that the priest, as he walks among his flock, carries himself as if he had positive and absolute authority over their thoughts and their consciences? Why is it that when you meet him on the street he tosses up his head as though he were a demigod, and hardly needed to tread on common earth? It is because he has the secrets of his flock, the personal and private life of those who have confessed, and those who have not confessed, whose servants and families have brought him the information. It is because he is virtually a spy in every home, and knows every heart; and knows that, if he wishes to, he can force them by his knowledge to yield to his power and come under his sway. No wonder that he carries himself in the pride of presumption and arrogance as a master; no wonder that from the altar he threatens them with cursing if they refuse to obey his will. And this, in my judgment, after careful study, is the reason for auricular confession in the church of Rome.

There is another point that I must touch before I part with this theme to-night, in order that I may get sufficiently along with the subject to meet the further demands of another occasion like this. All the confession of the penitent is declared to be absolutely secret and kept in the bosom of the confessor. That is the theory of the Roman Catholic Church. Every word spoken to the priest in the confessional is an absolute secret between him and the penitent; so that, I suppose, if a Roman Catholic priest in this city had knowledge of any matter whatever, whether relating to an individual or a community, delivered to him in the privacy of the confessional, he would not be compelled by any law of the State to tell what he knows, even though disclosure might lead to the protection of virtue or the

overthrow of evil doing.   Let me read you the theory
of the church in its own words : " It is not lawful to
reveal anything that is told in confession, though it
be to avoid the greatest evil that can happen ; or to
save a whole commonwealth from damage, temporal or
spiritual ; or to save the lives of all the kings in
Christendom.   The seal of confession must be maintained even by falsehood and perjury ; though the loss
of a man's life, or the ruin of the State, be the consequence : nor can the Supreme Pontiff dispense with
the obligation," says Dens, in his Theology.   " The
seal is an obligation of Divine right most strictly in
every case, even where the safety of a whole nation
is at stake," says St. Liguori.   " But, Father ! it
may happen that my confessor will make known my
sin to another.   What do you say ?   Know that the
confessor is bound to suffer himself to be burnt alive
sooner than disclose a single venial sin confessed by
a penitent."   Such is the theory of the Roman Catholic Church and under the pledge of such secrecy all
confessions are made.

Do you believe that they would be made if the
penitent were aware that the seal of the confession
was as easily broken as the other pledges of the
Roman Catholic church ?   Can you imagine that manhood and womanhood would make absolute surrender
of all the facts, the thoughts, the dreams of their
lives to another if they supposed that that other
would ever reveal those secrets ?   And yet I say
to-night, on the most unimpeachable authority, that
the secrets of the confessional, from Popes who have

been confessors down, are not only the subject of rude jest and free conversation and open comment; but they have been the means of working ruin to those who have made confession, by their betrayal to the civil and other authorities, even when such men have been only the friends of liberty and endeavoring to make free the State. So abundant is this testimony that I hardly know how to take hold of it, for the very brief moment which I can use to speak upon it. I find De Sanctis saying, on page 122, exactly what Father O'Connor said to me in New York only a few days ago, as follows : " But while the penitent arraigns his faults with all the fatuity of a simpleton, what is the confessor doing? Laughing at the simplicity of the penitent : and afterwards, in the priestly orgies that follow a morning of great confessions, in the hilarity that flows from wine, amidst coarse explosions of laughter, they describe the stupid folly of their penitents, and each priest vies with his brother in rendering his own penitents more ridiculous than the rest. To such a degree is the individual debased and degraded by confession."

Further I find upon turning to a historical authority, that Pius V., Pope of Rome, " for the punishment of certain offences, took advantage of the confessional, which ought to be an inviolable sanctuary." While he was Cardinal, the extraordinary apparent piety of his life made a great many flock to him for confession ; " but they grievously misreckoned when they confessed to a person who adroitly took care to assure himself of name and surname, which he committed to his memorandum book, probably with the intention of using the information at a fitting opportunity; as in fact he did. For no sooner was he made Pope, than he gave the Governor of Rome a list of five persons, three men and two women, supplying him with the requisite particulars for finding them. He took care, however, not to mention that they had confessed to him, though he positively assured him of the grave offence that each had committed. When the Governor replied that justice was not accustomed to imprisonment on informations, without the certainty of having witnesses, Pius answered: " When you have imprisoned them, you can then, on the assurance of our word and our conscience, put them to the torture: for they will assuredly confess the offences of which we inform you." This was the act of Pope Pius V.

Pope Sextus V. summoned confessors, and said, "That they could make a report to the Pontiff, without any danger attached to revealing a confession, he giving them absolution for the whole." That is, the Pope, considering the fact that the confessors had taken the oath of secrecy, absolved them from the oath, and compelled them to tell the secrets of the confessional to him, in order that he might enchain the freedom of the mind, and in order that he might destroy heretics. Page after page of testimony here follows. Citations from historians of the highest reputation are given to show how numerous the instances, how unnumbered the occasions, on which the confidence of the penitent has been betrayed rudely by the confessor. "The general opinion of Roman Catholics is, that priests do not think of, nor recollect, the sins they hear in confession, and much less talk of or relate them to others; but, with the greatest regret, I can assert the contrary, and prove the fact. Some lay people informed me, that they heard several priests in company relating some sins of a delicate nature, of which the said clergy acquired knowledge in the confessional, under the seal of their sacred tribunal, at which they were greatly scandalized, but had not fortitude enough to reprimand, or sufficient knowledge to report them to their superiors, who ought to suspend them perpetually from their office. I have been present in company at different times, when I witnessed priests revealing heinous sins sacramentally made known to them; some priests informed, without the least necessity, of some enormous crimes they heard in confession, perpetrated between . . . There it stops very properly. (Rev. L. Morissey, Parish Priest, etc.)

Moreover, "several priests vie at times amongst themselves, to know which of them can relate and inform each other of the greatest and most odious sins communicated to them in the sacred, confidential tribunal. They take a secret pride in having it in their power to make such communications." A bishop informed me of the sins of one of his penitents, told him in confession, who was a respectable lady, and an acquaintance of mine. He even mentioned her name. Some coolness existed between a certain priest and myself, to whom I was in the habit of going to confession previous to our misunderstanding. In the course of some time after, he revealed my sacramental confession to others in my presence." So he goes on to say : "I shall only say, that this sacrament was considered before now as the pillar of the Roman Catholic Church, through which grace was conveyed and salvation obtained ; but now it is considered by many priests and prelates as the pillar of the Holy Inquisition, the source of genuine information for sanguinary purposes, the security of absolute and universal influence, and the extermination of heretical pravity." (*Ibid.*)

The following are the words of one who was himself a Popish priest for some time. Referring to another priest, whom he occasionally met, he says : "All our conversation ran upon the stories he heard in confession. But he is not the only person who is free in what he has heard, for it is the ordinary discourse of the priests, when they meet, to inform one another of what they have heard in confession. This I can assert, because I was often present at such conferences, where the conversation was so indecent that even an honest pagan would have blushed." (See Elliot, "Delineation of Roman Catholicism.")

"Every day they [the Dominican monks] came, and talked most licentiously, relating things that had happened at the Holy Office at Perugia, confessions they had heard, etc." This is from the bishop of Pistoia, Scipio de Ricci, whose memoirs were so scandalous that the Italian Government caused them to be printed in order to give a reason why the Government had seized the property of the church, and turned out the monks and nuns from the houses which they had disgraced. My friends, only the lack of time is a bar to my reading to you for half an hour the most astonishing and undeniable testimony on this subject. We have here an Italian patriot telling us how the names of the patriots were discovered through the confessional; how the priests delivered them up to the secular power and the Inquisition; and how, as a result, these men were imprisoned and exiled.

I will not take time to read you in his words the fact that De Sanctis himself, when the Inquisition was broken up and free Italy resumed control of the Roman States, found in the library and archives of the Inquisition volumes like ledgers, in which were the names of the persons, whose confessions were on adjacent pages, and there was the secret history of their lives, written out for the use of the Papal power, in order to the suppression of any revolt against its authority. I have not time to tell you how often the confession is betrayed; how small a tax is necessary in order that the priest may be excused for it: nor have I time to tell you how the priests bring their influence to bear upon the penitents to get permission to reveal what they are determined to reveal, whether the penitent shall give his consent or not: for if the penitent refuses to give his consent to the revelations of the confession, then the priest refuses absolution, and the poor person stands, as he supposes, in danger of immediate and final damnation.

What does the confessional do? These are proofs of the manner in which its secresy is violated. Are there Roman Catholics in this house to-night? are there intelligent people here, members of that Church; who, unaware of the manner in which their confidence is betrayed, have believed that this priestly absolution was simply the purpose of a good man to deliver them from their sins? My friends, you are greatly mistaken. The purpose of auricular confession is so to enchain you that you shall not dare to break away from the power of the priest; and that you shall not dare to think for yourselves in matters of religion or anything else. It induces immorality and crime. It degrades the priests and the penitents. It ruins the State and assaults liberty. It plunders families by means of the last and dying confession of their members; so that their wills are made in favor of the church. It renders impossible religious progress. It blights domestic happiness. It enchains all its devotees; and the truth of this statement I shall vindicate by ample proof hereafter.

I turn from a picture so revolting — from a scene so sad — remembering that multitudes of our fellow-men are in this bondage: I turn to one of many radiant lines of light from the Scriptures of Divine Truth, which I pray you to carry with you in your recollections of this hour. "Two men went up into the temple to pray; the one a Pharisee, and the other a publican. The Pharisee stood and prayed thus with himself: God, I thank Thee that I am not as other men are, extortioners, unjust, adulterers, or

even as this publican : I fast twice in the week, I
give tithes of all that I possess. And the publican,
standing afar off, would not lift up so much as his eyes
unto heaven, but smote upon his breast, saying,
"God be merciful to me a sinner."   And what said
the Great High Priest of time and eternity concerning
this confession?   " I tell you, this man went down
to his house justified, rather than the other : for every
one that exalteth himself shall be abased ; and he
that humbleth himself shall be exalted."   O friends !
will not you preach this doctrine to our brethren of
the Romish Church?   Will you not carry this Bible
truth to those who sit in the shadow of religious
tyranny?   Will you not tell them out of your own
heart, from your own experience, that the man,
however sinful, wherever he may be, who, in the
presence of God, smites upon his breast in humble
penitence, and confesses sin, praying " God be merciful to me a sinner," that man, by word of Jesus
Christ, is a justified man.   Oh that the day may
come when the slaves of Rome shall have this justification through Jesus Christ ; and when you and I,
and all of us, can tell them, that we, for our part,
know what it is by a blessed experience.   Amen.

Sermon XIV.

THE ROMISH CONFESSIONAL, WHAT IT IS, AND WHAT IT DOES.

The Romish Confessional cannot have the sanction of God.

We find the words of our text to-night, as we pursue the subject of the Roman Catholic Confessional, in the Second Epistle General of Peter, the second chapter, and the nineteenth verse: "While they promise them liberty, they themselves are the servants of corruption; for of whom a man is overcome, of the same is he brought in bondage." The eighteenth verse reads: "For when they speak great swelling words of vanity, they allure through the lusts of the flesh, through much wantonness, those that were clean escaped from them who live in error."

Every person in this congregation, I hope, at some time has thanked God for the story of the Prodigal Son. Of all the words of Jesus Christ, the good Shepherd of the sheep, who sought after us to save us, there are none more tender than these. Many of this congregation know, by personal experience, the history of a youth who wasted his substance with

riotous living, and awoke to his shame in a strange
land.   Kneeling on the ground, with no great cathedral roof above him, with only the swine for company, and God over all, this boy turns his heart and
thought and prayer toward home, and says : " I will
arise, and go to my father; and will say unto him,
Father, I have sinned against heaven, and in thy
sight, and am no more worthy to be called thy son."
The father's heart never had ceased to long for his
son, and ere the penitent reached the paternal man-
sion, the swift feet of love had met him, and fallen
on his neck, and kissed him ; had given orders that
the best robe should be put upon him, the shoes and
the ring, and that the feast should be prepared, and
had directed that merriment and gladness should
reign around ; " for this my son was dead, and is alive
again ; he was lost, and is found."

If the Romish confessional were necessary in order
that men should get back to their Father, this story
would never have been written.   If there need be
the interposition of a priest, who should hear in his
ear all the sin and sorrow of a wandering man, this
story of the Prodigal Son would never have been
spoken ; and perhaps the good God gave us this story
in order that, at this time, in the nineteenth century
of Christianity, we might lift up our voices against
the claims of ecclesiastical power, and the hindrances
which priests put in the way of those who will seek
their God, and say : " As came the prodigal to his
father ; so, my brothers, let us come to God."

The Bible is self-consistent in every part; and therefore the theory of confession and pardon which you
find in one place must be congruous and harmonious
with that you find in all places. The prodigal came,
exactly as we were saying on last Sunday night that
they come who pray the Lord's prayer, and say,
"Forgive us our trespasses as we forgive." The
prodigal came precisely as the publican smote upon
his breast, and prayed, "God be merciful to me a
sinner." Nor can there be any contradiction from
Holy Scripture of this method of confession, and of
its acceptability to God against whom we have sinned.
This Bible theory of confession is taught by all
Protestant Christians,— that I may come to God
anywhere, at any time, without any interposition
but that of Jesus Christ; and may have as definite
assurance that God the Father receives me as that
prodigal had of parental goodness, who felt the
arms of love about his neck, and the pressure of
love against his bosom, while the old man rejoic-
ingly said: "This my son was dead, and is alive
again; he was lost, and is found."

But there are two passages of Scripture which, as
used by Romanists, are in diametrical contradiction
to this form of true confession. On those two,
more than on any other, they build up the alleged
Scriptural authority for auricular confession. The
first of those passages is in the 16th chapter of the
Gospel according to St. Matthew, where it is said by
our Lord, addressing Peter: "I will give unto thee
the keys of the kingdom of heaven; and whatsoever

thou shalt bind on earth shall be bound in heaven; and whatsoever thou shalt loose on earth shall be loosed in heaven." The Roman Catholics who are in this congregation, know that from this statement the deduction in all the Roman Catholic books is this: The power of the keys given to Peter, the power of binding and loosing sins, is now solely in the Roman Catholic Church. The rights that Peter had by this promise were handed down to Popes following him, and bishops and priests, so that only by them can the kingdom of heaven be opened or closed, and only by them can the souls of men be bound or released.

But the Roman Catholic Church itself says that this promise was fulfilled as recorded in the 20th chapter of St. John, where, in the 19th verse, it is said that our Lord met his disciples, while they were assembled secretly for fear of the Jews; that he breathed on them, and said: "Receive ye the Holy Ghost: whosoever sins ye remit they are remitted unto them; and whosoever sins ye retain, they are retained." The Roman Catholic Church, De Sanctis says, tells us that this is the fulfillment of the promise. Here you will observe that at the fulfillment of this promise all the disciples were present; not Peter only, not the apostles only, but the one hundred and twenty men and women who constituted the infant church; and that the power of "binding and loosing," to use the Roman Catholic phrase, was given to every one of them, to all the Christians present. There can be no controversy whatever as to this fact, if people are disposed to be fair. The assumption, then, that Peter had this power alone, is plainly contradicted by the fact that our Lord gave it to all his apostles, and to all his disciples equally with the apostles ; that is to say, the power of opening heaven is in the Church as such, and as a whole ; and the power of binding and loosing, as it is called, is equally with every Christian, as with every other Christian.

What, then, is that power? What is the key? What is the binding, and what the loosing? Simply and only,—and it is as plain as day to any who do not want to corrupt the Word of God,— that the Gospel of the Lord Jesus Christ, which is given to all men if they will receive it, looses from sin those who take it, and binds with a deeper condemnation those who reject it. This is the condensed and concentrated statement. There is no other key, excepting the Gospel, for heaven, and deliverance from sin.

There is no other unloosing, except the unloosing which you can give, as well as I, if you have this Gospel to teach and preach. There is no binding, except the binding that you can give as well as the Pope, if you choose so to do, laying on men's consciences the Word of God, and holding them to it as the only way of salvation. And yet upon a childish perversion, superstitious, subtle, selfish, of these texts of Holy Scripture, has been built up the most colossal system of presumption, immorality and tyranny that the world ever saw. I say this deliberately, and I shall prove every word of it.

By the misuse of these texts, Rome has locked up men in the prison-house of superstition; has bound the human mind with chains of darkness; has shackled states and imprisoned free thought; has shed the blood of men whose lives were freely given for conscience and for principle. It has loosed no one; it has chained the world. The only governments that Rome has ever favored were tyrannies. Has the Pope ever pronounced his benediction on republics? Has he ever espoused the cause of the people against their oppressors? Why, the other day, this old man of the Vatican, supposing the people were all as blinded as Romanists would make them, began to prate about the slave trade; and the Worcester papers, that dare not say that we are here on Sunday night, said the Pope was moving in the direction of the suppression of the slave trade. How long ago was it that Protestant Christians, through their legislatures, denounced the slave trade? How many years have the guns of our navies on the coast of Africa delivered the slave and smitten his captor and kidnapper? And that old man has just woke up and asked these powers to combine against the slave trade! Father Leo, if you are really against the enslavement of mankind, get down on your knees like a sinner, as you are; ask Almighty God to forgive your presumption, and let go free the millions of Rome who are the slaves of superstition!

This utterly false and wicked idea of priestly confession puts bonds upon men and women, soul and body; binds their spirit, conscience and mind;

grasps their family, their social system, and their business; seizes their property, and pursues them into their graves with rapacious demands for money; robs them in such a way as monopolies never robbed the people; or rather, as a monopoly, would make it appear that they monopolize Heaven's gifts; assume that heaven is Rome's gift, while hell is its standing threat.

Now, instead of taking away sin, I am prepared to show, God being my helper, and the devil and the Pope to the contrary notwithstanding, that instead of diminishing sin, which all true confession ought to do, there is probably no force operative in the world that has created more crime and more sin than the Romish confessional. I use the language of one of the most intelligent ex-priests in the world, who gives it as his opinion that the social vice, at the name of which we shudder and grow sick at heart, has not created, in its common form, more immorality, or dragged down more people, than the Roman Catholic confessional. It is an author of sin, instead of a saviour from sin. It creates sin, instead of releasing men from sin.

I propose to show to-night, if I have time, first, that it is a system of falsehood and hypocrisy, producing crime and sin; second, that it is a system of spies, of espionage upon homes, persons and governments; third, that it is against the peace, purity and welfare of the family: fourth, that it is the opponent of liberty in the State; fifth, that it is the foe of pure religion and of religious progress.

1. I say, first, it is a system of falsehood and hypocrisy, producing crime and sin.

I have little less confidence in reading from De Sanctis, who will be my chief authority to-night, than I should have on matters of fact in reading from the Holy Scriptures; for while I believe them to be true, most amply vindicated, I believe the same of this distinguished man who was emancipated from the Roman Catholic Church. When I say that the confessional is a system of falsehood and hypocrisy, I mean to say, that I do not think that a large majority of the priesthood give any evidence of believing that they can free men from sin by their absolution, and that they regard the whole thing with a mixture of superstition and contempt.

De Sanctis says, after speaking of the character of the confessors: "While the penitent arraigns his faults with all the fatuity of a simpleton, what is the confessor doing? Laughing at the simplicity of the penitent; and afterwards in the priestly orgies that follow a morning of great confessions, in the hilarity that flows from wine, amidst coarse explosions of laughter, they describe to each other the stupid folly of their penitents; and each priest vies with his brother in rendering his own penitents more ridiculous than the rest. To such a degree is the individual debased and degraded by confession."

The ex-priests with whom I have talked, say to me, that there are honest priests, and a good many of them, who feel thoroughly degraded by having to sit in the confessional and take the confessions that are

given them. Some of them have said that the ear of
the priest is the sewer into which flows all manner of
evil and vicious conversation; and that while the
priests sometimes in public, because of their fear of
the Church, praise and laud the confessional, those
same priests in private bitterly lament their own
degradation, in that they are compelled to take the
confessions of those that come to them. It generates
hypocrisy and recklessness in the penitent. Of that
there can be no question. Listen to De Sanctis, who
was so many years a confessor in Rome. He says,
on the 108th and 109th pages of his book :

" The facilities for obtaining pardon of sins, by
relating them to a priest, too often a boon companion
in the excesses of the penitent, pave the way to the
commission of new sins. ' Sin confessed, sin forgiven ;' ' Confessing a hundred sins is as good as
confessing a hundred and ten,' are popular proverbs
in Italy. But I take for an example Rome, the city
which boasts to be the centre of religion, the seat of
the pretended Vicar of Jesus Christ; the city where,
more than in any other place, confession is largely
practised. I likewise take Rome as an example,
because of that city I speak with certain knowledge.
That city was my native place, and I discharged in it
for fifteen years the ministry of hearing confession : I
fulfilled in eight years the duty of a parish priest ;
these facts give me sufficient knowledge to speak
with certainty.

" Rome is the city which surpasses all the other
cities of Italy in immorality. But perhaps the blame

ought to be imputed to the Roman people? No. The Roman people, noble and generous as its fore-fathers, would be the people of the greatest virtue, a heroic people, if it were trained to virtue, if it were educated in the Gospel. But all the fine quali-ties of that people are stifled by the teaching of its Church, and the people are brutalized in guilt. Blasphemy against God is the predominant vice of the Roman; but the blasphemer confesses, departs absolved, and is no sooner out of the church than he begins to blaspheme anew. Drunkenness, murder, theft, fraud, adultery, are crimes incessantly repeated; but whoever commits them, confesses, and believes himself absolved; and immorality is not only arrested, but, by the facility of pardon at the cost of a few prayers, is committed again without scruple. There is no society that had not annually, (at least up to 1848) its spiritual exercises to pre-pare for confession; the number of individuals who did not confess at Easter in so vast a city never amounted to fifty; yet, with so many confessions, immorality was ever on the increase, and vice ever triumphant; and the increase was greatest (I speak of notorious facts) in those who were most regular in confession; and to them is Rome indebted for the current proverb, ' Better an unbeliever than a bigot.'"

He then goes on to give criminal statistics of the most startling character. For instance, he says: "Let statistics be appealed to, and it will be seen that if Catholic criminals are in ratio to the population as ten to a thousand, for instance; Protestant criminals are only one to a thousand. Let Protestant England be attentively regarded, and compared with Catholic Ireland; the Protestant cantons of Switzerland with the Swiss cantons; the country of the Waldensians with the rest of Piedmont. Let statistics be consulted, and the difference will be seen at a glance between Protestants who do not confess to a priest, and Catholics who do; it will be seen that the latter are much more criminal and immoral than the former." The man who had heard confessions for so many years ought to know what the effect of the confessional is. When I find that the Protestant Irishman is so noble a specimen of Christian morality, I want to know why it is that men of the same blood are furnishing so vast a proportion of our criminals. We have not found out the reason yet; unless we trace it to the Romish Church as a cause and a source. Please to notice : " Those most regular in the confessional," says De Sanctis, " are the most notoriously irregular in their lives."

We have supposed, in our simplicity, resulting from our lack of attention to this matter, that the confessional caused a good deal of restitution to be made in cases of theft, robbery and the like. What does De Sanctis say of that, on pages 126-27? I have never believed that the confessional favored honesty ; but now I know it does not. De Sanctis says : " The much-vaunted restitutions are, after all, mere dust thrown in the eyes of simpletons " (rub the dust out of your eyes my friends,) " that they may not observe the peculations of the confessor: so rare are they, so insignificant, that they do not restore even a thousandth part of the plunder. To these insignificant restitutions, which yet would be an advantage to society, is to be contrasted the encouragement given to theft, as to every other crime, by the facility of obtaining pardon; and the absolutions given to robbers, usurers, murderers, without their having made any restitution whatever. They repair to the confessor, present him with a goodly offering for a mass; or, if they are robbers of celebrity, men abounding in wealth, they found a chapelry, a benefice, or something of the kind; and who is the confessor, to resist the force of such powerful arguments, and send away the penitent without absolution? At Rome, the public robbers who are in the galleys confess, all of them, once a year, and even oftener; but never from those places does there come a restitution, though it is known that the objects stolen are secreted; yet they confess and communicate." Now further: "At Rome, for instance, every one knows that Pius VII. granted to all who hear confessions in the Holy house Ponterotto, the privilege of absolving *from the obligation of restitution* all who have defrauded the Rev. Apostolic Chamber, or the Government; and all defraud, and run there to receive absolution. But this is not enough. Leo X., in his Bull beginning with 'Postquam ad Apostulatus,' gives confessors the privilege not only of absolving robbers, but of permitting them to retain, in all good conscience, the fruits of their usury, robberies, thefts, etc., on condition that part of the goods be given to the Church." That is one way to get off, is it not? The robber, the murderer, seizes his victim, his plunder, and according to the Apostolic Bull of an infallible church, by paying a portion of this to the infallible church, has the power of binding and loosing applied to him, and the key turns which opens the kingdom of heaven, and he goes in, red-handed and black-hearted! I myself have seen in the chapels of Rome, on the altars of their churches, in more than one instance, the daggers of assassins which had been placed there as an offering to the saint who had helped them, as they supposed, in the murder of their enemies.

2.   It is a spy system in the interests of tyranny. You remember the martyrdom of Bishop Latimer, who is one of the uncanonized saints of the English church, whom Romanists burned at the stake. Years ago in England, he said, in his sermon on Matthew viii., concerning the confessional : "And so they came to all the secrets that were in men's hearts, so that emperor nor king could say nor do, nor think anything in his heart, but they knew it, and so applied all the purposes and intents of princes to their own commodities.   And this was the fruit of their auricular confession."   That was said some centuries ago in old England.   They knew it then, and it has been known ever since.   It is a system by which the priest who desires it, if you have a servant in your house who goes to the confessional, knows what you think and say and do ; as on the 132d page of this book of

De Sanctis : "Confession in relation to society may be defined as an universal spydom, organized and complete.   Confessors are not content to know the sins of those who confess ; but they must learn the regulation and management of the family : and when an ingenious youth or an innocent maiden comes under the fangs of a knavish confessor (and which of them is not a knave?) they do not escape till they have first revealed the secrets of the family circle — without, however, being aware of it," (and then follows a passage which I cannot read to you).

Now the testimony as to their espionage, and of their reports to head-quarters concerning such action everywhere transpiring, · is so voluminous that it is almost impossible to take out from it a little abstract for this occasion.   I read : " They were further enjoined," (that is, the Jesuits), "in all cases of doubt or difficulty, in which a sovereign sought their counsel, to refer the matter to their superior and obtain his decision, before giving their own reply : in reference to which it must be mentioned, as an essential part of the system, that the confessions of sovereign princes were at all times communicated to the General of the Order."   Further it is stated, that " By means of the religious Orders submitted to its power and discipline, the Holy See was enabled to penetrate into the secrets of the laws, and the feelings of the people.   The confessional of every Catholic monarch found its corresponding echo beneath the dome of the Vatican."   Further, we are told, that the messenger between the Council of Trent and the

Jesuits of Paris, whose name is given, had for part of the instruction given him this: " To take notice of the confessions of the people of France, and especially of the nobles and gentry, and in case they suspect anything detrimental to the Holy See of Rome, then to confer with three or more confessors of the suspicion, and so take memoranda to be asked of the party so suspected the next time." And so the history goes on multiplying the proofs. We are told that even the boys in certain schools in Rome are encouraged to write out as a confession, at a certain time in the month, all that they are, or think, or feel, or dream; and this is laid with ceremony on an altar provided for the purpose; remains in the hands of the confessors for a month; is copied into books; and so the secrets of ingenuous youth, and the households to which they belong, become the property of the most unscrupulous spies of the most unscrupulous power that the world ever knew. There is authority given for breaking the seal of the confessional, as I told you last Sunday night, and as I need not now repeat. I presume that in three-quarters of the homes where Roman Catholic servants are employed who go to the confessional, your business, your words, your attitudes, your secrets, as far as known, have become the property of the priests. What do they do with them? They lay the astutest and profoundest plans that they can possibly contrive for gaining such knowledge and influence as will be to the advantage of the Church, without reference to the advantage of anybody else; for the confessions that are recorded in the confes-

sionals of Rome are always in the interests of oppression and tyranny.

3.   But I must hasten to show, that against the
peace, the purity and welfare of the family, the confessional continually conspires.   Do you suppose
that Roman Catholic men know the questions that
are asked their wives and daughters in the confessional?   I do not believe they do.   Father Chiniquy
says, they do not.   He says, in a startling passage:
" But the betrayed husband knows nothing of the
dark mysteries of auricular confession; the duped
father suspects nothing: a cloud from hell has ob-
scured the intelligence of them both, and made them
blind.   On the contrary, husbands and fathers,
friends and relations, feel edified and pleased with
the spectacle of the 'piety' of their wives and daughters."   (I have to read very carefully here.)   " The
wife is brought under apostolic control, and so all the
family.   In the Church of Rome, if the husband ask
a favor from his wife, nine times in ten she will inquire from her father-confessor whether or not she
can grant him his request; and the poor husband will
have to wait patiently for the permission of the master,
or the rebuke of the lord, according to the answer of
the oracle which had to be consulted.   If he gets
impatient. under the yoke, and murmurs, the wife
will soon go to the feet of the confessor to tell him of
the fact."   And this man was a priest of Rome, and
took confessions for twenty-three years; and lives to-
day to defy the power of the Pope, notwithstanding
the most strenuous efforts to kill him.

What is the influence on the home? He says again : " Thus it is that that stupendous imposture, the dogma of auricular confession, does completely destroy all the links, the joys, the responsibilities and divine privileges of the married life ; and transforms it into a life of perpetual, though disguised, adultery. It becomes utterly impossible in the church of Rome that the husband should be one with his wife, and that the wife should be one with her husband : a ' monstrous being' has been between them both, called the confessor. Born in the darkest ages of the world, that being has received from hell his mission to destroy and contaminate the purest joys of the married life, to enslave the wife, to outrage the husband, and to damn the world."

Turning to another authority, I find a similar statement in regard to intervention in family life, as follows : " In important questions affecting the family welfare — the education of his children, the professions of the sons and the marriages of the daughters,— the father finds his rightful authority superseded by the silent encroachments and underhand influences of the confessor. The mutual confidences of home disappear : its tenderest sympathies are destroyed ; its fondest associations are marred and disfigured ; and the cold shade of the priest casts a withering blight over its best and purest affections." " The Confessional of De Sanctis," says his translator, " will be at least a timely, and in many cases it is to be hoped an efficacious antidote." Father Hyacinthe, that famous priest of whom I told you on last Sun-

day night, quoted by Chiniquy in "Priest, Woman and
Confessional," says, concerning the character of the
confessors, that 99 per cent. of them live in sin with
their female penitents ; and Father Hyacinthe was the
greatest preacher in France, until he renounced
Romanism and left the pulpit of Notre Dame. I
would not dare to say as much as he said. I do not
know as much as he knew. But the man who was
the companion of Popes, of Archbishops and Cardinals, of priests and confessors, would not say that
unless he had great reason so to say. De Sanctis
adds : " How can it happen otherwise, if immorality,
thanks to confession, is reduced by Catholic priests
to scientific principles? The most shameless liber-
tine could not read, without blushing, the filth which
is contained in the books of moral theology. And
it is upon these books that the education of the
young clergy in the seminaries is formed."

He proceeds still further to show how true that is.
Discords are fomented in families, by the confessional, in the interests of the church ; as when it is
said : " From the confessional proceeds the most
serious discords in families : the priest is determined
to rule at all costs ; hence you must either fall into
his ideas, and thus make yourself his slave, or else
prepare to wage a family war. If you conform to
his ideas, you will no longer be master in your own
house ; you will no longer be able to do anything
without the *placet* of the confessor : he will thrust
himself between you and your wife ; and, heedless of
that sacred bond, a meddlesome priest will interpose

with his counsels, his insinuations : he will interfere
between you and your sons, and all your paternal
authority will only be allowed to exert itself in subordination to the dictates of your priest : he will
arrange the marriage of your sons ; he will preside
at their choice of a profession ; he, in short, will be
the true father of the family — you will only execute
his will. Suppose you determine to escape this
state of degradation, and propose to maintain your
position as father and husband, and then all family
peace is ruined : you will be looked on as an infidel,
and as such, with hypocritical compassion, the confessor will describe you to your wife and to your
sons."

Do you ask why Roman Catholic men do not escape
from the Church of Rome ? Do you not see how they
are bound ? " In continual contact with the priest,"
he says of women, lads and old men, "and feeble by
nature, they allow themselves to be imposed upon
by him, especially in matters of religion ; and husbands, fathers and sons dare not hazard a word in
the family circle with a view to exposing the abuses
of the clergy on religious subjects ; they dare not
read the Bible, dare not enter into religious con-
versations—both to avoid throwing a gloom over persons so dear to them, and for fear of being denounced.

For the priest cannot absolve a wife or a son, if,
with the knowledge that the husband or the father
speaks of the Gospel otherwise than in the sense of
the Church of Rome, they have not denounced him
to the Inquisition, where it exists, or else to the

bishop where the Inquisition exists no longer. Imagine, then, if religious progress is possible, where the discipline of the confessional exists."

We have a record here which I will state and not read, that in the days when Italy was struggling to throw off the yoke of tyranny, both papal and civil, wives, intimate friends, children, in the confessional, were compelled to denounce their husbands, fathers, lovers and friends as being liberals, in the sense of loving liberty, and the result was their banishment. or incarceration in the dungeons of the Inquisition, and sometimes death. "Yea, the time will come when he that killeth you will think that he doeth God service."

4. The greed of the confessors, in the matter of property, I must let you into the secret of. This eminent man says, that confessors, from being poor, become rich. "By confession, in fact, so many families are immersed in poverty; because the grasping confessor, taking advantage of the weak moments of a dying man, has had the will made to the profit of the clergy; and facts of the kind may be reckoned by the million. From confession arise so many separations of married people—frequent in proportion to the frequency of confessions."

Now you know, that where extreme unction must be preceded by absolution in the case of a dying man, the priest has a fearful control over that man; and that control has been repeatedly and continually used to extort from the dying a very large share of their property for the Church. De Sanctis says, that he has known confessors who were poor when they began to take confessions, and afterwards came to live in the splendid homes of families who were reduced to absolute poverty by the changes which those confessors made in the wills or minds of their penitents. For example, we have it recorded from very numerous authorities (this in De Sanctis; it is a historical statement supplemented by the names of the authorities), that the "grasping cupidity of ecclesiastical will-hunters, and the consequent ruin of innocent and helpless families, formed the subject of an indignant remonstrance of the German princes at the Diet of Nuremberg. That the Popes should have connived at these fraudulent artifices, need not be a matter of surprise; for a considerable number of the multitudinous clerical host must, no doubt, have died intestate, and all such property, by a decree of Innocent IV., was to escheat to the Pope. To such a length was this execrable practice sometimes carried, that the last sacraments were denied to the dying man till he consented to make a will in the priest's favor. To facilitate their nefarious designs, the clergy were provided with testamentary forms that might be executed at a moment's notice. For the further promotion of ecclesiastical interests, wills, before they were proved, were subject to a private preliminary examination in a 'special court' called St. Peter's Tribunal. And for still greater security, Popes are equipped with the power of altering testamentary dispositions in favor of the Church."

Robbers that they are! Equipped with power, from what source? From hell; whence lies, thefts, corruptions and murders, of which they have been among the chief agents in the history of time, have been vomited forth. Changing testaments indeed! Ay! they have changed the New Testament of our Lord and Saviour; they have changed the Old Testament; and they change the testamentary wills of men, that they may seize hold of their goods. " Wycliffe, on his death-bed, testifies that the priest attending on the dying, were commanded by the Pope to extract bequests in favor of the Church." Further, it is said: " How different the proposed reform is from the present corrupt state of the Roman priesthood, may be safely inferred from the numerous trials in Irish courts of justice, in spite of numbers of cases that are hushed up or compromised, where the inheritance of the deceased is disputed between the priest and the surviving relatives." When Gregory VII., with a power equal to that which any tyrannical ruler ever exercised, insisted on the celibacy of the priests,—when he separated the married priests from their wives and from their children, and forced with prodigious earnestness the bond of celibacy on the priesthood,— it was specifically declared, more than once, that the purpose was, that the estates of the priests might go to the Church, instead of going to the wives and children of the priests. And so one reason why the priests of Rome cannot marry, is that, grasping the property of their people, they hold it till they die, and give it to other priests for the Church. Thus the Church and its ecclesiastics abound in wealth, and their people abound in nothing but poverty.

5. The confessional is the assassin of liberty in the State. There can be no liberty (I have shown you that fully in preceding discourses) where the Pope of Rome has his way. There never has been, and there never can be. What does one say who well understands Rome, concerning the relation of the confessional to liberty? Father Chiniquy says: "Have not the Popes publicly and repeatedly anathematized the sacred principle of liberty of conscience? Have they not boldly said, in the teeth of the nations of Europe, that liberty of conscience must be destroyed, killed at any cost? Has not the whole world heard the sentence of death to liberty coming from the lips of the Old Man of the Vatican? But where is the scaffold on which the doomed liberty must perish? That scaffold is the confessional box. Yes, in the confessional, the Pope has his 100,000 high executioners. There they are, day and night, with sharp daggers in hand, stabbing Liberty to the heart." He says again: "In vain chivalrous Spain will call Liberty to give a new life to her people. Liberty cannot set her feet there, except to die, so long as the Pope is allowed to strike her in his 50,000 confessionals. And free America, too, will see all her so-dearly-bought liberties destroyed, the day that the confessional box is universally reared in her midst. Auricular Confession and Liberty cannot stand on the same ground; either one or the other

must fall. Liberty must sweep away the confessional as she has swept away the demon of slavery; or she is doomed to perish."

I refer again to the fact that Freemasonry has always been an object of intense antagonism to the Papal power, and you can see better now than at any former time why it is so. Freemasonry, in the old country, has been to some extent a refuge and sanctuary to men who were not in any sense political conspirators, but who had hope in one another and trusted one another; they dared to hold secrets one with another, which they believed for their mutual benefit and the welfare of the State, which secrets they would not tell in the confessional, and which even their wives and children could not know or tell in the confessional. But the penalty of belonging to that society; the penalty of harboring a member of that society; the penalty for failing to denounce a member of that society, by the word of the infallible Pope, was death. You know why, now. Because the Freemason could not, and would not, by his obligations, put himself under the power of the priest. I have often thought there were things about this great society that needed to be reformed. But I tell you, my friends, it may be that even the most earnest antagonist of Freemasonry may see in it one of the bulwarks against the power of the confessional and the Romish Church in this country. I do not say it will be so; but I tell you, it is getting to be easy for me to love what the Pope hates.

6. And now as I draw to a close, I must show that as the Papacy and the confessional are the enemies of liberty and the assassins of the same, so the confessional is the foe of pure religion and religious progress. Can anything be the friend of pure religion that creates immorality, that destroys liberty, that invades and plunders the home, that steals the property of the dying? Oh, do not talk to me, my Roman Catholic brothers,—do not talk to me about the glory that would come to God, through evil doing. There is no glory to God in evil doing. If the confessional, as seems obvious from those who know all the facts concerning it, is the friend of immorality and creates crime, as I shall have to show next Sunday night more fully than I can to-night, then it cannot be for the glory of God. God is not glorified by wickedness.

But there is other proof than this that the confessional is the enemy of pure religion. We are told that it advances infidelity and ignorance, by this most careful writer, De Sanctis, whom I quote once more: "The horrible consequence, however, for religion and for souls, is that infidelity advances with huge strides, especially in Roman Catholic countries. The enlightenment of the age no longer permits men to believe in the priests blindly, as in the times of ignorance. Free discussion alone could show that the doctrines of the Roman Church are not those of the Gospel; discussion, as it would prove their falsehood to a demonstration, would establish the truth of the evangelical doctrine. Discussion being prevented, it

follows that, seeing clearly the falsehood and iniquity
of the Roman doctrines, men believe them, because
they are not discussed, to be the doctrines of the
Christian religion, and abandon them, and live in indifference and infidelity. Rome sees, knows, and is
silent: she never quarrels with infidels, unless they
speak against her; but her quarrel rather is with those
who, laying bare her abuses, seek to bring back their
brethren to the Gospel, the religion of their fathers.
The unbelieving and the superstitious equally observe
the Church of Rome, and are equally beloved by it;
the Gospel alone it detests, and for the destruction
of the Gospel it instituted confession."

Furthermore he says: "If confession is naturally
ruinous to faith and morals, religious progress under
such a system is manifestly impossible. Confession
is the great obstacle opposed by the Popes to the
re-establishment of the Gospel; hence it is necessary
to demolish such an obstacle to religious progress."
And then he proceeds to the proof in great detail.

It was intended, especially at the outset, to uproot
heresy. The Popes' object for auricular confession
was more this than anything else. For example:
"Innocent III., the most knavish and the most audacious of all who have ever occupied the Roman See,
resorted to the remedy." In the fourth Lateran
Council after having proclaimed crusades, after having
canonized persecution against those who published
the Gospel, he instituted compulsory confession for
all the followers of the Church of Rome, as a measure
of preventive policy, to compel denunciation of

heretics under penalty of eternal damnation; and thus confession, which at first was free, became compulsory, and was afterwards converted, by the decision of the Council of Trent, into a dogma of faith and a sacrament. The aim of confession therefore, is to prevent all religious progress, and maintain ignorance and superstition." Has it practically and actually corrupted religion? There can be no doubt of this. A word or two more : "Nor can it be alleged that certain Popes have misused religion, and that the abuses ought therefore to be attributed to the individual and not to the system. From Sylvester to our time, all the Popes, some more, some less, have contributed to transform the religion of Jesus Christ, and to build up the system of oppression and political annihilation on the ruins of liberty and progress. Nay, the very Popes who have been most conspicuous in this work of destruction, are adored as heroes on the altars of Rome." Then, speaking of Gregory VII., he says : "Gregory VII. is on the altars of Rome," (that is, he is a canonized saint), "and the ferocious Ghislieri (Pius V.), who, in the name of God and of the religion of the Gospel, taught the despot Charles IX. that he could never obtain from God the pardon of his sins if he did not shed, without the slightest compunction, the blood of his subjects who asked for the pure Gospel,— is not he also on the altars of Rome?" See what they worship. "In canonizing such men, the Popes have canonized their doctrine ; hence it cannot be said that despotism, obscuration, oppression of nations, and hatred for any kind of

progress, exist through the mal-practice of any one
of the Popes; they exist by the very system of the
Papacy. But the Popes, to establish their dominion,
have butchered them by the million. But among so
many Popes, has there been one, one only, who has
deplored such abuses? Therefore the corruption of
religion ought not to be attributed to abuse of it by
the individual, but to the system; therefore the system ought to be reformed; therefore the Gospel
ought to reign in its purity, and ought to be delivered
from this great enemy; and Italy and Rome ought
to confer upon the world this great benefit of despoiling the Popes of their usurped power, and
re-establishing on the ruins of the Papacy the pure
religion of Christ."

We have come to the edge of a precipice. There
are, no doubt, in this church to-night, many brave
hearts, who, with strength from purity, will dare
with me to descend, scaling the face of this precipice,
into the fearful abyss below. My friends, I beg you
to remember as I close, that if we have shown the
immorality and the hypocrisy of this system of confession—if we have shown that it is a system of spies
for the overthrow of freedom—if we have shown that
it is a foe to the family and an assassin to liberty,
working the ruin of pure religion, in so doing we
have only touched on the beginnings of its actual
wickedness, and of the ruin which it works. And if
you have hearts bold enough to hear, and God gives
me judgment and wisdom enough to speak, I will let
you down into those nether depths where you can

see in all its horrors, the beastly immorality of priests and people, of Popes, Cardinals and bishops, of men, women and children, as the result of this wicked, ungodly, unscriptural, and unchristian system of auricular confession.

NOTE BY THE AUTHOR.—The Author begs to say, in closing this work thus abruptly, that already it has grown nearly 150 pages beyond expectation. Manifestly, the discussion is not here completed. The patient reader has noted the logical order of the book, and that up to the close, it is a compacted whole.

The Introductory discourse leads to the second; which, of necessity, finds in the Jesuits the controlling force of the Papacy; they furnishing, in their principles and history, the key to the Papal intention. Their pope is portrayed, in the third chapter, as the enemy of civil and religious freedom—as are they. And particularizing, the Papacy is shown, in the fourth and fifth discourses, to be antagonistic to the Constitution and to the Laws of the American Republic. Thus their hostility to universal education is manifestly based on irreconcilable animosity to the fundamental principles of our Government. The sixth, seventh and eighth chapters develope the purpose of Romanism to destroy our Public Schools; showing the alleged and actual reasons for their attempt. Claiming, as they do, to educate, naturally we ask and answer, in the ninth, tenth and eleventh discourses, the burning question, What do they propose to substitute for Common School education? or, "The morality which Romanism would teach American youth."

A few general observations previously omitted, upon parochial schools, make up the twelfth sermon. And then, to show how Roman Catholic peoples are suppressed and throttled; to show also why they yield though they protest, the Confessional is exposed to view as the place where Papal tyranny forges the chains which bind them.

Naturally, beyond these observations, much remains. The two discourses unveiling the confessional, spoken to men only, are needed to complete the picture. The dogmas, the priesthood, the financial greed and its impoverishing consequences, remain to be discussed, and sharp contrasts drawn between the policy of a true Christian Church, and this politico-ecclesiastical tyranny. These the author may sometime put before the public as complementary to the foregoing, believing that the free discussion of Romanism, in all its monstrous deformity, is sure to detach from it those who, in the growth of their knowledge concerning the true Christian religion, will behold in the Papacy the worst enemy of a genuine Christianity, and of the civil freedom of a Republic.

INDEX.

APPENDIX.

THE BALTIMORE CENTENNIAL AND ITS DECLARATIONS.

THE twelve hundred delegates of the Roman Catholic Church assembled at Baltimore, Nov. 11, 1889, listened to carefully prepared papers on many subjects, and to addresses by her most eloquent and distinguished sons. There are in these papers and addresses frequent expressions of loyalty to the country, its liberty, its constitution and laws, which are satisfactory in phrase and form, and which we would gladly accept as the policy of the Papacy.

The very fact of these calls attention to another of much greater significance, viz.: that no other body of professedly religious people, save the Mormons, have in a time of peace made such professions.

Their entire ecclesiastical system is now and ever has been so inimical to all that freemen hold dear, and their fundamental allegiance is so irreconcilably and transparently antagonistic to true fealty, that we can hardly be amiss in calling our readers' attention to a few fragments that embody the spirit underlying all the utterances of this assembly.

1. All the speakers avow absolute and unconditioned loyalty to the Pope, who is now agitating all Europe and America for the restoration of the temporal power.

Charles J. Bonaparte, in his paper "On the Independence of the Holy See," says, recurring to the past years of the domination of the church : —

"She needs now as she needed then, a chief ruler who for what he does or leaves undone shall answer at no human judgment seat."

This puts the Pope above the laws and the judiciary. Again, said Mr. Bonaparte,

" Catholics will never accept any law of an Italian parliament as assuring the independence of the Holy See. A law is the act of a sovereign affecting those who are his subjects, or at least under his legitimate dominion. That a national parliament should pretend to legislate regarding the Holy See is a denial of its independence."

Suppose that national parliament were the Congress of the United States ?

" If we admit that he (the Pope) is such a subject, then the laws of the Italian parliament bind him as much if he disapprove as if he approve them. But in this admission is contained what Catholics do not and never can or will admit. The matter of the law goes for nothing, etc., etc., and for the Catholics of America we say this now and here — a subject he cannot be."

Would Mr. Bonaparte and the Romanists who applauded these sentiments, to which he and they, in his closing utterances, specifically pledged the Catholics of America, support and defend the Pope in denouncing, annulling, and overriding the laws, legislatures and courts of the United States as he did in Austria, Sardinia, etc.? (see page 100). Is this their boasted loyalty ?

In addressing the assembled hierarchy, Archbishop Sotelli, as the representative of the Holy See, said : —

" The Pope doubts not that the Catholics of America will labor that he may once more reacquire that independence and liberty which by divine institution appertains to him as sovereign head of all the church and representative of the person and authority of Christ, and under which liberty and independence the power of the free constitution of the states are founded, are maintained prosperous, and their existence secured."

Are free American citizens expected to believe that these amazing assumptions can consist with a spirit of loyalty to our institutions ?

And finally, the whole Congress, in its last utterance in the platform of resolutions, declared itself as follows : —

" We cannot conclude without recording our solemn conviction that the absolute freedom of the Holy See is equally indispensable to the peace of the church and the welfare of mankind.

" We demand, in the name of humanity and justice, that this freedom be scrupulously respected by all secular governments.

" We protest against the assumption by any such government of a right to affect the interests or control the action of our Holy Father by any form of legislation or other public act to which his full approbation has not been previously given, and we pledge to Leo XIII., the worthy Pontiff to whose hands Almighty God has committed the helm of Peter's bark amid the tempests of this stormy age, the loyal sympathy and unstinted aid of all his spiritual children in vindicating that perfect liberty which he justly claims as his sacred and inalienable right."

This is treason in Italy. What is it here? Such an utterance should put every one on his guard against all the high-sounding professions of loyalty made at Baltimore.

Submission to the Papacy involves, of course, the endorsement of its ultramontanism, as represented by the Jesuits, whom Archbishop Ryan eulogizes, without a hint of criticism, as "the greatest society in the Catholic Church." Yet this society is dreaded, doubted, hated, by freemen everywhere.

Archbishop Ireland represented the Congress in its thought of America and Protestantism in such language as the following : —

"America is at heart a Christian country. As a religious system, Protestantism is in hopeless dissolution, utterly valueless as a doctrinal or moral power, and no longer to be considered a foe with which we must count. The Catholic Church is the sole living and enduring Christian authority."

Could assumption go farther ?
Dr. Clark affirmed : —

"The loyalty of the laity has been well exemplified by their devout acceptance of the dogmas of the immaculate conception and of papal infallibility, and in their docile support of the decrees of the American councils."

Could servility go farther ?
And Archbishop Ireland would have these dogmas accepted by everybody in the United States.

"Our work," he says, "is to make America Catholic. . . . Our cry shall be, 'God wills it.' . . . We know that the Church is the sole owner of the truths and graces of salvation."

Major Brownson of Detroit, speaking on "Lay Action in the Church," said boldly : —

"The American system is anti-Protestant, and must either reject Protestantism, or be overthrown by it."

Judge Dunne in his paper on "The State and Education" claims America now as Catholic. He says:—

"Why, then, should we not love this land? Is it not our own? Is it not Columbia, daughter of Catholic thought, of Catholic wealth, of Catholic courage? Is not this whole country really a Catholic land? Is it not under the care of Catholic saints? With a Catholic population, this land were surely Catholic. Well, we have twelve millions of Catholic people now, and of them the end is not yet," etc.

Daniel Dougherty, Esq., of New York, evoked the wildest enthusiasm by making similar preposterous claims. Seven and a half millions is an outside estimate for their population, while by more careful reckoning there is a population of over fifty million adherents to Protestant churches. This is not a Roman Catholic land, nor is it likely ever to be.

Judge Dunne fiercely denounces the State in its relation to public education; and time and again the different speakers outspokenly declare for the sole right of the Romish Church to educate their children, denouncing taxation for education as now laid equally upon all. Nevertheless, Americans, thanks to Protestant and State schools, can read, while Spanish, Italian, Mexican, and South American Romanists do not know their alphabet.

Many things said at this gathering need to be explained, and we may perhaps illustrate this by their references to the press and their professions of loyalty.

Dr. George D. Wolff, speaking "On the Catholic Press," said:—

"The Catholic press is to be the antidote for pestilential literature. Catholic editors are not the expounders of what the editors may think in doctrine. Editors and writers are to declare the doctrine taught them by the authorized teachers of the church."

On the 13th of April, 1887, Archbishop Corrigan of New York wrote a letter, of which the following is a copy:—

452 MADISON AVE., NEW YORK,
April 13, 1887.

Editor and Proprietor of Catholic Herald.

GENTLEMEN:—By this note, which is entirely private, and not to be published, I call your attention to the fact that the Third

Plenary Council of Baltimore, following the leadership of Leo XIII., has pointed out the duties of the Catholic press, and denounced the abuses, of which journals styling themselves Catholic are sometimes guilty. "That paper alone," says the Council (decree No. 228), "is to be regarded as Catholic that is prepared to submit in all things to ecclesiastical authority."

Later on it warns all Catholic writers against presuming to attack publicly the manner in which a bishop rules his diocese.

For some time past the utterances of "The Catholic World" have been shockingly scandalous. As this newspaper is published in this diocese, I hereby warn you that if you continue in this course of conduct, it will be at your peril.

I am, gentlemen, yours most truly,

M. A. CORRIGAN,
Archbishop of New York.

Does this consist with freedom of the press? As a significant commentary on their professions of loyalty it may be noted that, since the Baltimore Congress, the president of the Mormon Church has spoken, insisting that Mormons love the Constitution and the country, and are the most loyal of Americans. But to harmonize Mormon principles with Mormon professions is a far less difficult and complicated task, in view of the utterances of the Vatican in this generation alone, than to discover accord between the Pope's encyclicals and our laws; the papal canons and the American Constitution; Romish methods and civil freedom; papal history and American liberty; Romish hierarchical despotism and the progress and purpose of the United States.

Our final judgment of the utterances at Baltimore must be governed by such facts as these: —

In 1870 the seven hundred bishops composing the Vatican Council that declared the Infallibility of the Pope, reaffirmed the canons and decrees of the Council of Trent, and individually "swore adhesion to them, kissing the Holy Gospels in solemn token thereof."

This Council of Trent was the answer of Rome to the Reformation, and its canons and decrees, as also the Syllabus and Encyclicals of Pius IX. (see p. 73) are now of infallible authority.

www.ingramcontent.com/pod-product-compliance
Lightning Source LLC
Chambersburg PA
CBHW031058110726
47900CB00003B/977